Dr. Donald G. Herter

To Don with many
thanks
Walter H. Zoltai

Managerial Reform and Professional Empowerment in the Public Service

Managerial Reform and Professional Empowerment in the Public Service

Walter L. Balk

Foreword by **Frank J. Thompson**

QUORUM BOOKS
Westport, Connecticut • London

Library of Congress Cataloging-in-Publication Data

Balk, Walter L.
    Managerial reform and professional empowerment in the public service / Walter
  L. Balk ; foreword by Frank J. Thompson.
      p.   cm.
    Includes bibliographical references (p.) and index.
    ISBN 1–56720–011–7 (alk. paper)
    1. Organizational change. 2. Professional employees in
  government. 3. Whistle blowing. I. Title.
  JF1525.073B35   1996
  350.007′5—dc20   95–19463

British Library Cataloguing in Publication Data is available.

Library of Congress Catalog Card Number: 95–19463
ISBN: 1–56720–011–7

First published in 1996

Quorum Books, 88 Post Road West, Westport, CT 06881
An imprint of Greenwood Publishing Group, Inc.

Printed in the United States of America

The paper used in this book complies with the
Permanent Paper Standard issued by the National
Information Standards Organization (Z39.48–1984).

10 9 8 7 6 5 4 3 2

Contents

Tables and Figures

Foreword

Democratic government and its relationship to professionals in the public service has been one of the major preoccupations of public administration. Much of the literature is fixated upon the needs of higher-level policymakers—upon ways to direct subordinate action and motivation. Walter Balk goes counter to this trend as he considers approaches for agency insiders to motivate managers and other policymakers to initiate critical reforms. In so doing, he faces head-on the paradoxes of government organizations including the difficulties posed by administrative beliefs that originate in the private sector.

The author's unusual background has prepared him to grapple with these perplexing and wide-ranging issues. As an engineer and manager in the corporate world he gained practical experience with large work organizations. Later, in his public administration teaching, research and consulting capacities he got to know public agencies and, along the way, became increasingly concerned with the dilemmas of public service careers.

At the heart of this book is a model of public agency democracy that accommodates the benefits of bureaucratic processes along with the disruption of change. To better understand its implications and potential the author has synthesized an extensive amount of knowledge about the field of public administration, the meaning of effectiveness, management persuasions and individual motivation. A creative and unusual approach emerges that may well overcome some of the paradoxes and frustrations that typify so many government careers. All of this is backed up by specific ways to combine ethical purposes with expert action.

This book should be of great interest to students, practitioners and others who wish to shape the future of the public service. Balk's thesis that public agency democracy can narrow the gap between generating and implementing effective government policy deserves to be taken seriously indeed.

Frank J. Thompson

Acknowledgments

I hope that what follows will encourage the reader to question many ingrained government administrative beliefs and values. If the discussion encourages innovative approaches to agency reform, if it helps to establish a better sense of common purpose among public service professionals, so much the better.

This book went through repeated changes and I appreciate the help of colleagues. Don Calista of Marist College provided insights and suggestions over a longer period than most would endure. Phillip Cooper (University of Vermont), Charles Goodsell (Virginia Polytechnic Institute and State University), James Kent (Marist College) and Frank Thompson (The University at Albany, State University of New York) generously shared their time and knowledge.

Among my associates at the Graduate School of Public Affairs, Donald Axelrod helped me to apply for a Ford Foundation grant that was instrumental in developing the idea of agency democracy. John Gunnell, James Heaphey, Joseph F. Zimmerman and Virgil Zimmermann increased my understanding of public administration philosophy, applied theory and practice.

I am also indebted to graduate students who over the years criticized the themes, models and approaches used in this book. I am especially grateful to Alain Belasen, James Feldt, Al Mauet, John Rogone, Gail Samuelson, Robert Smith and Tim Winchell.

Addie Napolitano managed the processing of and countless revisions to the text. Her expertise, patience and good humor has seen many of us through the turbulent, at times frustrating experiences of publication.

Finally, I dedicate this book to Ann Heins Balk, whose wisdom and support have caused so many good things to happen to those in the light of her presence.

Walter L. Balk

Chapter 1

Theory and Action

What is a democracy, Lysis? It is what it says, the rule of the people. It is as good as the people are, or as bad.

Mary Renault

This book is about the reform of government agencies by insiders. It explains why so many professionally trained experts find it difficult to take purposeful action at crucial times. Ways are suggested for these "silent intermediaries" to prevail in the face of bureaucratic resistance.

All government employees are charged with promoting and protecting the public interest. They have important citizen obligations at their workplace toward elected officials and the community at large. Occasionally these responsibilities require subordinates to go far beyond conventional practice since public servants are expected to question harmful policies, resist wasteful practices and disclose unlawful acts. Under such circumstances it may become necessary to bypass regular hierarchical and procedural channels so as to motivate higher authorities to do the right thing.

Yet when agency insiders exercise their citizen duties, they raise perplexing issues and disconcerting sentiments. Political and bureaucratic authorities usually do not take kindly to persistent reform efforts on the part of subordinates. It is then that activists are open to retaliation, even when their endeavors result in highly favorable outcomes for the public. On the other hand, management must use valuable time and resources in order to sort out reasonable from unreasonable demands. To what extent should agencies expose themselves to disruptive endeavors that could threaten essential bureaucratic order? Who is to tell when subordinates are using citizen obligations as a disguise for their own self-interest? Such dilemmas become especially visible during whistle-blowing episodes, but there are many other kinds of reform initiatives, far removed from the public eye, that involve similar quandaries.

This topic is of crucial importance to government agency professionals be cause the ability to initiate change is at the heart of their career identity and purpose. Yet there is little in the literature concerning efforts on the part of subordinates to energize their hierarchical superiors or the public in order to bring about necessary reforms. Accounts of whistle-blowing are to be found, but in-depth research is rare. The topic of employee-motivated organizational change has only recently aroused the interest of management theorists and philosophers. Even so, except under controlled circumstances involving management-directed participation or union negotiations, small consideration is given to what should and could be constructive hierarchical responses to spontaneous internal efforts to bring about significant change. It will be shown why the academic fields of administrative science and public administration are singularly ill equipped to provide answers.

The theory and practice of public agency democracy as discussed throughout this book has important implications for the way that government service is envisioned because it requires thinking through conflicts of loyalties and values, conflicts due to inescapable differences between bureaucratic agency and democratic political purposes. On the one hand agency people must have a predominant commitment toward structure and processes aimed at tangible, well-defined outcomes. Therefore it is necessary to give high priority to agency goals and loyalty toward organizational superiors. On the other hand for lower-level public servants to become, however briefly, preoccupied with essential reform endeavors may involve enduring discordant, open-ended democratic action frequently accompanied by a switch of allegiance to actors and values external to one's functional unit and even one's agency. I will argue that resolving such conflicts of trust and loyalties need not paralyze beneficial employee initiatives; nor is it necessary for reason to be distorted by deeply felt longings to act in assertive, ethical ways.

Any discussion of reform initiated by public agency insiders should be useful to policymakers, educators, and other citizens striving to improve government effectiveness. Two groups of readers will find the topic of direct personal significance. The first consists of students who are considering careers in the wide spectrum of government agencies. The second group includes practitioners, ill at ease, often disillusioned with the "politics" of their agency workplace. My intention is to help these readers predict career crises and grapple creatively with the problems of initiating action. Unfortunately, there are no simple prescriptions because reform action is fraught with paradox. A good deal of reflection will be necessary to integrate several kinds of knowledge which are normally considered either in isolation one from the other or passed over in the press to fulfill other education program requirements. Because of the emphasis upon specialized expertise, many professionals have not had sufficient opportunities to consider the deeper, subjective, necessarily contradictory, and ambiguous aspects of their commitment to the public service . . . only to pay a heavy price for this oversight at a later date.

What follows has been deeply influenced by my experiences as a practitioner, faculty member and consultant. Four inadequacies of government operations are of major interest. All have profound influence upon the revitalization and well-being of the public service.

UNACCEPTABLE IMPACT AND FREQUENCY OF ERRORS

The past two decades have been far from reassuring to those interested in the effectiveness of government operations. While they represent but a small fraction of all activities, significant failures are regularly reported by the media; these occur at every level of government. They involve blatant tolerance of waste, poor planning, insensitivity to citizen needs and outright malfeasance on the part of public servants. The incidence does not appear to slacken, and the magnitude of these scandals is alarming not only because of the sorry misuse of money and talent. Massive mistakes engender public distrust and cynicism about all that government does and represents; for the great majority who perform their agency responsibilities in a competent and caring manner, these failures diminish the meaning of their working lives. Spectacular misdeeds such as Watergate and the Iran Contra scandal may come to mind, but they appear to be more political executive than bureaucratic agency shortcomings. In its own perverse way the widespread condemnation of these acts has reaffirmed the strength of democratic institutions to make public, condemn and begin to correct bad judgment and wrongdoing at highest government ranks. Unfortunately they have overshadowed the interest in failures at the agency workplace.

It is said that the incidence of bureaucratic error and corruption is no worse, even less than in the past, but this is of small comfort, given the extent and magnitude of agency breakdowns that capture public attention. Some will point out that most of government works quite well and that political along with other influences beyond the control of agencies are the real cause of mishaps. Yet others will ask what we expect since the general public neither cares nor is informed about the public service; outstanding performance receives little citizen gratitude, and the distribution of rewards is at times inconsistent with accomplishments. But minimizing internal agency shortcomings by blaming others only causes those within these agencies to become passive and illogically defensive. Most importantly, the serious inadequacies of public agencies remain unopened to the potential for insiders to bring about meaningful reform.

What is the basic problem? One prevailing notion is that the public service does not attract the requisite talent such as innovative management, knowledgeable staff members and skilled employees. So the usual response to government failure is to advocate educating and electing more dedicated, competent, honest people who will, in turn, run more effective operations. Surely progress must continue along these lines. But no matter how gifted our political and agency leaders, they share the normal inadequacies of other humans. These include leanings toward self- rather than community interests as well as a limited capacity to absorb and act upon the seas of information that they are exposed to. At the same time we should question the general feeling that, if government does not attract "excellence," then the private sector does. The ongoing record of business failures, errors and malfeasance fails to support this conclusion.

It is probable that many bureaucratic mishaps occur because the times require increasingly complex economic and government services. Modern society has fallen into the grips of intricate, intertwined systems that rational design, responsible management and decentralization efforts can never totally master. A seminal thought is found in the work of Charles Perrow regarding the "normal accidents" that are predictable in complex technological and social arrangements.[1] To parallel his line of reasoning, administrative systems failures are usually corrected by tighter procedures and more complex interactions. However, these adjustments often create unforeseen conditions that result in unpredictable breakdowns. It seems logical then, since upgrading skills and intense redesign efforts do not preclude systemic mishaps, that many errors may be caught and corrected through unorthodox subordinate initiatives before they become overwhelming predicaments. The drive to make things right should be powered by strong ethical concerns. Unfortunately, the motivation for insiders to become seriously involved in protecting the public interest is far from assured.

PASSIVE PROFESSIONALS

Cynicism and disillusionment are common among government agency employees but rarely adequately accounted for by empirical research. One reason is that job satisfaction surveys, for a variety of reasons, are not designed to tap the complex dimensions of the phenomenon. Another is that we too readily accept disaffection as an inevitable and natural outcome of working within government bureaucratic environments.

In my discussions with practitioners, a major source of frustration is the sense of powerlessness to bring about necessary improvements in agency performance. When asked to elaborate, professionals focus upon the covert machinations of "politics," the lack of attention by higher-ups to agency operations and the "irrational" nature of government bureaucracy. In their eyes public agencies do not compare well to business enterprises and they envy what appears to be the freedom of action of those in the private sector. While displeased with the unfairness of the generally negative citizen perceptions of government employees, they express feelings paralleling the public anger at bureaucratic waste and ineffectiveness. Many have firsthand knowledge of agency failures, at times more serious than those ordinarily made public.

There is a curious ambivalence toward top policymakers. Professionals identify with popular management values but are frequently troubled by the quality of line supervisory skills and the lack of upper-level attention given to agency performance improvement. For such reasons they feel that making progress in preventing the misuse of resources and improving the quality of services within a political environment is indeed dubious. It is possible that contemporary movements such as the Total Quality Management and "reinventing government" programs will alleviate some of these concerns, but, as will be discussed, these do not get to the roots of error and passivity.

Managers at higher agency levels try to act like and often show admiration for their counterparts in the private sector, but matters concerning agency operational effectiveness are regularly overshadowed by other priorities. Most will accept the notion that innovative improvement action, especially in a political environment, involves tension and conflict. Yet there is little curiosity as to what are constructive levels of and innovative channels for tension within their organizations. In practice resistance to the status quo on the part of subordinate professionals is quietly and tightly regulated. Executives tend to value muted contention around means, not ends, so it is not considered appropriate to question higher-level goals, priorities or behavior. Strongly enforced norms regulate the expression of disagreement. The first stipulates that, no matter how hard the infighting, agency members must present a unified, "all is well" front to the outside world. Powerful norms make it strictly out of bounds for subordinates to overtly challenge the actions or motives of others in the agency. Behaviors counter to these rules of the game are traditionally seen as simply unprofessional, as stemming from a lack of emotional control. The erroneous assumption is that "real" professionals should never become engaged in subjective judgments; rather they must confine themselves to the "facts" so as to act as neutral sources of competence within their scope of responsibility.

INADEQUATE APPLIED THEORY

My concern over theories as useful guides for action rose as I became involved in research directed at increasing government productivity. The usual approach is to rely upon "generic" organizational initiatives that involve changes in process, structure, technology, employee motivation and controls. Scientific methodology directs the collection and interpretation of facts around a basic input-throughput-output model. At the same time, while the volume of organizational research and literature has exploded over the past thirty years, much of this has been at the expense of practitioner involvement and comprehension.

The premise that organizations share common attributes in the private and public sectors has been a mainstay of public management over the years; but

Values

beliefs

this is insufficient when it comes to improving public agency effectiveness. While organization theory is primarily derived from business economic institutions, government organizations are part of political institutions, so they operate under markedly different sets of rules and values regarding their purpose and relationships toward society than do those in the private sector. Therefore the intrinsic meaning of organizational effectiveness differs. If business and economic concepts do not suffice, it should be possible to derive a solid applied theory from political institutional premises, but there is a long and unsuccessful history of attempts to tie in political with administration philosophy. The key, according to most, in relating government agencies to their political context is to create a viable theory of democratic administration,[2] but in so doing most theorists make gross assumptions about the nature of bureaucracies. Since there is a tendency to pin all hopes for significant change upon improving the ability of higher management to inspire and engineer progress, the potential for subordinates to generate significant reforms receives scant attention.

Such inadequacies help to explain why major theories and prescriptions in the literature fail to capture the imagination of the more seasoned agency professionals. Practitioners reason that textbook organizational learning is perhaps fine for business, but people in government face unique conditions and constraints that do not predict success. To better understand these reservations our graduate students examined actual needs for improvement with professionals at middle and lower agency levels so as to design resolutions at the work site. These projects, which will be examined later, provided useful information regarding the dilemmas of initiating action from lower professional levels.

It seems that top policymakers and most professionals are locked into a web of unrealistic expectations and perceptions. The former expect compliance alongside subordinate candor without the necessary costs of tension and conflict. Professionals want to be influential without taking the risks of moving out of safely defined specializations or dealing with essential political institutional ambiguities. Both appear to lack the guiding theory and action alternatives to work out of the snare. The impasse takes its toll not only in terms of agency effectiveness. It also strikes at feelings of self-worth with especially detrimental effects upon the majority of professionals who do not generate high-level policy. They see themselves as unable to respond to challenges, frustrated at attempts to initiate action and dependent upon seemingly irrational forces. They feel trapped by an oppressive bureaucratic "political" system. Too often the choices are either to leave the public service or to withdraw into the safety of isolated routines and the temporary relief of cynicism and apathy. For many of those who remain, this leads to serious discontent with the purpose and meaning of their professional careers. As a result, badly needed creativity and commitment are lost that could have been directed toward the public good.

It is time to question some common beliefs that guide applied theory, such as the assumption that all professionals should be considered as naturally on the same team as those at the top of the hierarchy. In reality there are significant differences in interest that create stresses essential to change. For instance, because of their strategic location and knowledge, lower-level professionals will at some times be most capable of initiating sizable improvements; they will at other times have a clearer sense of social need and accountability than will their agency superiors. To put abilities of this sort to use from within the agency often calls into question existing agency priorities and engenders struggles for temporary relocation of power. The energy generated by such turbulence can be used to affirm and improve political institutions or it can remain, as at present, a corrosive, muted force often inimical to the public interest and to large numbers of professional careers.

A WEAK SENSE OF INDIVIDUAL INTERNAL RESPONSIBILITY

Lasting, effective government institutions depend upon the ethical exercise of power. Laws serve to persuade, compensate or even coerce citizens to act in the common interests. They also establish the legitimacy of agency operations under a network of substantive and procedural mandates.[3] Therefore emphasis is put upon external responsibilities for professional behavior such as neutral competence in an area of expertise, maintaining smooth operations, deferring to executive/legislative authority and following due process in the resolution of disputes. At the same time relatively little attention is given to the internal, often conflictual, moral responsibilities that professionals are expected to abide by. These include (a) serving the best interests of the public, (b) improving overall agency effectiveness, (c) enhancing the proper role and function of government, (d) judging when to comply with or resist directives and (e) protecting critical social and group values.[4]

One possible reason for the lack of sustained attention to matters of internal responsibilities is that tangible rewards like salaries and promotion are connected mostly with external responsibilities. Since these usually are of most immediate interest, concerns over personal, internal ethical responsibilities at subordinate levels may seem only to muddle the external, "objective," highly rationalized administrative world. Another possible reason for the lack of focus upon internal responsibilities could be that it is assumed that matters of commitment toward the public interest and personal ethics are just matters of plain decency, impossible to articulate because individuals vary in what they value. Finally, there is a tendency to avoid internal motivation in management training except when these energies can be harnessed to control subordinate behavior.

As a result most professionals, having been conditioned to divorce external realities from internal values, tend to leave matters of organizational morality to those in charge. While specialized professional training may incorporate some values regarding what is ethical, the more democratic aspects of personal responsibility receive scant attention. When it becomes all too easy to put aside complex matters of right and wrong, professionals then feel free to put their efforts into activities that have a tangible payoff in terms of pay and status. However, the longer-run costs build up as professional careers lose their deeper meaning, as action at the workplace becomes separated from life's larger purpose and as agency effectiveness goes into decline. To begin to grapple with these consequences of passivity and inadequate theory, better ways must be found for subordinates to take principled action, action sustained by a strong, shared sense of internal responsibility.

THE IDEA OF PUBLIC AGENCY DEMOCRACY

Consider the nature of theories directed toward social action. These are inventions that attempt to explain phenomena; some are better than others, but they are essential to define desirable behavior and predict its consequences.[5] Theory as a guide for action should view desirable practice as an ethical, community-directed effort aimed at satisfying the deeper individual needs of those involved. This is why subjective meanings, feelings of personal responsibility and the initiation of action will be emphasized in this book.[6] By now some general concepts and terms associated with an applied theory of public agency democracy should be of interest. Elaborations will be made in subsequent chapters, but for the time being an overview of the theory will serve to guide the way.

To begin, consider the nature of democratic, person-to-person behavior found in daily life. What distinguishes desirable democratic relationships between the masses of American citizens and those in government positions? Successful relationships depend upon the ability to mediate a delicate interplay between harmony and contention. Harmonious, law-abiding behavior assures social predictability and stability. Yet contention, so often the leading edge of citizen-inspired social change, serves as a moderating influence upon elected and appointed holders of political power. These two major forces, in continuous motion, define an underlying process of cooperation with as well as responsible opposition to government control.

Power, vested in formal positions of government authority, is required so that policymakers and implementors of these policies can guide the majority. Citizens rather reluctantly accept the fact that important aspects of their lives must be influenced by government functionaries responsible for the community good, but one of the conditions is that ways must exist to insure a measure of citizen power over choosing leaders and generating broad social goals. Consequently —and this is of major importance—citizens have to be able to demonstrate ambivalent feelings toward policymakers and take appropriate action to minimize dangers of errors in judgment, corrupt practices and oppression.

These desirable aspects of political authority relationships with citizens stem from the fact that policymakers may at times act against or fail to act in the interests of those they are elected or appointed to represent. It is then that these officials must be redirected or opposed. So there is a necessary association between citizen compliance toward and opposition to authority.[7] These paradoxical relationships are essential to the survival and betterment of democratic political institutions in the United States. Contention and opposition are held in high regard, alongside order and consensus. This critical balance between appropriate harmony and appropriate resistance provides social stability while ensuring the ability to engage in the disruption and turmoil of required change.

It is also of major importance that the impetus for change is commonly undertaken by responsible, informed people quite remote from individuals in high policy-making positions; ordinary citizens who must and do take the lead in tempering and altering the behavior of the powerful few. In other words the survival of political democracy is based upon tentative trust by the public in those who occupy high leadership positions, as opposed to unquestioned acceptance and conformity. Feelings of loyalty toward political officials are contingent upon the performance of these leaders.

Turning now to government administration, the main question regarding the visualization of agency democracy is this: Can and should the general citizen behaviors described above be replicated in some appropriate manner within agencies? The basis for order and consensus within public agencies depends upon networks of role-directed responsibilities and behavior. Agency members must operate according to rules and established expectations the great majority of the time. While the forms and patterns of organization may differ, there is an inescapable requirement for structured, hierarchical relationships since this kind of order is frequently essential for (a) the efficient use of resources, (b) the implementation of policy along with appropriate designation of responsibility and accountability and (c) assurance of fair, impartial treatment of citizens and government employees. Therefore agency employees are logically expected to follow instructions, demands and suggestions from on high. In other words professionals must normally direct their energies toward performing their established roles in order to ensure the predictability and effectiveness of government operations. Trust as well as loyalty on the part of subordinates is required toward those who command. Yet in a democratic society an obsession with harmony can smother the creative potential that comes with the necessary questioning of that order.

Under what conditions is contention appropriate and desirable? In principle it is only required when existing agency behaviors and policies are clearly not fulfilling their purpose in political institutions. For example, agency actions that are seriously adverse to the public good must be corrected; functionaries behaving in unlawful ways have to be brought to account; massive waste of resources must be curtailed. Employees within agencies are often the first to know of and frequently the most capable of understanding the reasons for such failures. Preferably corrective action will be taken by acting within the formal or informal confines of one's role. However at crucial times reformers must by necessity act out of role in unusual ways. They should then be able to choose between two identities; one will be called "proactive citizen professional" the other "reactive agency professional." Reactive professionals respond in customarily conforming ways consistent with hierarchical and procedural bureaucratic demands. Proactive professionals initiate important changes and reforms that involve taking actions beyond their formal role responsibilities.

The underlying rationale behind public agency democracy is that any complex system requires constant internal corrections to adapt to new circumstances and cope with its inherent weaknesses. Reactive corrections involve customary changes to established goals, structure, procedures and motivations. Proactive corrections tend to question or work around normal administrative systems through actions that are less constrained by, less consistent with, formal roles. The first kind of corrections are in-role initiatives, the second out-of-role initiatives. Within these categories several alternative paths of action exist. More detailed elaborations are found in chapter 4 along with an in-between category called borderline-role initiatives.

The most essential requirement for proactive behavior is that it must be in accord with "regime values" dedicated to maintaining fundamental, constitutional political order.[8] When these lawful procedures, values and ethics are paramount, logical and essential attitudes toward agency authority on the part of subordinates follow. It follows that loyalty toward any given hierarchical order, its goals and means is contingent upon the subordinate's careful assessment of a given agency's effectiveness in serving the public interest and what is being done to correct major shortcomings. Therefore trust in agency leadership is tentative, depending upon its perceived ability to respond to needs for change. While these attitudes toward authority are at the root of all democratic behavior, they create paradoxical tensions as well as hazards which need to be understood by and adjusted to by many actors within and surrounding government agencies.

THE PLAN FOR THE BOOK

There are many reasons why most professionals enter their government agency careers with an inadequate understanding of public administration as a field of endeavor. The specialized education of some (e.g., engineers and scientists) has not touched upon the unique nature of bureaucracies in political institutions. Others have but a primitive view of organization design and behavior. For instance, those in special governmental professions (e.g., social welfare and criminal justice) may acquire tightly focused perspectives that do not readily lend themselves to more general governmental agency philosophical and ethical considerations. Even the small number with degrees in the field of public administration are prone to reflect less upon the deeper aspects of their chosen careers as they become involved with specific agencies and the immediacy of specialized tasks. Consequently it is not easy for professionals from one government field to identify with professionals in other fields experiencing similar frustrations. It will also be argued that educational and other cultural forces have joined to create romantic notions about the supremacy of rational techniques and the promise of higher management leadership. These, in turn, produce an impatience with the complexity of public agency relationships, especially the necessity to cope with ambiguous events and feelings.

Given these diverse professional backgrounds, it is first essential to cover some common terrain so as to establish a footing to go on to the detailed workings of agency democracy. Chapter 2 defines the characteristics of principal actors such as "intermediary professionals" and "policy elites." It shows how the vast majority of professionals in the public service act as intermediaries, as mediators between the desires of top policymakers (policy elites) and those who turn these policies into reality. A discussion of various movements, along with their values and attitudes, will serve to better understand the problems of and potential for professionals to act as agents of reform. Chapter 3 examines public administration as a field of endeavor, a field fraught with long-standing dilemmas. Many of these remain unresolved to this day because of the difficulties of dealing with democratic action at the agency workplace. These discussions of professionalism and public administration serve to better understand the operational model of public agency democracy developed in chapter 4. A wide range of democratic behaviors is defined in detail. Aimed at "hands-on" matters, the applied theory associates agency reactive with citizen proactive endeavors.

Together, the first four chapters introduce concepts essential to encouraging responsible citizen initiatives from within agency walls. At first glance, the model of public agency democracy could appear logical, even conservative in nature; but the thrust is not in accord with established administrative beliefs and practices. These deeply ingrained convictions make it difficult to envision democratic change action in parallel with the ongoing necessity to fulfill regular, in-role responsibilities. It will present a challenge for most readers to give serious thought to such paradoxical relationships in view of their past experiences. Therefore the next three chapters are devoted toward better understanding various aspects of common administrative mindsets which inhibit constructive reform on the part of insiders.

Chapter 5 shows how the visualization of organizational effectiveness has become so closely integrated with economic institutional values and why this bias falls short of meeting needs of those in government. Discussions of public sector productivity help to illustrate the issues. Chapter 6 addresses common theories of organization and management which are at the heart of administrative practice. The traditional emphasis upon business applications does not permit a full understanding of change in the public sector. Significant weaknesses stem from management beliefs which are based upon military metaphors. Chapter 7 discusses aspects of proactive subordinate motivation which tend to run counter to management desires to shape and control motivation. This second part of the book concerning effectiveness, organization theory, management beliefs and motivation should be of special interest because it clarifies why it is necessary to grapple with the paradoxes that require the exercise of public agency democracy.

Having proposed various alternative democratic behaviors and explored some common inhibitions to action, it is time to examine specific aspects of various proactive initiatives. Chapter 8 reviews a study that helps to clarify the workings of borderline-role initiatives aimed at resolving agency predicaments. Chapter 9 discusses various practical issues associated with out-of-role activities such as processes of resolution and sustaining motivations to initiate reform. The last two chapters focus upon some benefits and problems of public agency democracy in order to better understand the realities of implementation. Chapter 10 proposes ways for professionals to increase their proactive potential and become less dependent upon unrealistic expectations regarding technical rationality and leadership perfection. This new identity will, over time, require shifts in educational, associational, hierarchical and other professional influences. The final chapter considers professionals as part of a network of influential actors, all affected by efforts to turn public agency democracy into reality. A "stakeholder" approach suggests revisions in outlook and behavior so as to better integrate proactive considerations into daily activities with its beneficial effects.

A persistent theme in this book is that government agency policies will become more effective and resources more wisely used as subordinates become more influential. Many difficulties exist today because of the nature of democratic political institutions and ingrained management inhibitions to react positively to reform initiatives. The applied theory of public agency democracy provides a systematic way to analyze appropriate behaviors. Resolutions are possible, but these entail significant shifts in orthodox administrative and professional beliefs. Some will question the need to become concerned with the realignment of agency power relationships at a time when so many other priorities confront government. Involvement in these matters could seem risky because of the potential for disruption and confusion. It may even be argued that when issues of agency authority remain somewhat murky and unexamined, this permits flexibility, it enables everyone to get on with their job rather than becoming bogged down. More direct paths of action could appear to have higher priority such as improving the design of operational systems, devising new organizational structures, generating clearer mission statements and developing more highly trained, more competent employees.

Without denying many other needs, consider the thrust of two contemporary movements which have been enthusiastically accepted by public management practitioners. Modern information technology and Total Quality Management (TQM) proponents call for more rapid, effective response to "customer" needs, empowerment of employees, more subordinate creativity along with greater independence of work groups. Managers are urged to change their traditional ways, to develop two-way communications and rely less upon coercive relationships.[9] It is recognized that such improvements call for a fundamental shift in the exercise of authority, yet little has been done to think through the real implications of these calls for action. Insufficient attention has been given to the ways that hierarchical and subordinate actors are conditioned to resist change. Fundamental operational differences between public and private sector organizations are not clear. Few concrete proposals have been made to bring about lasting revisions in government management cultures. What follows is directly concerned with overcoming these difficulties. Resolutions, however, are not self-evident, and a good deal of ground must be covered in order to support the specific recommendations that appear in the last chapters of this book.

The topic of this book has a long history in the field of public administration: It was put in the form of opposing arguments almost fifty years ago in a classical debate between Carl Frederich and Herman Finer.[10] Should a sense of subjective, or personal accountability or a sense of objective, or rule-directed accountability guide the behavior of administrative officials? Frederich's argument in favor of subjective accountability was that administrators will at times, because of their technical and situational knowledge, have a deeper understanding of the public interest than will others; therefore, they must initiate political action. Finer's response was that objective accountability is the only path to follow since those within agencies are obliged to be subservient to the popular will as expressed by the mandates of political officials and agency executives.

Over time both objective and subjective accountability have been vindicated. They persist in uneasy association, though the tendency is to downplay the importance of the latter in favor of an administrative myth striving for pure, objective accountability. Two fundamental revisions to orthodox practitioner perceptions will be proposed. The first raises subjective agency accountability to a formal level of visibility by providing an applied theoretical rationale. Then the realm of public administration discourse is extended well beyond conventional management philosophical domains so as to recognize employees as legitimate, proactive actors, citizens with a powerful commitment to the values and actions essential to democratic political institutions.

NOTES

1. Charles Perrow, *Normal Accidents* (New York: Basic Books, 1984), chapter 1.
2. Robert B. Denhardt, *Theories of Public Organization* (Monterey, CA: Brooks/Cole, 1984), pp. 186-87.

3. Alan W. Lerner and John Wanat, *Public Administration* (Englewood Cliffs, NJ: Prentice-Hall, 1991), pp. 219-27.

4 Phillip J. Cooper, *Public Law and Public Administration* (Englewood Cliffs, NJ: Prentice Hall, 1988), pp. 355-63.

5. See Daniel Robey, *Designing Organizations* (Homewood, IL: Irwin, 1982), pp. 40-44. Robey, in addition to invention/discovery differences, also makes the distinction between "pure" and "practical" theory whereby the latter injects an ethical component.

6. Michael Harmon, *Action Theory for Public Administration* (New York: Longman, 1981), chapter 1.

7. Peter M. Blau, *Exchange and Power in Social Life* (New York: Wiley, 1964), pp. 313-38. Blau uses the terms dominance and opposition.

8. John A. Rohr, *Ethics for Bureaucrats* (New York: Marcel Dekker, 1978), pp. 2, 59-61.

9. See John Tapscott and Art Caston, *Paradigm Shift* (New York: McGraw Hill, 1993). Part 1 discusses the premises of information technology and needed changes in administrative orientations. Total Quality Management will be discussed in more detail in subsequent chapters.

10. Herman Finer, "Administrative Responsibility in Democratic Government," *Public Administration Review*, vol. 1, no. 4 (1941): 335-50. Carl J. Frederich, "The Nature of Administrative Responsibility," *Public Policy* (1940): 3-24. Both articles are reprinted in Peter Woll, ed., *Public Administration and Policy* (New York: Harper Torchbooks, 1966).

Chapter 2

The Silent Intermediaries

For better or worse—or better and worse—much of our government is in the hands of professionals.

Frederick Mosher

The general theory of public agency democracy is based upon the assumption that subordinate professionals have a major, logical potential to press for some changes traditionally seen as the responsibility of upper management. This goes counter to the belief that the specialized knowledge of professionals sets firm, immutable limits upon their activities. The assertion that experts should only serve in ways stipulated by their administrative superiors through formal role structures is now open to examination. Who are these professionals? Why is their potential not fully realized?

This chapter reviews various characteristics of the professional movement, along with some aspects of government settings. The nature of professional power and its strategic potential in mediating roles is then considered. Terms that will be used in a more detailed model of agency democracy are defined in more detail. It should then be interesting to examine ways of initiating action which involve coping with management norms of loyalty and harmony. Other issues concerning public administration professional identity are also discussed.

THE PROFESSIONAL MOVEMENT

In order for any bureaucracy to achieve its purposes, it is evident that some internal authority and predictability are necessary. Difficult goals are attained when specialized tasks are performed by highly trained and competent people. Over time these positions, called roles, have become increasingly professional-ized and imbued with the power of knowledge.

Professions are activities normally learned through and enhanced by formal higher education. They are envisioned as occupational fields that frequently serve as lifelong careers. Some educational experiences prepare one to directly assume a professional role (e.g., engineer). Others serve as a basis to acquire the professional role through on-the-job experience (e.g., political science as a foundation for public administration). To qualify formally as a member of a professional group involves recognition by other professionals and/or by a recognized accreditation body. Today's professions, more in some cases and less in others, incorporate ethics of service which are intended to take precedence over self-interest. Beyond such generalizations, defining the nature of professionalism has been subject to a good deal of controversy. Some reasons are to be found in the historical development of various specializations.

Before the rise of modern professionalism, the "learned" or classic professions (e.g., law, medicine, clergy) had their roots in medieval universities and the church. There then was a rapid evolution propelled by the scientific, technological and organizational revolutions of the nineteenth and twentieth centuries. Increasing numbers of experts were needed to bring about economic changes essential to goods and services production. These new professions developed a market among the general public by helping to resolve needs which required the mastery of (a) technologies of energy production and information processing, (b) methodologies of empiricism, experimentation and theory construction and (c) changing time perspectives from the past toward adapting to the present and the future.[1] Professions continued to be self-regulating as scientific values replaced those of the older moral order.[2] Along with the acceleration of technological and social change, the variety and intensity of specialization of professions continues to increase.

It is uphill work to define the common characteristics of all professions. There are, for example, sharp differences between professional tasks that intrude into the private world of others and those that facilitate technical control of bureaucratic endeavors. On the one hand, physicians, lawyers and members of the clergy require a high degree of client confidence because the relationship involves intimate knowledge about their private lives. This is paralleled by reasonably explicit ethical values, large status differences in client-professional relationships and a reliance upon client feelings of trust. On the other hand, professionals employed by bureaucracies, such as program administrators, engineers, and accountants, are in a management-employer contractual relationship that normally calls for proof of technical competence rather than individual blind confidence.[3] Consequently ethical stances and expectations meant to govern the exercise of self-interest on the part of professionals in bureaucracies are usually not a major focus of attention. The reason could be that unethical conduct in bureaucracies is considered more controllable and less damaging than in relationships requiring intense personal trust on the part of the client.

Increases in scientific and technological knowledge during the twentieth century have been accompanied by a proliferation of professional titles and roles.

Along with the steady movement toward greater professionalization of work, debates have cropped up over the nature of a "true profession." Some, for instance, see teachers, nurses and social workers as "semiprofessionals" since their tasks involve less training time, legitimate status and autonomy from supervision than do those of the "full" professions.[4] Such distinctions aside, the advent of modern professionalism has received mixed reactions. Talcott Parsons once wrote that the professional complex has begun to make obsolete "the primacy of old issues of political authoritarianism and capitalistic exploitation." His reasoning was that competence through scientific formal education and skills in problem solution would include powerful ethical orientations advocating social responsibility. Therefore, professionals would become a major and increasingly benign influence upon society.[5] Others, expressing a more contemporary, less sanguine view, do not agree. Most professions, for instance, have had little trouble supporting repressive political regimes which were based upon the undemocratic use of power.[6] Parsons' emphasis was upon functionalism, wherein members of individual professions are seen as sharing a cohesive identity through common values, roles and interests; but systematic studies of work activities, methodology, collegial associations and power relationships show that modern professions are segmented and in conflict. Therefore internal discord and hierarchical struggles within and between professions are reported.[7]

Given the shifting nature of professionalism, how will it be defined in this book? A highly flexible interpretation will be used whereby a "professional" is an agency employee who (a) has completed four years or more of higher education, or its equivalent, (b) acquires the requisite skills for and commitment to an area of expertise and (c) identifies formally or informally with a national association of specialists (e.g., the International City Management Association). Some professionals are seen as qualified to do a particular type of work because they have passed formal education requirements; others also have to pass standardized examinations as evidence of competence (e.g., attorney bar examination and architect licensing). While most require a higher education degree as an entrance prerequisite for a particular position, it stands to reason that a small number will qualify as professionals as they learn a specialization through work experience and less conventional ways (e.g., workshops and self-directed studies). The category of "manager" comes to mind since individuals are commonly promoted into this specialization and many improve their skills through additional education while on the job.

[handwritten margin note: a definition of professional]

GOVERNMENT PROFESSIONALS

In his influential book *Democracy and the Public Service*, Frederick Mosher devotes a chapter to what he calls "The Professional State."[8] The author explains why governments and the professions are interdependent. While governments regulate and subsidize some professions, they are a prime source of employment as well. The professions provide skilled people, specify the content of specializations, determine employment criteria and influence policy. His basic definition of a professional also includes a higher education requirement, "at least through the bachelor's level."

Mosher observes that many categories of professions have their origins within government, for example, city manager, environmental analyst, public works engineer, social welfare counselor and foreign service officer. People in these and other more general areas of expertise, trained in colleges and universities, dominate the generation of policy and the running of programs in areas such as health, urban renewal, welfare and transportation by:

- being elected and appointed to high political and judicial office
- monopolizing key administrative positions
- controlling other levels of government than their own through the allocation of grants (e.g., federal categorical grants-in-aid to cities)
- influencing the decisions of political executives and legislators

In this manner society has been undergoing a fundamental change wherein the boundaries between the responsibilities of government and those of the leading professions are becoming increasingly blurred. These developments are worrisome because, since the professions determine the nature of specializations and regulate qualification standards for entry, control of basic personnel policies is moving out of the orbit of government. The civil service system is based upon ideals of neutral direction, competitive merit and equality of opportunity, but government is turning over its personnel policies to biased outside professional interests which favor curtailment of competition and restrictive selection. It is this propensity toward self-regulation in the professions and the potential to capture political power that could put democratic open government at risk.

Mosher is also apprehensive about the inadequate moral grounding provided in the education and socialization of professionals, given their profound influence upon society. Scientific values, rigid attitudes toward clients and limited service philosophies prevail with minimal attention given to broader ethical issues, especially those involving public dedication and citizen responsibility. The quandary is that major hopes for democracy must rest with the education system; yet most professional schools appear unprepared to actively reinforce democratic values.

Today these generalizations are tempered by the fact that there exists today a great variety of professions, some more, others less open to charges of amorality. Agencies vary in their vulnerability to dominance by professional groups. Mounting popular concern with general ethical issues during the 1980s and 1990s could be having a beneficial impact upon the training of larger numbers of these specialists. It is also possible that the growth, fragmentation and subdivision of interests within major professions has mitigated their undesired influence upon government. Yet Mosher made penetrating observations regarding the tendencies toward isolation, self-preoccupation and inadequate ethical grounding of professionals which remain valid today.

How many professionals are there in government? Given the definitional problems and the nature of available data, only rough approximations are possible. To put the matter in perspective, it is interesting to consider why the total number of government employees has grown more than two and one-half times since 1955. Some plausible reasons are (a) total population growth and its greater complexities, (b) the popular demand for new services and (c) increased necessity for public services which support private sector needs. Table 2-1 shows that state and local government have more than tripled over a thirty-eight-year period.[9] Federal civilian employment increased less than 40 percent over the same time span and began to taper off during the 1980s; 1995 levels are expected to be less than those of 1994.

In September of 1994, 6.3 million at local levels and 1.8 million at state levels were employed in education occupations alone.[10] They represent about 50 percent of the combined populations of state and local government.

The composition of the national workforce in terms of occupations has changed rapidly with respect to educational background. By 1992, more than 26 percent of the entire civilian workforce had at least a four-year college education compared to 14 percent in 1970.[11] In 1994 executive, administrative and managerial ranks employed 13.5 percent, while "professional" specializations came to 14.2 percent of the 123.8 million total employed.[12]

It is a complicated, convoluted exercise to derive an approximation of the number of professionals employed in government agencies. Some years ago, the director of the U.S. Census Bureau, after excluding functions found in the private sector (e.g., education and health) projected a total of 5.95 million government employees for 1990. Of this total 21 percent fall into professional specializations (e.g., engineer, computer specialist, accountant, lawyer) while 11 percent are managers and administrators.[13] He noted that, compared to national employment, professionals have a 50 percent higher representation in government. Other sources show that 1.3 million were hired for federal, state and local hospital services.[14] This raises the total of government employees (excluding educators) to about 7.3 million, of which 32 percent or 2.4 million fall into the public administration professional category.

Another way to arrive at the total of professionals in civilian government is to subtract the 8.1 million employed in education from the total employed by government. This yields about 11 million which, multiplied by the 27.7 percent of professionals and managerial people in the national workforce, results in a rough total of 3.0 million. There is then a spread between the two figures which appears to be accounted for by different component populations and times that the studies were made. Since it is not necessary to arrive at a precise number, it seems reasonable to average the two numbers and conclude that about 2.75 mil-

Table 2-1
Civilian Government Employees
(In millions, numbers rounded)

	FEDERAL	STATE	LOCAL	TOTAL IN GOVERNMENT
1955	2.2	1.2	3.6	7.0
1960	2.3	1.5	4.6	8.4
1965	2.4	2.0	5.7	10.1
1970	2.7	2.7	7.2	12.6
1975	2.8	3.2	8.8	14.8
1980	2.9	3.6	9.8	16.3
1985	2.9	3.8	9.7	16.4
1990	3.1	4.3	11.0	18.4
1994 (Sept)	2.9	4.6	11.7	19.2

lion government agency employees fall under "professional" designations as defined in the previous section.

What proportion of government professionals enter into the workforce with competence in public affairs and government? Again, only very rough estimates can be made. The data in table 2-2 are of interest because they show significant shifts in proportions of specializations that have had deep effects upon public service professional employment.[15] Most of those with an educational background in government are found in social science (political science) and public affairs ranks. Note how the business majors have more than doubled as social science ranks dropped by well over 20 percent. While public affairs degrees have more than doubled over the sixteen-year period, they still represent less than 3 percent of the total degrees conferred.

Since government must draw upon available skills, it is evident that great numbers of highly educated people enter the public service with minimal knowledge of political institutions, processes and ethics. There are then two predictable consequences: (1) most employee socialization about and knowledge of government will be gained on the job and narrowly related to a particular agency and professionally specialized role, and (2) whatever concepts new employees have regarding administrative processes and purposes will be heavily based upon the needs and values of the private sector. We will return to these realities later since they contribute to important aspects of the public agency democracy and professional citizen predicament.

Other noteworthy aspects of the constantly changing national workforce which still prevail today were already evident in the 1980s:[16]

Table 2-2
Higher Education Degrees Conferred Nationally by Selected Specialization
(in thousands, rounded)

	1971	1991
Total Bachelor and Master's Degrees Conferred	1,070	1,432
Business and management	141	329
Social sciences	172	137
Engineering	67	94
Public affairs (includes public administration)	14	35

- Over 20 percent of craft workers and 10 percent of blue-collar workers have at least four years of college.
- College graduates show increasing concerns with the quality of their worklife— over 50 percent feel underutilized.
- Professionals and white-collar workers identify less with management than in the past. They are more conscious of their rights concerning matters of dignity, respect and discrimination.
- Unions are on the decline nationally but continue as a powerful influence in the public sector.
- The average age of the workforce will rise, with larger shares of women, minorities and immigrants.

A more recent assessment of the new American workplace notes the (a) continued shift to a service economy, (b) needs for general upgrading of skills, (c) movement toward project teams with less hierarchical management authority, (d) presence of a growing multicultural workforce and (e) increasing single-parent and greater numbers of husband-wife earners in the same family.[17]

In the face of these changes, while more educated, younger people will change the nature of government workforces, they could encounter fewer opportunities for rapid advancement because of the aging workforce combined with curtailed government growth and technological change. Meanwhile, it is clear that professionals will play an increasingly important role in meeting contemporary challenges to the public service as a good place in which to invest one's future.

PROFESSIONALS AS POWER INTERMEDIARIES

A crude way to visualize power within any large government agency is to think of the organization as some form of a hierarchical triangle. People at the top are high-level administrators and their staffs. Then a larger middle layer of managers and specialists is found; thereafter, a zone of other employees makes up the more heavily populated base of the triangle. Those in the middle layer are, for the most part, professionals because advanced education and special experience are required. Many are found in what have been called the bureaucratic professions (e.g., administration, engineering, accounting, social work). Smaller numbers are in older, more traditional specializations such as law and medicine. The proportion of professionals vis-à-vis other employees keeps growing as more routine jobs are automated and operational complexity increases.

reconciliation function

The middle stratum of professional employees serves a broad reconciliation function between the objectives specified by groups at the organizational apex and the delivery of services. Those within this intermediate zone (a) design, plan and supervise work, (b) coordinate activities internal and external to their particular agency and (c) perform direct, sometimes confidential services for citizens. Typical titles are administrator, manager,[18] supervisor, lawyer, engineer, social worker, accountant, systems analyst and training specialist. As go-betweens they make crucial decisions usually directly geared toward getting specific tasks completed and services delivered. In their agency mediating position professionals are quasi-elites characterized by unusual knowledge qualifications and important operating responsibilities involving access to specialized information. Because they know how to translate policy intent into reality, professionals have a unique potential to initiate action; they are a force that can be turned toward improvement of agency performance as well as, at crucial times, the modification or even redirection of policy decisions. All of this explains why the term *intermediary professional* will be used to identify these individuals throughout this book.

intermediary professional

Individuals at the top of the agency triangle are also professionals. Normally directly subordinate to outside political executives, these executives along with other influential people set broad policy by determining action priorities, issuing directives, starting new programs and allocating resources.   Titles such as commissioner, secretary, director, deputy and chief, along with designations for closely associated line assistants are common for those who head public agencies. Their main function is to implement and interpret policy mandates as well as to suggest, maintain and develop initiatives for political figures such as president, governor, mayor, legislator, judge and board president. Bureaucratic and political high-level decision makers are supported by powerful staff members who plan, monitor information, analyze situations, perform liaison duties and propose new policy. Common titles are counsel, budget director, policy analyst, chief economist and public relations director. The process of arriving at policy decisions is fraught with stresses and ambiguities that will be discussed in the next chapter. For instance, there are often sizable tensions between political appointees to higher agency positions and the more permanent career executives. As an entity, political, bureaucratic and staff people, all engaged in generating and directing major political priorities and action, are low in number compared with those they influence. Since they possess an enormous amount of power and status, all of these highly placed individuals will be called *policy elites* throughout the remaining chapters.

Organizational layers of influence can be better understood by taking advantage of some of the nomenclature developed by Henry Mintzberg. The makeup of organizational structure can be usefully defined by configurations of various types of tasks. A predominant structure found in big government today is the one called *machine bureaucracy*, characterized by high formality, large size, task specialization and centralized authority.[19] A machine bureaucracy rendition of Mintzberg's configuration is shown in figure 2-1.

At the top of each agency is a group called the Strategic Apex (A) linked with various forces in the political environment. They are "managers of managers" who, through a Middle Line (M) managerial component, direct the activities of those in the Operating Core. The operating core consists of people who do the basic work of rendering services. These three components define the line organization since they include the formal flow of authority. In addition two major staff components are found in machine bureaucracies. The technostructure (T) consists of analytical professionals and their clerical support who help develop policy, design workplans and perform training functions. Another component, the Support Staff (S), performs various services to keep the agency going (e.g., public relations, payroll, legal counsel, mailroom).

Consistent with the previous discussion, policy elites occupy positions in the Strategic Apex as well as in the turbulent political environment. Some will also be found in higher Middle Line positions with designations such as assistant, director and deputy. Also at the summit of the staff components, additional policy elites are found whose function is to direct as well as to provide technical and support advisory functions to policy elites.

Intermediary professionals populate the Technostructure, Support Staff, lower Middle Line and Operating Core. Some are required in staff positions; others are first-level line supervisors and managers in the formal line structure. Finally, significant numbers of professionals occupy positions in the operating core as experts rendering direct services (e.g., social workers, foresters, lawyers). The general territory of intermediary professionals is shown by the shaded band. It is a mediating zone because much of the conflict between worker needs, client requirements and policy elite directions occurs and is routinely resolved within this arena.

To perceive professionals as mediators assumes that they attempt to reconcile differences between parties. In order to satisfy this function, professionals require some independence from policy elites as well as others who are potentially in discord with policy elites. Where, then, do professionals look for the authority and standards to perform as mediators? Traditionally, their organizational

Figure 2-1
Professionals as Agency Mediators

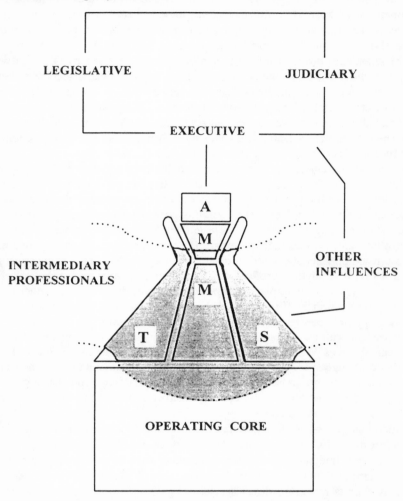

role and specialized skills have been seen as providing the required power and knowledge base. One problem is that the organizational power base of professionals is largely defined by the very policy elites who may want to prevent unconventional, "disruptive" intermediary professional initiatives. Another concern is that professionals are trained to rely upon special categories of facts and objectivity as the basis for decisions, but few matters at the workplace can be dealt with in a detached, value-free manner. This is not just because professionals may disagree among themselves over what directions to take, but it is also evident that public agency decision making rarely takes place in an atmosphere that is conducive to carefully garnered data and scientific objectivity.[20]

Unfortunately most professionals are not trained to act as brokers in these subjective and dynamic political environments. Yet the great bulk of professionally qualified people wind up in mediating roles between policy elites, the operating core, other agencies and the public. In the previous section an estimated total of 2.75 million professionals in government was arrived at. If we assume a rough ratio of one policy elite professional for every twenty other professionals, the total number of intermediary professionals should be around 2.6 million. Given their numerical prominence, why are the predictable tensions and frustrations of intermediary professionals not discussed more openly? Why has so little attention been given to mediating functions and their importance?

Critical question

The presence of a trichotomy of management, other professionals and workers is briefly considered by Frederick Mosher but not pursued since he sees a "mutually supportive relationship" between professional managers and professional employees often dominated by what he calls an "elite" profession. Natural tensions and conflicts between management, workers and professionals are not of major significance in his opinion because of the common objectives of those within bureaucracies and the elite professions. He suggests that the composition of a professionalized government agency can be seen as an interaction between political appointees, staff professionals, members of the elite profession, supporting line professionals, administrative professionals and workers. Each has varying degrees of access to agency top management levels called the "elite of the elite."[21] Following his reasoning, the most important stresses are conflicts (a) between elite agency professionals and appointed officials (who usually also have professional qualifications), (b) between a dominant profession and other professions and (c) between segments within a dominant profession. Principal tensions are thus "horizontal and diagonal rather than vertical." These include struggles over content of the personnel system regarding, for example, entrance requirements, work content and promotion criteria. All of this occurs within a general context of professional aversion and suspicion toward politics and government.

Mosher's thesis of horizontal contention between professional segments differs from the basic premise of this book, which emphasizes intermediary professionals as a category of employees in necessary stress with as well as in requisite harmony with elite policymakers. Mosher concludes that interests between enclaves of top management and other professionals are mutually supportive. This is often the case, but it is more probable that both vertical and horizontal tensions are significant. The ingrained, persistent vertical tensions between elites, mediators and operators are difficult to ignore. There is abundant proof that differences in interest are continuously at play between policymakers and lower-level implementers within the same profession. Social

workers, for example, regularly voice strong public disagreement with their professionally trained superiors over case loads. More importantly, there is the
inescapable evidence provided by the unionization and other work place associations of professionals at intermediary levels. Organizational researchers and
theorists have recognized the presence of vertical conflict for a long time. The
debilitating effect of bureaucratic structure upon employees and their ability to
cope has been of major concern.[22] Some have noted the struggle between the
authority base of managers and the knowledge base of specialists.[23] Others
conclude that rigid hierarchical structures are likely to alienate professionals
when these are seen as constraining action and resulting in impersonal relationships.[24]

So, while horizontal conflicts between specializations, within specializations
and with political appointees are a reality, clearly vertical tensions between policy elites, professionals and workers are also highly significant. Why, then, is
there such little mention of this phenomenon? Hierarchical structure with its
narrowly defined roles, numerous rules and regulations helps repress signs of
contention, but the least discussed and arguably the most convincing reason is
the extremely high priority put upon unconditional loyalty toward those at upper
levels.

NORMS OF LOYALTY AND HARMONY

A predominant and constant concern of political power holders is allegiance
to their leadership. Incumbent executives, along with those in legislative bodies,
have to get visible results over short periods in order to stay in control. At the
same time it is necessary to ward off attacks by the opposition. Consequently,
political leaders prize loyalty in their associations with other policy elites. A
joint commitment to specific outcomes calls for exchanges of public esteem and
material advantages, all dependent upon mutual trust. These systems of reci-
procity are extremely complex and frequently implicit, so the notion of
"loyalty" within agencies has an air of mystery. Clearly, however, the objective of high-level power holders is to create predictability at subordinate levels
by promoting compliance, if not heartfelt cooperation, at critical times.

Requirements for loyalty extend to and through public agencies because these
implement and maintain political directives. The outward behavior of agency
members has a direct impact upon citizens in that it affects public perceptions
and attitudes toward policy elite political programs and purposes. Managers at
upper agency ranks are politically appointed not only to make certain that public
administrators respond to executive direction, but also to ensure smooth and
harmonious appearances of agency operations. Agency policy elites who have
worked up the ladder as civil service careerists have powerful incentives to re-
frain from visible contention with appointees above them. There is not only a

tradition of loyalty to superiors, but being responsive to their direction is a highly esteemed quality.

Consistent with the demands for leadership, communications and cooperative exchanges within work organizations, policy elites interact with intermediary professionals in order to develop policy. This is because their subordinates' skill and advice are essential in order to predict implementation difficulties and to flesh out procedural details. At other times professionals are in a position to propose new approaches in order to resolve agency difficulties. Such upward influence does not normally occur without adjustments involving stress, dissent and occasional confrontation; but strong pressures exist to keep these differences within agency walls, for the power base of agency and political policy elites is reduced when discord is made visible. This containment is seen by policy elites as essential since to air questions, doubts and uncertainties cannot only result in confusion and loss of public credibility; it also provides ammunition for the political opposition. For such reasons, when intermediary professionals question the need, morality or even the legality of a directive, it is more often than not a lonely and risky endeavor. To go the next step by engaging in public dissension compounds the danger because this violates norms of harmony, loyalty and conventional professional conduct, all seen as essential to the maintenance of policy elite power, as synonymous to what is right and proper in organizations. Professional traditions of confidentiality and deference toward their employers also contribute toward the silence of intermediary professionals. When policy elites are considered to be the client/employer, then an "us versus them" mentality evolves. "Them" are all others except other relevant professionals and the client; consequently, agency workers, the media and other citizens are routinely excluded from necessary inside knowledge.

The twin needs for secrecy and compliance carry strong sanctions against what is perceived as disruptive dissent. Despite government merit systems based upon civil service examinations and qualifications, promotions to executive and higher staff ranks are eventually dependent upon subjective evaluations by policy elites already in place. There are compelling reasons for the latter to want to keep any evidence of waste, corruption or mismanagement within agency walls until, if ever, action can quietly be taken. Conforming to these norms of discretion and silence is an important measure of how well candidates for higher posts fit into networks of managerial authority. At the same time, the policy elite capacity for retaliation against public dissent on the part of individual agency members is impressive. For this reason, repeated attempts have been made to provide legal protection for "whistle-blowers" because dissenters, even those espousing the most worthy causes, court demotion and unchallenging work assignments, if not the loss of their jobs.

The presence of threat and secrecy that surrounds policy elite retaliation is constant and subtle. It prompts employees to be overcautious and conservative in their actions since it is difficult for them to grapple directly with the causes and effects of demands for harmony and loyalty. No records are kept, but negative feelings toward dissenters become fixed in the memories of policy elites, who are regularly in quiet and informal consultation. Within this environment of confidentiality and veiled threat, it should not be surprising that intermediary professionals consider the attitudes of their agency leaders a mystery. When subordinates try to account for unfavorable developments in their careers, the real reasons are often difficult to find; for it is close to impossible to determine whether higher management is retaliating because of past actions that could have violated norms of loyalty and harmony. Since the process of influence is ill defined and informal, it is virtually unthinkable for concerned professionals to engage in frank exchanges with their agency superiors about how such perceptions affect their advancement. Therefore, most subordinates tend to play it safe in the face of the prevalent, if opaque, danger of policy elite sanctions. These dark corners of organizational life are known to all, but rarely brought to light. Rather than accepting stoic silence as the destiny of subordinates, we might wonder if all this secrecy is necessary. In any event the demands for conformity, combined with retaliatory power, reinforce an ideal of organizational harmony wherein the desired outward appearance is one of agreement in feelings, actions and priorities.

A final reason for the mute compliance of intermediary professionals is that ideals of harmony and response to authority remain the bedrock of orthodox management theory and practice. Discord and dissension between policy elites and all other agency employees are seen as aberrations to be overcome by intensified efforts to specify missions, improve human relations and sharpen techniques of motivation, bargaining, compromise. These are accompanied by norms of managerial conduct promoting public attitudes of optimism, fortitude and good cheer. The constant purpose is to make employees' goals more congruent with those of the organizational policy elites, thereby decreasing what are perceived as the disruptive effects of uncertainty and conflict. While varying amounts of tough-minded, confrontive behavior between policy elites and intermediary professionals may be briefly endured behind agency walls, the compulsion is to reduce public differences, to rationalize dissent, and eventually to bring about more harmony. In this manner, public impressions of successful, steady service help maintain an image of agency mastery, control and predictability.

Persistent pressures for loyalty along with cultural and organizational conditioning, combined with the enigmatic nature of retaliation, tend to encourage professional overconformity. A few may accommodate with ease because they prefer authoritarian direction. Others identify heavily with policy elites and obey without reservation. Most, however, though perturbed and ambivalent, keep a low profile because being at the forefront at the wrong time in the wrong place can have unhappy consequences.

While requirements for internal agency loyalty and harmony seem logical, too little attention has been paid to the toll upon intermediary professionals as a group. They become vulnerable to feelings of anxiety regarding their upper-level relationships not only because promotion and recognition are at stake. Many cherish a special sense of purpose beyond material career rewards. This is because they have gone into the public service seeking to be influential in society, not necessarily within the authority structure so closely monitored by agency policy elites. At critical times intermediary professionals will have the knowledge and skills necessary to initiate important changes, but reasonable overtures may be rejected. When there is no individually reaffirming outlet, no general ethic of legitimate resistance to the domination of hierarchical superiors or even getting their attention in quiet ways, then professional talents and energies are dissipated. This is because many become disillusioned and cynical about political institutions and agency work which leads to withdrawal or other aberrant behaviors destructive to individual careers, counter to good government.

There are then powerful reasons why the majority of intermediary professionals has elected to remain silent over a wide variety of issues such as improving operational effectiveness, threats to public safety, dangers to community welfare, agency mismanagement, purchasing scandals and criminal conduct within government. Yet, given their expertise and situational knowledge, great numbers of professionals deep within agencies should have the capacity to influence such adverse events before they get out of hand. Their initial impressions may not always be correct, their diagnoses and prescriptions subject to error, but it should be made easier for intermediaries to explore valid concerns, to become influential in more meaningful ways. Awareness of serious shortcomings in government should be less smothered by the wraps of agency loyalty and harmony, less inhibited by conventional management beliefs. For these reasons it is crucial to understand and remove roadblocks that hinder a more open and constructive approach to proactive behavior.

DIFFERENT VIEWS OF PROFESSIONALISM

What agency controls over agency employees and their autonomy are necessary in order to ensure political democracy? Two issues have been mentioned; each calls for a different perception regarding the role of intermediary professionals. The first centers upon the worrisome potential influence of the professionally trained upon political democratic processes. The administrative state requires ever-increasing numbers of professionals in order to run its bureaucracies. These specialists may at times attempt to acquire power that will be used primarily to serve their own self-interests. There is then danger of a lack of accountability to elected officials if agencies are permitted to grow into fiefdoms which interpret and influence public policy to the advantage of professional enclaves rather than that of the community. Therefore the fundamental problem is seen as one of controlling the potential damage by rules, regulations and other outside controls.

These concerns have shaped the ways that professionals are perceived by others. Some judge their training and motives inadequate for ethical self-direction; therefore it is essential to make them narrowly reactive to hierarchical demands. While it is recognized that intermediary professionals will naturally experience tensions and conflicts as they perform their mediating functions, these must be resolved within the limits set by orthodox values of agency harmony and loyalty. Since professionals retain the specialist label as a core identity, the purpose of their working lives is seen as one of fulfilling role obligations effectively and legally, to do a job within their own sphere of competence as in any large organization. It just so happens that government is the employer. Within this framework, Mosher's work helps us understand some major problems with professionalism in government that call for a general ethic of democratic responsibility, but the importance of subordinates as citizen activists has not been adequately examined.

The second perception, the one of major interest to this study, relates to the deeper purpose of professionals in government and political democratic society. We begin with the assumption that the majority have chosen to work in government because they want to bring some meaning to their working lives that goes beyond material self-interest. There is a desire to become influential, to be proactive in ways that at times will transcend specific jobs and responsibilities. While professionals know when these yearnings are frustrated, only rarely do they make the connection between being proactive and the legitimate need for democracy at the workplace. There are two reasons for this failure of insight. Few are knowledgeable about broad political institutions even when they have a profound knowledge of their agency's operations. It is erroneously assumed that formal professional training is naturally compatible with political institutions. The second reason for the lack of effective proactive behavior is that agency hierarchical power does not readily adapt to it.

In order to take advantage of their citizen potential, intermediary professionals would have to know when it is necessary to engage in stressful exchanges with policy elites. This calls for a different type of self-image, one that does not assume that professional technical training alone is adequate to satisfy the drive to become meaningfully influential. There is a real need for self-awareness as a product of reflection about one's citizen obligations toward the broader purposes and values of democratic government, but to press for reform often requires confronting agency values of harmony and loyalty. Solidarity and cohesion among intermediary professionals help to protect those who become proactive. At the same time policy elites should agree that orthodox hierarchical norms have to become less of a barrier toward desirable change. While institutional constraints and narrowly focused professional reactive behavior are essential, it is also necessary to make proactive behavior more acceptable from within bureaucracies. There is a need to arrive at a satisfactory resolution, but is this recognized by the field of public administration in the visualization of professional roles? Is a superordinate identity evolving that could incorporate reactive and proactive behavior?

Darrell Pugh sees a core of knowledge, a social ideal, ethical standards, associations and a "hall of fame" of outstanding leaders that bode well for public administration professionalism. He acknowledges the dangers of displacement of public interests by professional ones and the inadequacy of theoretical grounding. These problems in the eyes of the author, are an "exciting, even uplifting challenge to practitioners and academicians alike." The real problem of professionalism is not image but rather the need to strive for broader purposes such as competency, valuing civil servants and legitimate participation in policy making.[25]

This point of view, which seems representative of contemporary thinking in the field of public administration, bypasses two important realities. The first is that the majority of practitioner professionals have little knowledge of public administration philosophy, ethics or the major issues found in the literature. An indirect indicator of interest in such matters is to consider how many join the American Society for Public Administration (ASPA). The total paid circulation for its professional journal was about 14,000 during 1994, which includes a very high representation of higher education faculty and libraries.[26] It is troubling that the major nationwide professional organization dedicated to improving knowledge about and cohesion around common goals in the public service is represented by well under 1 percent of the professional population in the public service. An obvious conclusion is that there exists a substantial communication gap between practitioners and those promoting common visions of desirable professional action and ethics in public administration. Prospects for relating the minority educated in the academic field of public administration to the majority of other professionals remain unexplored. Consequently professionals by and large identify with their specialized degree (e.g., social worker, psychologist, accountant) and narrow agency operating goals. Another concern is that most concepts of professionalism in the public service infer a natural, all-encompassing communality of interest between agency policy elites and intermediary professionals. This ignores the very real and necessary vertical tensions that are the central preoccupation of this book.

Given these problems of government agency professional action and identity, there remains much to be done to ensure a sense of profound involvement in democratic institutions. A good way to begin is to agree that all intermediary professionals as public administrators are, without exception, engaged in some kind of political action. It is the nature of the job. "A professional public administrator can no more 'not govern' than a professional physician can 'not heal' a patient."[27] To fully understand this statement it will be helpful to consider the nature of public administration activities, how these mesh with the political environment and what effect this has upon professional identity in government agencies.

NOTES

1. Magali Sarfatti Larson, *The Rise of Professionalism: A Sociological Analysis* (Berkeley: University of California Press, 1977), pp. 9-18.

2. Eric Helderbrand, "Philosophical Tensions Influencing Psychology and Social Reaction," *American Psychologist*, vol. 42, no. 2 (February 1987): 111-12.

3. William J. Goode, "The Theoretical Limits of Professionalization," in *The Semi Professions and Their Organization*, ed. Amitai Etzioni (New York: Free Press, 1969), pp. 266-313.

4. Amitai Etzioni, ed., *The Semi Professions and Their Organization* (New York: Free Press, 1969), pp. v-xviii.

5. Talcott Parsons, "Professions," in *The International Encyclopedia of the Social Sciences*, ed. David Sills (New York: Macmillan & Free Press, 1968), pp. 545-46.

6. *Ibid.*, Larson, p. 246.

7. Gerald L. Geison, ed., *Professions and Professional Ideology in America* (Chapel Hill: University of North Carolina Press, 1983), pp. 3-11.

8. Frederick C. Mosher, *Democracy and the Public Service* (New York: Oxford University Press, 1982), chapter 5.

9. *Employment and Earnings* (U.S. Department of Labor, Bureau of Labor Statistics), October 1994, vol. 41, no. 10, table B-1, p. 45.

10. *Ibid.*, table B-12, p. 77.

11. U.S. Bureau of the Census, *Statistical Abstract of the United States: 1994*, 114th ed. (Washington, DC, 1994), table 614, p. 397.

12. *Ibid.*, *Employment and Earnings*, table A-17, p. 28. Not all had four-year higher education degrees, but other college-educated people occupy "administrative support positions" that are not included in managerial and professional categories.

13. Vincent Barraba, "Demographic Change and the Public Work Force," prepared for the Second Public Management Research Conference on the *Changing Character of the Public Work Force*, Washington, DC, November 18, 1980, table 4, p. 34.

14. *Ibid.*, *Employment and Earnings*, table B-12, p. 76. Educators employed by government are excluded from consideration in this total because arguably, their institutional values and norms are unique, not directly connected to political institutions and operations.

15. *Ibid.*, *Statistical Abstract*, tables 293 and 294, pp. 184 and 190. Doctoral degrees are not significant for the purposes of this study since their totals only increased from 32.1 to 39.3 thousand. See the National Commission on the Public Service Task Force Report, *Leadership for America* (Washington, DC, 1989) which expresses concern that incoming federal service professionals are "often untutored in the most basic structural, procedural and institutional knowledge of government," p. 133.

16. See William B. Johnson et al., *Civil Service 2000* (The Hudson Institute: June 1988, prepared for the U.S. Office of Personnel Management) as well as Rosabeth Kanter and Barry Stein, *Value Change and the Public Workforce: Labor Force Trends, the Sali-*

ence of Opportunity and Power, and Implications for Public Sector Management, prepared for the U.S. Office of Personnel Management Public Management Conference, Washington, DC, November 1980.

17. Willa Bruce and Dorothy Olshfski, "The New American Workplace," in Marc Holzer, ed., *Public Productivity Handbook* (New York: Marcel Dekker, 1992), chapter 20.

18. The term *manager* in this context refers to positions closer to the middle and lower chain of command levels, which include a formal responsibility to direct the activities of others.

19. Henry Mintzberg, *Structure in Fives: Designing Effective Organizations* (Englewood Cliffs, NJ: Prentice-Hall, 1983), pp. 163-86.

20. George W. Downs and Patrick D. Larkey, *The Search for Government Efficiency* (New York: Random House, 1986).

21. *Ibid.*, Mosher, chapter 5.

22. Chris Argyris, *Personality and Organization* (New York: Harper, 1957).

23. Victor Thompson, *Modern Organizations* (New York: Knopf, 1961), pp. 156-57.

24. Richard H. Hall, *Organizations: Structure and Process* (Englewood Cliffs, NJ: Prentice-Hall, 1977), pp. 167-70.

25. Darrell Pugh, "Professionalism in Public Administration: Problems, Perspectives and the Role of ASPA," *Public Administration Review*, vol. 49, no. 1 (January/February 1989): 1-8.

26. See the "Statement of Ownership Management and Circulation," of ASPA's journal, *Public Administration Review*, vol. 54, no. 6 (November/December 1994), last page (unnumbered). An enrollment of about 18,000 was reported in December of 1989.

27. Phillip J. Cooper, "Defining PA Professionalism," *The Bureaucrat*, Spring 1982, p. 52.

Chapter 3

Dilemmas of Democratic Administration

The challenge of public administration is to demonstrate conclusively whether big government can be controlled, which controls are the most effective and what new controls might be needed.

Gerald E.Caiden

Public agency democracy is a logical way to improve the effectiveness of government political institutions and their policy-implementing agencies. In order to better understand why this is so, this chapter presents some general aspects of American democracy along with controls over bureaucracies and the reactions of agency insiders to these constraints. This will lead to a discussion of the restless search for public administration meaning and identity. My purpose is to integrate themes, events and trends in a manner relevant to the concerns of intermediary professionals.

RULE BY THE PEOPLE

Americans are attached to an ideal of pluralism in government aimed at accommodating the interests of different groups. Designed to prevent the accumulation of excessive power by one faction, the responsiveness of the state to the needs of many factions is envisioned as the basis for political liberty. Among the major characteristics of this pluralistic model are (a) citizen voting rights along with freedom of association and expression, (b) checks and balances between legislative, executive and judiciary functions and (c) an electoral system with competing parties. Throughout, a prime purpose of government is to reconcile and adjudicate differences in expectations between factions.

Since power is shared between widely diverse groups, an underlying value consensus is assumed along with agreement on procedures and policies, all guided by a desire to limit government intrusion into private lives. A sufficiently influential citizenry, through voting and other ways of sharing and bartering power, is essential in order to attain political stability alongside of necessary change. Critics of contemporary pluralism see the ideal falling short of its promise because of the bias toward corporate power, tendencies of politicians and governmental units to become self-serving and the prevalence of debilitating power contests (versus desirable sharing and bartering). Another concern is unequal citizen involvement and access due to great differences in socioeconomic power and insufficient openness in government.[1]

Over 80,000 often-overlapping governments in the United States are held together by a federalist network. Each has varying degrees of influence one over the other as power is shared between units at federal, state and local levels. The resulting interdependence in matters involving political, legal, administrative, public policy and citizen rights culminates in large numbers of shifting, difficult issues in continuous interplay. A good deal of coordination is required between national and state governments, among individual state governments, and between individual state governments and their local governments. The amalgamation has been defined "as a contest or tension between fragmentation and diversity on one hand and coordination and uniformity on the other."[2]

As with other nations, one of the major aspects of the evolution of American government has been the proliferation of bureaucracies. Table 3-1 compares total economic with government purchasing growth.[3] Government purchases in 1990, as a rough indicator of the "rise of the administrative state," show more than a sevenfold increase over 1935. Total expenditures for government goods and services hover around 20 percent of GNP over the fifty-five-year period. This can be interpreted as a consistent effort on the part of government to keep pace with national economic growth and social complexity.

At one time most citizens saw the administrative state as "an instrument of social betterment, an indispensable weapon against evil." The feeling was that national problem solving by government agency professionals had great promise. However, as society's dependence upon the administrative state grew, government began to show disturbing signs of weakness, reflected by overloaded bureaucracies, skyrocketing costs and conspicuous program failures. Public perceptions appear to have changed over the decades in that (a) the administrative state is no longer seen as "inevitable or necessarily beneficial," (b) politicizing certain issues such as moral decay and the control of crime "does not guarantee their solution," (c) strong executives tend to become arrogant and abuse their power, (d) "professionalization does not guarantee competence," (e) people do not conform as readily to governmental requirements and (f) citizens increasingly resent the control of bureaucracies over their lives while suspecting the motives of civil servants.[4]

To be sure, criticisms regarding bureaucratic failures do not appear fair or balanced at times. For instance avid protesters against government waste rarely

Table 3-1
Gross National Product and Government Purchases in 1982 Dollars
(billions)

		GOVERNMENT PURCHASES		
	TOTAL GNP	FEDERAL	STATE & LOCAL	TOTAL
1935	580	34	79	113
1950	1,204	117	114	231
1965	2,088	244	242	487
1980	3,187	247	373	620
1990	4,153	349	482	832

recognize that many government agencies provide benefits essential to their communities and the nation in an effective manner. Yet it is a fact that since public agencies have amassed a great deal of power over the past few decades, they are seen by a significant portion of the population as a potential threat to traditional democratic ways. Citizens feel that they are overly dependent upon mastery over events of government bureaucrats. There is a perceived loss of control over one's destiny because of bureaucratic powers of rule making, adjudication and regulation.

CONTROL BY ELECTED REPRESENTATIVES OF THE PEOPLE

The growth of the administrative state, a response to the historic transformation of political/economic conditions, raises the concern that bureaucrats, not elected by the people, will make important political decisions and exercise undelegated power. Given the power that government agencies have over citizens, how can public agencies be better controlled by and made more responsible to the public?

The underlying premise is that bureaucrats must be subordinate to the will of the people as expressed by their elected public officials.[5] Politicians curtail bureaucratic power by:

- passing legislation setting boundaries, defining procedures, limiting authority, delimiting tasks; controlling resources (fiscal and personnel) through the appropriations process and using legislative veto powers to govern detailed agency decisions and regulations
- using legislative committees to investigate agencies and their policies by holding hearings and using staff audits
- maintaining informal contacts with administration officials to give advice and

engage in reciprocal support. Agencies frequently provide specific suggestions for legislation and data to support legislative changes.

These relationships vary in effectiveness since legislators are frequently pre-occupied with other issues, have limited resources and information and may use their influence with bureaucracies to enhance their personal power. Judicial controls over bureaucracies determine whether administrative agency actions are consistent with legislative intent and agencies are at times brought to task if they misuse their authority.

Elected executives must also curb the independence of their bureaucracies; therefore:

- They order agencies to comply with directives since bureaucracies are subordinate in the chain of command.
- They "set the tone" for their administrative units through leadership.
- They appoint line officers to policy-making and support positions. Executive staffers help control agency actions and reorganize agency functions and programs.
- Their budgetary powers can be directed at enlarging or restricting agency programs, thus serving as rewards or punishment for agency cooperation.

The effectiveness of these restrains is tempered by the restricted time that executives have to devote to bureaucratic problems, so their ability to acquire and absorb knowledge about agency performance is severely limited. At times bureaucracies develop close relationships with legislative bodies which can dilute the executive's control.

Legislative, judicial and executive ways to confine bureaucracy power, known as "overhead democracy," are used at all levels of government. These controls are far from tidy, not well understood by most. Wary of the power of the big government, unhappy over its size, expense and its visible failures, voters and their representatives engage in sporadic reform endeavors. Intermediary professionals are toward the end of the chain, constantly affected by these dynamic processes of power sharing. What are their reactions?

REACTIONS

A striking characteristic of the public service is the inconsistent performance and high fragmentation of top agency leadership. There are "limits imposed by the agency's power setting" and "the discontinuity of leadership at the top of the organization," all related to the difficulties of career employees at lower levels to press for beneficial change. It has been suggested that "debureaucratization" may help employees to see unfavorable organizational conditions as problems that they can resolve internally,[6] but this has its limitations.

Citizens distrust and resent their government because they observe a lack of effectiveness in agency operations. One reason for the problem is that the same political and judicial processes that create policies to be implemented also "tear away at executive authority and force the manager to share control." When senior federal officials want to get results, they habitually substitute process, organization and technique rather than individual management in order to coordinate the authority and resources in different branches and levels of government.[7] It is not surprising that increasing controls results in agency tensions. David Rosenbloom proposes three ways to visualize public administration processes.

- *Management approaches* emphasize businesslike effectiveness along with clear goals and hierarchical functions. There is an impersonal view of clients.
- *Political approaches* stress political responsiveness and accommodation to pluralistic citizen interests. Agencies are part of a collective, constituency-oriented system.
- *Legal approaches* put weight upon individual rights, equity and fairness in conflicts between citizens and government. People are seen as unique in unique situations.

The political approach tends to relegate efficiency to a secondary position because it requires agency consultation with agency "outsiders" interested in political priorities. Thus conventional managerial controls may be bypassed. The legal approach also downgrades the "cost/benefit reasoning associated with the managerial approach." At odds with the values embodied in the other two, it "militates against efficiency, economy, managerial effectiveness, representativeness and political accountability."[8]

Most of the literature concerning the impact of outside controls upon agencies centers upon the federal government and the effects of (a) rapid turnover of high-level leadership, (b) struggles between political appointees and career executives, (c) dilution of managerial power and (d) tensions between internal administrative objectives. Similar effects are experienced at state and local levels, and they help explain why it is so difficult to establish a public administration professional identity. While there are understandable needs to regulate the administrative state, the outcomes have a profound impact upon those within agencies. They perceive

- themselves as held on a short rein that limits their flexibility and at times makes them feel untrusted.
- a great degree of movement and change among policy elites resulting in a lack of communication and continuity.
- that high-level policy elites may not understand legitimate administrative problems and dilemmas; therefore, meaningful relationships are difficult to establish.
- a pervasive tendency for the public to unfairly question the competence of those in public agencies.

- that their jobs involve a good deal of tension, different than what is found in the private sector.

Consequently "many practitioners today are experiencing discouragement, frustration and exhaustion." Though agency people may feel that something is wrong about their situation, they have difficulties in articulating the reasons why. This seems to be because of a "misguided framework for action"; so there is a need for better applied theories to guide practice.[9] The next sections briefly discuss some efforts along these lines.

THE SEARCH FOR MEANING AND ACTION

A common approach to understanding public administration is to study its historical evolution. The United States has a "mixed, cumbersome and confusing lot of concepts about its public service." A series of "waves" over time, successively emphasized government by gentlemen, the common man, good people and efficient people. As public agencies became initiators of change and acquired political sophistication, "government by managers" took hold, a theme which continues at present. Thus the two administrative "deities" of political neutrality and efficiency complement and support each other.[10]

The birth of public administration's self-awareness is commonly credited to Woodrow Wilson's influential essay "The Study of Administration," which appeared in 1887. He envisioned government administration as "a field of business" whereby its connection with political life is "only as machinery is part of the manufactured product." Civil service reform makes public service nonpartisan and opens the way for "making it businesslike" and "capable of improving its methods of work . . . . Administrative questions are not political questions."[11] These pronouncements have been used to argue that politics and administration are separate activities. If so, this strengthens the case for administration as a generic activity common to business and government.

But Wilson, even as he wrote his influential article, experienced a good deal of ambivalence over the politics/administration dichotomy. Since the term "management" was not yet popular, was Wilson using "administration" in the contemporary management sense or did he have something else in mind? That possibility is reflected in other parts of his essay. At another time he defined public administration as a subfield of public law; all of this shows that the issue of reconciling democratic political ideology with administrative practice was an open one to Wilson, but many of these subtle aspects of his argument appear to have been lost over the years.[12]

There is a tendency among some academic public management "purists" to deplore the domination of political science when the field was a subdivision of this academic discipline. On the other hand it has been reasoned that the connection was a response to the inadequacy of early business-oriented administrative thought as a viable foundation for professional identity. Why didn't a more integrated and universally appealing public administration paradigm and identity evolve under the leadership of political science? There was a hopeful tone to the literature of the 1950s in that public administrators were seen as becoming "more temperate" about the promise of scientific management and therefore more open to new approaches. Also the increased importance given to human aspects of the administrative process held possibilities for cross-fertilization of knowledge.[13]

During this time Dwight Waldo wrote that the groundwork had been laid for a unique democratic administrative theory. There was a recognition that public administration had, in a sense, been false to the ideal of democracy because it had considered it "peripheral to administration." But all that was changing; the politics/administration dichotomy was rejected; efficiency was no longer the central preoccupation, and there was movement away from the doctrines of unity, centralization and simplicity. There was then hope for the development of a "democratic administrative theory," the problem being how to reconcile the "desire for democracy with the demands of authority."[14] With the approach of the 1970s, however, Waldo saw public administration as having a "second class citizenship status." The public administrator's counsel "is little sought by his political science colleagues," even though it is respected and well rewarded by others.[15] One of the striking changes during this period of turbulence was the decline of administrative law as a central interest of political science and public administration. Even though the importance of law has recently reemerged, the impact of the decline has been a severe one for professionals trained in public administration.[16]

There are patterns over these years that should be of special interest to professionals in the public service. Simpler times permitted simpler approaches. The politics/administration dichotomy was surely a useful distinction early on because it permitted the necessary introduction of business efficiency improvement techniques and management thought into government agency operations. But the "government by management" wave was only a partially adequate response to rapid growth and complexity, for by then the public service had entered territory that increasingly denied the logic of the politics/administration dichotomy. Scientific management concepts alone no longer served to give form and purpose to the field of public administration. This seems to explain why the intellectual development of the field remained for many years with political science. There were efforts to associate political processes and values with administration actions; but philosophical inadequacies and lack of attention to the needs of professionals resulted in a movement toward public administration separatism.

Rather gloomily James Perry and Kenneth Kraemer see the period of political science domination as one during which public administration "lost any unifying focus and, as a corollary, its identity as a distinct discipline." They then praise the emergence of a "competing paradigm," centered upon generic organization theory, organization behavior and management science. Recognizing the danger that unique aspects of public administration thought could be engulfed by business orientations, the authors propose a new vision called "public management." It would accommodate two polar perspectives, those of management as a generic activity and public administration as a special activity. In this manner, they state, the search for identity has "returned full circle to the foundations laid by Wilson."[17] While the authors assert that a viable paradigm must incorporate normative institutional concerns alongside of tangible administrative competence, their answer appears problematical since it does not cope with the inevitable paradoxes. A return to the ambivalent Wilsonian "foundations" serves to encourage the outworn political-administrative dichotomy, and the dilemma remains unresolved to this day.

THE SEARCH FOR INTEGRATIVE THEORY

The Frederich-Finer debate mentioned at the end of chapter 1 keeps reappearing in the literature because it put two views of democratic administration in sharp contrast. Finer, it will be remembered, took the position that objective means of accountability should be the prime concern. His reasoning was that agency actions must be controlled by external forces, and this chapter has shown how legislators, the judiciary and political executives have devised numerous ways to prevent government bureaucracies and their nonelected officials from subverting democratic government processes. Such perceptions are compatible with formal, structured, in-role, reactive aspects of bureaucracy.

Frederich raised the basic political need for initiation of action from within agencies to enhance democratic objectives. Favoring subjective accountability, he argued that professionals within bureaucracies can understand public needs in ways that outsiders cannot. Therefore they must take action depending upon an internal, personal sense of what is right. For instance, "street-level bureaucrats" (e.g., social workers, law enforcement officials and health workers) play a critical political role because of their intimate association with the public. Since they have considerable discretion, these professionals can greatly enhance individual citizen lives and opportunities. Or, if poorly trained and motivated, they can turn government into a detrimental force. There is no way to specify through general regulations how each case should be handled; as a result those at street levels control the meaning of democracy and citizenship to large numbers of people. Their accountability must be to a great degree subjective, which is to say dependent upon a sense of morality, appropriate judgment regarding the initiation of beneficial action and the presence of an "inner check" so as not to overreach one's responsibilities.[18]

In line with the Frederich position, while political science was still the predominant influence upon public administration thought, a significant development called the "new public administration" emerged. The main themes were characterized as debates centering upon (a) developing ways for public organizations to better represent constituent needs, (b) understanding the effects of administrative actions, (c) increasing the knowledge of interorganizational relationships and (d) gaining better insight into the "normative shortcomings of public organizations, administrators and policies." Much emphasis was put upon the necessity for public administration applied theory to be relevant to practitioners, so personal morality and organizational integrity were stressed throughout the proceedings. There was a pronounced shift from ideals of administrative science value-free research toward less tangible concerns, such as social justice. It was urged that more attention be given to theories and organizational forms that permit constituent participation, confrontation and involvement in social purpose. The needs of clients would direct the definitions of program and agency loyalties. This would be accomplished by more situationally adaptable organizations emphasizing noncompetitive, trusting social relationships and inviting client-centered services.[19]

During the same era Vincent Ostrom delivered a series of lectures which became another important milestone in the search for public administration identity. His concern was over the fundamental intellectual crisis emerging from an inadequate professional theoretical framework. The traditional theory of public administration, he proposes, has been erroneously based on the provision of public goods through attempts to elaborate and improve bureaucratic structures. This direction was reinforced by the work of applied theorists which centered around ways of designing organization structure to parallel managerial functions found in business. This left open an emphasis upon increasingly centralized, larger and more elaborate bureaucracies, considered by Ostrom as inherently inflexible, costly and error prone; unsuited to principles of management of public goods based upon individuals pursuing their own interests. Ostrom proposes a new paradigm to encompass a "democratic administration." It does not preclude a theory of bureaucratic administration, but rejects the assertion that it is "the only theory of good administration for all governments alike." His paradigm encourages public organizational diversity, decentralization, influence by citizens, overlapping jurisdiction and fragmented accountability. The role of the professional administrator should be one of advancing and serving "the interests of the individual persons who form his relevant public." The author's rationale revolves around the core notion that "the public servant in a democratic society is not a neutral and obedient servant to his master's command."[20]

These attempts to reconcile subjective with objective accountability and action were aimed at overcoming the damaging effects of the politics-administration dichotomy upon public administration purpose and identity. Yet the public administration movement, under way since the beginning of the century, has not to this day generated a working theory of practice. This confusion around the meaning and direction of public administration professionalism is in striking contrast to that of traditional business administration.

After four decades as a prominent scholar and government practitioner, Dwight Waldo concludes:

> I do not believe that it is possible to solve the problem of relating politics and ad-
> ministration in any way that is systematic and generally acceptable in and for the
> United States under present conditions and in any foreseeable future.[21]

Another renowned scholar and past president of the American Society for Public Administration summarizes the professional field in this manner: "Public administration theorists seem to dispute endlessly about their work, hence there seems little possibility of developing anything approximating a paradigm in the field."[22]

Meanwhile the relentless push since the 1970s toward "generic" management-oriented administrative thought continues as the core for a public administration theory of practice. Some years ago, a Delphi exercise involving scholars from seventy schools of public administration yielded these perceptions of the future perceptions which have become increasingly influential:[23]

- an instrumental approach will emerge that will "soften" value orientations
- a movement toward generic management thought and political economy will occur along with a shift toward social technology
- an emphasis upon public policy will evolve with a focus upon policy analysis and the "normative supra framework of policy sciences"
- future boundaries of public administration will be more blurred and political science will continue to lose ground as the "mother discipline."

It is difficult not to conclude that efforts to define public administration as a profession have resulted in a trend toward simpler resolutions with a proven record of failure. The break from political science has been followed by higher acceptance of the "high-tech," politically isolated replay of past themes that have provided so few answers to dealing with professional career identity paradoxes. The drift toward the past and its applied theoretical inadequacies continues today.

CONTEMPORARY PERSPECTIVES

In an effort to satisfy the pragmatic concerns of practitioners, increasing attention has been given to the public management movement, which emphasizes generic concepts of management while expressing concern for normative institutional matters. This appears to be why political economy, organization design and policy sciences are of growing popularity in schools of public administration. The influence is beneficial because it brings implementation knowledge up to date, increases analytical competence and expands the multidisciplinary character of the field. It is disturbing, however, to see that "soft" normative concerns continue to be crowded out by the emphasis upon "hard" scientific inferences. Furthermore, the movement away from political science and its essential constitutional, philosophical, value-laden concerns can only result in a critical loss of perspective.

A reassessment of the new public administration was made twenty years after the first conference at Minnowbrook of 1968. Individuals representing the 1960s cohort were joined by others who entered public administration in the 1980s. The majority of participants had political science backgrounds and held academic positions. Over a period of several days, numerous papers were discussed in an effort to better understand the future of public administration as well as determine whether there were differences between those who entered the public service in the 1960s and those who entered in the 1980s. At that meeting major themes of the first Minnowbrook conference which seem to have prevailed over the years were reviewed. These include a shift from management to policy issues, an increased emphasis upon social equity, a return of ethical concerns, change (versus growth) as the more critical theoretical issue, a heightened interest in an active and participative citizenry and finally a questioning of the "correctness of the rational model and the usefulness of the strict concept of hierarchy."[24]

Some remarks of participants strike directly to the concerns of this book. One commented that while most of the attention of public servants must be given to the "practical day-to-day operations of government," they have to achieve "civic autonomy" by (a) forming and expressing independent moral and technical judgments and (b) exercising "discernment" as compared to routine applications of rules.[25] A tendency toward "technicist consciousness," or what could be called the objective search for hard facts, is seen by another as displacing the public interest as a unifying moral symbol in public administration. This has happened because of the virtually uncontested acceptance of the *decision* as the primary focus of analysis in organization theory. An *action* or process alternative is proposed that (a) combines values and facts, (b) includes morality as an essential part of social interaction, (c) sees organizations as contexts for making sense of events and (d) does not artificially distinguish decisions from the "ongoing flow of social process." All of these should result in a fusion of fact and value that must be considered as inherent to social relationships.[26]

It was noted by others that there is "a longing for the feel of an emotion and passion, for a direction and completeness." While the first conference "represented a well intentioned but flawed optimism," the new realism of 1988 "might more effectively serve the public and the public sector for the next two decades." Finally, the increased complexities of the past twenty years means that "bureaucrats must have a commitment to dialogue and negotiation. . . . They must be able to operate interorganizationally and inter-group . . . practicing public administrators must be more proactive in the performance of their duties."[27]

I have referred to this conference and its papers at some length because it covers a wide range of perceptions and points of view that help to summarize the disarray of public administration theory today, along with the yearnings to break out of the obsession with neutral competence. Since the importance of a theoretical concept is often measured by the arguments and creative perspectives that it generates, then the new public administration movement has without doubt been a great success.

At present the literature centers upon two divergent points of view. The first considers professionals as primarily constitutional agents whose major responsibility is to maintain and improve the viability of political systems. This is done by supporting hierarchical superiors, maintaining the integrity of policy formulation and effectively implementing those policies. Governance and normative issues are the prime concerns. Consequently individuals at higher policy managerial and staff levels are seen as true professionals, in contrast with the large numbers in coordination and technical functions.[28] The public management identity appears to be a reaction to the above since it is driven by the desire to recognize the majority of those professionals involved in implementation operations. Its focus is upon agency effectiveness through resource controls, cost containment, service quality and rapid, timely responses. The ideal is to apply politically neutral specializations to agency operational missions; success will help assure political values.[29]

While the "sturm und drang" of the academic world has not affected most agency practitioners, these diverging perceptions of professional identity are disturbing. Without doubt the majority of today's professionals are attracted to the second vision that relates agency mission to specialized knowledge to valued business management techniques and beliefs. This comes at a high cost since the silent intermediaries are not encouraged or prepared to take an active hand in shaping the meaning and future of the public service.

RELEVANCE TO PROFESSIONALS

Various aspects of the accountability of public agencies toward political authority have been discussed. Overhead democracy makes agencies responsive to legislative, judicial and executive control. This legitimates the prevailing emphasis upon formal structure and authority. The logical assumption is that hierarchical processes and professional expertise will carry out the implementation of democratic purposes through efficient performance of politically defined agency functions and routines. However, simplistic perceptions of this view of accountability do not recognize that overhead controls are not always consistent, agencies perform political functions, and bureaucracies must take politically significant change initiatives.

Public administration philosophers have attempted to keep the meaning of the public service abreast of changes in size and complexity of the administrative state. Ways have been proposed for agencies to become more proactive toward democratic processes. Various points of view have been put forth that are fragmented and inconsistent. Two major attempts at theory integration, stressing subjective accountability, have not resulted in general agreement. There was a feeling of movement during Minnowbrook II days, but the tendency of some was to relegate administrative routines, hierarchies, the stress upon operating effectiveness and other reactive in-role behavior to a position of theoretical and intellectual, if not moral, inferiority.

Some have placed the reason for lack of progress squarely upon public administration theorists. Evidently practitioners have valuable, untapped forms of knowledge, but academic theorists do not permit these to emerge since they consider themselves uniquely qualified in theoretical thinking and, as experts in the analytical model of science, have mastered an approach assumed to be the only way to discover the "truth." Also they surmise that "insight into how people think is more easily possible from the top down rather than from the bottom up or the side in."[30] On the other hand professionals rarely generate and articulate innovative approaches to organizational knowledge. While Total Quality Management and the reinventing government movements are exceptions, these will be shown to be rather limited as enduring foci for professional identity in the public service.

It is difficult not to agree that progress has been limited by two obstacles. The first is an overemphasis upon the relationship between agencies and legislatures which does not properly encompass the moral and political purposes of public organizations. The second is the uncritical adoption of business managerial values by government agencies.[31] Clearly today's assortment of philosophical orientations has limited appeal to practitioners, the bulk of whom do not see themselves as policy makers or academic intellectuals. Most are intensely preoccupied with performing their roles in a conventional professional, reactive manner. They have little inclination to ponder the unresolved issues being voiced in educational circles and lean toward isolating administrative from political concerns. Therefore pressure has been put upon public administration and other professional academic people to provide practitioners with what is seen as more direct and meaningful knowledge. In so doing a drift has occurred toward "generic" management and the "hard facts" of administrative technology and policy science accompanied by reduced interest in the confusing, "soft" value orientations so often espoused by those removed from daily agency operations.

Public administration educators who stress political normative concerns tend toward the use of deductive theory, stemming from the global values of political institutions. Their calls for proactive behavior, aimed primarily at policy elites, urge more dedication to community interests and civic virtue. Following the deductive thought style, bureaucracies are seen as socially irrational, mechanistic arrangements potentially destructive toward democracy. What is buried in this perspective is the obvious fact that hierarchical, routine-oriented responses also serve democracy. Understandably, practitioners will find it difficult to relate to theorists who put little value upon the role-oriented, reactive, technical skills that they have worked so hard to acquire. Many professionals believe, with good reason, that they implement democratic purposes by norms of impartiality and neutrality. Their view of the agency world is inductive in that the main interest is in doing a particular job well and then going on to more responsibility in another specific job. What is lost in this perspective is a larger sense of democratic purpose that is so essential to bringing about change and giving intrinsic value to one's career.

More adequate concepts of public administration are needed that serve to close the gap between educators and practitioners, orientations that relate democracy to administration, citizenship to professionalism. The challenge is to prevent one perspective from overwhelming the other. Rather these seemingly contrary forces need to be used as essential, reinforcing relationships that can work to the advantage of internal reform. The next chapter translates this desirable association into concrete behavior.

NOTES

1. This discussion of major characteristics of democratic pluralism is derived from chapter 6, "Pluralism, Corporate Capitalism and the State," in David Held, *Models of Democracy* (Cambridge, UK: Polity Press, 1987).

2. David H. Rosenbloom, *Public Administration* (New York: Random House, 1989), p. 121.

3. *Statistical Abstract* (U.S. Dept. of Commerce, Bureau of Census) 1990, 110th edition, table 690, p. 425, and *Economic Indicators* (prepared for the Joint Economic Committee by the Council of Economic Advisors, 102nd Congress, 1st Session, U.S. Government Printing Office, Washington, D.C.), July 1991, p. 2.

4. Gerald E. Caiden, "The Challenge to the Administrative State," in *Current Issues in Public Administration*, ed. Frederick Lane (New York: St. Martin's, 1986), pp. 469-78.

5. The rest of this section follows the reasoning found in chapter 6 of Kenneth J. Meier, *Politics and Bureaucracy* (Monterey, CA: Brooks/Cole, 1987).

6. Donald P. Warwick, *A Theory of Public Bureaucracy* (Cambridge, MA.: Harvard University Press, 1975), chapters 10 and 11.

7. Laurence E. Lynn, Jr., *Managing the Public Interest* (New York: Basic Books, 1981), pp. 4-9.

8. David H. Rosenbloom, "Public Administration and the Separation of Powers,"

Public Administration Review, 1983, vol. 43, no. 3 (May/June): 219-26. These views are elaborated in Rosenbloom, pp. 14-29.

9. Robert B. Denhardt, *Theories of Public Organization* (Monterey, CA: Brooks/ Cole, 1984), p. 186.

10. Frederick C. Mosher, *Democracy and the Public Service* (New York: Oxford, 1982), pp. 74-82.

11. Woodrow Wilson, "The Study of Administration," *Political Science Quarterly*, vol. 2 (June 1887): 197-222.

12. Phillip J. Cooper, "Public Law and Public Administration: The State of the Union," in *Public Administration, the State of the Discipline*, eds. Naomi B. Lynn and Aaron Wildavski (Chatham, NJ: Chatham House, 1990), chapter 12, p. 256.

13. Roscoe Martin, "Political Science and Public Administration: A Note on the State of the Union," *The American Political Science Review*, vol. 46, no. 3 (September 1952): 660-76.

14. Dwight Waldo, "Development of Theory of Democratic Administration," *The American Political Science Review*, vol. 46, no. 8 (March 1952): 81-103.

15. Dwight Waldo, "Public Administration," *The Journal of Politics*, vol. 30 (May 1968): 443-79.

16. Phillip J. Cooper, "The Wilsonian Dichotomy in Administrative Law," chapter 4 in *Politics and Administration*, ed. Jack Rabin and James S. Bowman (New York: Marcel Decker 1984). This chapter is also of interest since it shows how clearly ambivalent Wilson was over the politics/administration dichotomy. See also Rosemary O'Leary, "Response to John Rohr," *Public Administration Review*, vol. 49, no. 2, (March/April 1988): 115.

17. James L. Perry and Kenneth L. Kraemer, eds., *Public Management* (Palo Alto, CA: Mayfield, 1983), preface.

18. Michael Lipsky, *Street Level Bureaucracy* (New York: Russell Sage Foundation, 1980).

19. Frank Marini, *Toward a New Public Administration* (Scranton, PA: Chandler, 1972), p. 15.

20. Vincent Ostrom, *The Intellectual Crisis in Public Administration* (University, AL: University of Alabama Press, 1973), pp. 26-29 and 131.

21. Dwight Waldo, *The Enterprise of Public Administration* (Novato, CA: Chandler, 1980), p. 77.

22. Denhardt, p. 150.

23. Emanuel Wald, "Toward a Paradigm of Future Public Administration," *Public Administration Review* (July/August 1973): 366-72.

24. H. George Frederickson, "Minnowbrook II: Changing Epochs of Public Administration," *Public Administration Review*, vol. 49, no. 2 (March/April 1989): 95-100.

25. David Hart, "A Partnership in Virtue Among All Citizens: The Public Service and Civic Humanism," Frederickson, *Public Administration Review*, vol. 49, no. 2 (March/April 1989): pp. 101-5.

26. Michael Harmon, " 'Decision' and 'Action' as Contrasting Perspectives in Organization Theory," Frederickson, *Public Administration Review*, vol. 49, no. 2 (March/April 1989): pp. 144-49.

27. See comments in "Minnowbrook II: Conclusions," Frederickson, *Public Administration Review*, vol. 49, no. 2 (March/April 1989): pp. 218-22.

28. Richard T. Green, Lawrence F. Keller and Gary L. Wamsley, "Reconstituting a Profession for American Public Administration," *Public Administration Review*, vol. 53, no. 6 (1993): 516-24.

29. Anthony P. Carnevale and David G. Carnevale, "Public Administration and the Evolving World of Work," *Public Productivity and Management Review*, vol. 17, no. 1 (1993): 1-14.

30. Ralph Hummel, "The Crisis in Public Administrative Theory," *Dialogue*, vol. 11, no. 4 (Summer 1989): 1-4.

31. Robert B. Denhart, "Public Administration Theory: The State of the Discipline," in *Public Administration, the State of the Discipline*, eds. Naomi B. Lynn and Aaron Wildavsky (Chatham, NJ: Chatham House, 1990), chapter 3, pp. 65, 66.

Chapter 4

A Model of Agency Democracy

Bureaucratic and democratic ideals should not be thought of as competing perspectives but as part of one belief system that legitimates the entire political system.

Kathryn Denhardt

This chapter translates the general theory of public agency democracy into an operational model and considers some of its implications. As a first step basic kinds of reactive and proactive behavior are associated with appropriate choices and performance alternatives. Comparisons with other theories of organizational participation and democracy help to clarify the nature of the model. The discussion ends with propositions derived from what has been covered in the initial chapters of this book.

The underlying mechanism of democratic social systems was described early on as an interplay between harmony and contention. Harmony within government agencies is ensured by behavior reactive to in-role responsibilities, aimed at agency stability and predictability. Constructive contention, often the leading edge of change, is facilitated by proactive behavior. Revising goals, jobs, operations and control systems along with motivating employees is usually emphasized, but tempering the decisions and behavior of policy elites is also an important important aspect of reform. These principles will guide the generation of a model that will include major types of change initiatives:

- Specific reactive and proactive behaviors must be defined so that they cover most of the possible alternatives open to agency insiders.
- Desirable relationships between reactive and proactive behavior must be specified.
- Behaviors should be credible; this means that adapting to the model must be organizationally and psychologically realistic.
- No proposed behavior should threaten existing political institutions.

Three major categories of agency member actions will now be described.

IN-ROLE REACTIVE BEHAVIOR

The main purpose of organizational structure is to assure predictable, effective performance. Therefore a network of positions directs streams of activities toward accomplishing shared purposes. These positions are called "roles" and their tasks, grouping and hierarchical arrangements, which is to say "structure," is a predominant concern of organization designers.[1]

The idea of "role" is based upon desired behaviors which accompany specific organizational positions and status. These are arranged in clusters with reciprocal rights and duties so as to make social relationships more predictable and reduce uncertainty in the analysis and implementation of decisions.[2] The term "bureaucracy" describes a formal order of roles which establishes patterns of specialization and authority, frequently represented by organization charts. Bureaucracies are typified by formal specification of areas of competence and authority, high degree of specialization, rules and impersonal judgments. While the purpose of bureaucratic organization is to create a machinelike social arrangement specifying how, when and by whom tasks are to be performed, human interactions require outlets for spontaneity, differing personality needs and special group characteristics that are not included in conventional organization descriptions. Since all contingencies cannot be predicted by formal structure, informal role arrangements exist paralleling the formal ones so as to accommodate other individual and group needs. Let us now consider three major types of reactive behavior.

The most common and necessary type of activity involves *following systematic responses to familiar situations, known as routines.* This does not mean that professional routines are simple or mechanical since there is usually wide discretion as to what to do under various circumstances. Administratively, however, professionals are seen as problem solvers by policy elites; problem solvers with the skills and necessary judgment to apply these in the right manner. Under these assumptions professional activities are considered appropriate so long as they (a) fall within the prescribed role of the individual, (b) are tied into agency goals as defined by policy elites and (c) do not violate prevailing legal, ethical and moral standards. Contemporary organization theory and design is largely aimed at producing systematic responses. This is done by defining feasible organizational goals; connecting these to appropriate networks of tasks; monitoring performance and shaping the behavior of organizational members to accommodate to organizational needs.

Another type of in-role behavior involves *responding to special policy elite directives.* At times intermediary professionals suspend their usual activities in order to help resolve unique, specific problems defined by their superiors.

Typically these are centered upon new priorities and contemplated changes to established routines; expertise is needed to introduce new technology, redesign formal structure and rearrange agency processes. Professionals are key actors in defining and resolving such problems within the existing agency system and/or with the agency environment. It is at times necessary to bend or ignore rules and formal procedures, a talent common to many "can do" experts. Agency policy elites accept such necessities, and transgressions are readily forgiven provided that they do not have unexpected, adverse public consequences.

A third type of in-role behavior occurs when professionals *spontaneously suggest resolutions to discrete problem areas* that have been identified by management as sources of agency operations inefficiency and ineffectiveness. Since the purpose is to improve policy implementation, success in taking the initiative is valued by both professionals and agency policy elites. Faced with the necessity to take action, managers will usually accept forceful and persistent initiatives on the part of subordinates. An individual record of favorable performance in these last two types of behavior is frequently seen as not only proof of technical competence but also creative administrative ability.

These features are common to all three types of in-role behaviors: They are reactive in that behavior is based upon an assessment of needs as defined by agency policy elites. They are oriented to problemsolving in that efforts are made to resolve specific conditions of explicit concern to agency policy elites. Action, in the three classes of behavior, is bounded by the official role responsibilities of participants, though informal role behaviors become increasingly important in responding to the last two types of reactive conduct.

BORDERLINE-ROLE BEHAVIOR

The second broad category of logical agency behavior involves making an independent assessment of and proposing resolutions to situations that are *judged by intermediary professionals* as needing correction. These situations are typically ill-defined clusters of intertwined problems that cross organizational boundaries and may even transcend specific agency interests. Permeated with feelings of ambiguity as well as uncertainty, they are predicaments, rather than reasonably well-defined problems amenable to in-role treatment. Their most distinguishing feature is that they are impossible at the onset to disentangle from human sentiments. Therefore, predicaments are not initially subject to linear, rational analysis by an impartial observer;[3] they are agency political situations requiring political skills in order to make progress toward their resolution.

Imagine, for example, that professional "A" observes a high and costly incidence of errors in a particular operation because employees are not well acquainted with procedures. Contacts with other professionals in other areas of expertise show that (a) procedures need to be better defined, (b) the operation could then be automated, (c) the systems analyst who is best acquainted with the operation is working on another job in an adjacent department and (d) professional A's direct supervisor shows little interest in the problem. There is no way to immediately resolve this matter in a conventional, technically rational manner because employee sentiments, diverging professional specializations, effort priorities and differing responsibilities are involved.

Professionals who set out to locate, define and suggest resolutions to predicaments require specific talents. They will be curious about knotty human, organizational and technical relationships and have special abilities to engage in subjective, nontechnical relationships with others who can help define the nature of a predicament under consideration. Only then are technical skills needed to understand in what ways corrective action can be taken. It follows that predicament resolutions call for special negotiating abilities to get the attention of policy elites and to guide the process of introducing change.

Another major characteristic of predicament resolution is that analytical and change investigation can rarely be confined to activities defined by clearly established organizational positions. Those involved have to work at the borderlines of their formal roles, at times "transgressing" into the turf and specialized interests of others. All of this is quite different from the third type of in-role spontaneous activity described in the previous section because now professionals "presume" to judge the importance of predicaments. In so doing they infringe upon activities that are often seen as the traditional preserve of "management" and policy elites (e.g., social intuition, interorganizational coordination, problem definition, priority setting).

Research on borderline role behavior will be discussed in chapter 8. It shows that, when provided with the proper orientation and conceptual tools, intermediary professionals have the capacity to locate and design resolutions to a wide range of predicaments. This is because they are best acquainted with specific organizational events and often have the unique skills and perceptions which are essential to successful change endeavors.

OUT-OF-ROLE BEHAVIOR

The third and last category of professional behavior is intensely proactive in that it usually involves aborting one's traditional agency role and immediate organizational hierarchical loyalties in the interests of what are perceived as higher political institutional causes. Three major types of behavior prevail.

When professionals see a compelling necessity for change and are not supported directly and formally by management, then they may *form action coalitions* within their agency and, sometimes, with others outside their specific agency. Efforts by law enforcement professionals to oppose the regressive influences of the National Rifle Association, when the safety of citizens and police is at risk, is one illustration of coalition formation. Such efforts have been undertaken with a sense of accountability to the community at large in order to, for instance, restrict the availability of assault weapons, pistols made of all-plastic components and teflon-coated bullets that can penetrate protective vests. These temporary affiliations are not based upon formal role relationships; rather they are spontaneous attempts to influence public opinion so that political policy elites will take corrective steps. Under other circumstances, action coalitions may be formed inside agencies to bring management's attention to and suggest remedies for undesirable situations.

The next two types of out-of-role behavior are mostly solitary activities involving resistance to specific policy elite practices. One of these, called *urgent individual representation*, consists of questioning, blocking or distorting desired responses to directives. Consider the dilemma of a professional who is ordered to engage in marginally ethical or outright illegal behavior. One response is to argue forcibly against the behavior. Another is to refuse to obey. Yet another is to drag out compliance by "forgetting" or inventing obstacles while quietly appealing to higher authority inside or outside a specific department. In clear-cut cases professionals may be supported by their superiors. But since most of these situations are not readily amenable to impartial gathering and analysis of facts, they usually involve tolerating high degrees of ambiguity and stress for all concerned until resolutions are arrived at. A regulatory agency engineer, for example, finds that a recent directive creates unforeseen dangers for the public. She then chooses not to implement these policies while striving to bring about changes internally through the regular chain of command. As another example, a professional attempts to stop unlawful and/or abusive peer practices by going to a top agency official. This has occurred in police agencies when colleagues who are drug users and traffickers are turned in by other agency members.

A different kind of urgent individual representation initiative occurs when government employees act as anonymous informers. Unsigned letters or disguised telephone messages may be directed at authorities to indicate that unlawful practices are being engaged in. At times "hot lines" are set up to encourage such contacts and to assure the protection of the informant. While disclosures of this kind are sometimes necessary, they are not compatible with the openness necessary for democratic interactions. More will be said about this in chapter 9.

The most taxing kind of out-of-role behavior is known as "*whistle-blowing*." The term is used in many ways, but for our purposes it will be defined as making public an agency situation that a subordinate considers as highly injurious to the public welfare. Since it is in direct contradiction to norms of bureaucratic harmony and loyalty, strong opposition along with retaliation is predictable. This lonely and hazardous initiative will also be discussed in chapter 9.

Several common aspects of out-of-role behavior are of interest. In the first place the reform effort frequently transcends the direct mission or responsibility of any one agency unit or agency. A deep commitment to broad political institutional values based upon one's judgment as to what is to the public interest triggers action. This sense of moral and ethical responsibility goes well beyond conventional in-role obligations. The second characteristic of out-of-role behavior is that it is narrowly issue-oriented since attention is focused upon a restricted set of circumstances connected to distinct, unwanted effects. Group and individual sentiment rather than extensive, formal, objective analysis energize action. Finally, while the outcomes of most out-of-role behavior are difficult to predict, they often involve risk to initiators of action as they confront influential powers inside and outside of agency walls.

PUBLIC AGENCY DEMOCRACY

Having defined general categories and some internally related types of behavior, it is now possible to construct an integrated model and its connecting logic. Note that all of the behaviors discussed in the previous sections have and are occurring daily in agencies at all levels of government. While there are inevitable requirements for proactive alongside reactive behavior, professional errors of judgment in choosing the wrong alternative to deal with a specific situation can work in opposition to the public good. For example, individuals within agencies cannot excuse reactive conduct patently harmful to innocent citizens by claiming to have only followed orders. On the other hand, whistle-blowers who defame blameless people and create unwarranted turbulence cannot justify their behavior by saying that they meant well.

A reasonable assumption is that, when applied to the appropriate situation, all reactive and proactive behaviors discussed above are legitimate and necessary to the effectiveness of political institutions. Table 4-1 lists and orders the major categories of agency behavior and the types within each. The character of choices and some probable effects can be gauged by these criteria:

- *Desirable Frequency*—the prevalence of one type of behavior over the other for any given agency population.
- *Issue Specificity*—the extent to which a behavior is directed at an uncommon or unique situation.
- *Career Risk to User*—the degree to which engagement in the behavior jeopardizes one's chances for promotion, continuation of employment or even, in rare cases, one's physical safety.
- The probable amount of *organizational disruption* involved in facing specific issues which detract from performing established routines and attaining policy elite priorities.

Descriptive weights allocated to these attributes are "ideal" in that they assume general types of bureaucratic operations under normal conditions. Basi-

Table 4-1
A Model of Agency Democracy

| Alternative Behaviors | Attributes | | | |
	Desirable Frequency	Issue Specifity	Career Risk to User	Organizational Disruption
IN-ROLE				
Follow Routines	Very High	Low	Low	Low
Respond to Directives	High	Varies	Low	Varies
Suggest Resolutions	Moderate	Varies	Varies	Varies
BORDERLINE-ROLE				
Analyze Predicaments and Propose Changes	Low	High	Varies	Varies
OUT-OF-ROLE				
Form Coalitions	Very Low	Very High	Varies	Varies
Urgent Individual Representation	Very Low	Very High	High	Varies
Whistle-blowing	Very Low	Very High	Very High	Very High

cally, the model is directed at making agency actors better aware of some of the circumstances that shape their ability to engage in change activities. As discussed, values are not seen as separated from facts, and ethical judgments are visible influences in choosing performance alternatives. Another feature is that the model is descriptive as well as normative. It is a reasoned set of logically coherent and necessary behaviors derived from common observation. Models of this type are essential predecessors to the more detailed empirical investigations that will be discussed in the last two chapters.

The construct fits reasonable expectations, similar to those of citizens at large. Most of us would like to live in a society wherein the great majority of relationships with government authority are routine, predictable and acceptable. We want our relationships with officials to be forthright and amicable; we want them to listen and respond to our suggestions for improving the effectiveness of government. While we do not wish to be encumbered with many restrictions upon our behavior, we react favorably to laws and the influence of government functionaries when these are seen as advantageous to us personally as well as society at large. Such feelings provide a sound footing for sentiments of trust in and loyalty toward authorities. All told, this can be labeled the ideal citizen reactive stance, based upon assumptions of mutual good will and norms of social harmony. These are all typical of effective "in-role" behavior.

At important times citizens find it to their individual and group advantage to make independent assessments of government predicaments and suggest remedies, to form temporary interest groups, to resist unreasonable directives and speak up as individuals. These are citizen rights protected by democratic institutions. Yet it is also evident that excessive and poorly reasoned proactive behavior can tear a society apart even to the point of endangering the overall political system. There is, therefore, a tacit lower limit put upon the incidence of proactive behavior as compared to harmonious behavior reactive to authority.

Clearly, agency democracy is a very conservative interpretation of wider democratic relationships; conservative from the point of view that there is no desire to challenge the core philosophy or fundamental ideals of the state, nor to distort lawful processes of government decision making, nor to engage in partisan political activities. In sum, proactive alongside of reactive behaviors are seen as ways to better articulate and attain established political institutional purposes already directed toward the public good. Having said this, extremely adverse political changes can be imagined under which bureaucratic employees would be morally justified to resist the state. These possibilities are not considered in this book since our purpose is to envision agency behavior well within the experience of today's American political institutions. The underlying assumption is that existing regime values have the requisite characteristics for fairness and benevolence toward the public.

Returning to the principles that were used to generate the model of agency behavior:

- The ranges of behavior are intended to encompass all major types of reactive and proactive alternatives.
- They are highly consistent with existing processes and values of American political institutions.
- Desirable incidence of types of behavior has been indicated. There are logical associations between issue specificity, degree of risk to initiators and probable amount of disruption attendant to each behavior.
- The behaviors are realistic in that all continue to occur in practice, with somewhat predictable degrees of acceptance and resistance on the part of those in charge.

Since the model is legitimate, which is to say consistent with the constitutional values and purposes of political institutions, it helps close the gap between general theory and concrete action. Logical sequences of reactive-proactive behavior escalation are suggested. Imagine, for instance, that a professional finds during the course of responding to a directive that some aspect does not appear to satisfy the intent of an established policy. Impartial observers would agree that the issue, if unresolved, would do significant harm to the public. He suggests revisions which are not accepted by his supervisor. Then the professional along with colleagues, using role-borderline approaches, analyzes the order as a predicament, calls for changes to the directive and suggests resolutions. Ignored by those in the chain of command the professional attempts to form a coalition of peers. When this proves ineffective, response to the directive is blocked while he attempts to reason with higher agency authorities. Finally, out of deep ethical conviction, whistle-blowing is resorted to. The sequence of behaviors should be permissible when it is logically linked to the public interest, but it does not preclude other circumstances which would require going directly from in-role behavior to, say, whistle-blowing if the issue is of such a critical nature that immediate and drastic action is required. Since the model is but one way of defining democracy at the workplace, comparisons with other studies should be instructive.

OTHER THEORIES OF WORKPLACE PARTICIPATION AND DEMOCRACY

All concepts of democracy at the workplace are based upon the idea of a lower-status, more numerous employee group becoming influential in decision-making processes that are normally in the hands of a small group of power holders. Certainly this is a premise of public agency democracy, but it is interesting to compare it to other movements which share three characteristics. First, the main concern is with business settings, though attempts have been made to fit some of the approaches to government work. Second, the principal actors are "management" and workers. Finally, it is assumed that more power equalization between the two groups will result in benefits for society at large, the enterprise and/or those at the workplace.

The most common approach is often called "democratic management." High-level policymakers invite workers to share in some decisions. This involves obtaining agreement upon objectives, expressing an openness to worker feelings, rewarding employee suggestions for improvement, delegating responsibilities, decentralizing decisions, redesigning jobs and engaging in the joint investigation of specific problems. All of these practices tend to dilute the formal power of managers over workers. Participation is seen as beneficial to workers since it can result in material rewards, higher job satisfaction, greater feelings of being influential, being in control of one's destiny and providing opportunities to demonstrate one's competence. In so doing, personality needs for affiliation, esteem and recognition are better satisfied, all essential toward "self-actualization" or, broadly speaking, the necessity to fulfill one's potential in life.

Why do managers go through the trouble of creating this particular kind of collaboration/consensus "democratic" environment? Not only do time and attention have to be devoted to power equalization, but there are other potentially costly outcomes. Employees may, through experiences in participation processes, decide to resist management goals. They can also develop expectations to be consulted on a wider range of matters than management is prepared to engage in. Some employees can become resentful because their ideas are not acted upon by others.[4]

Management takes these risks for the very pragmatic reason that they are seen as a path toward higher productivity and attaining other organizational goals. By increasing employee motivation to perform creatively, management enhances the effectiveness of the enterprise. While democratic management has overtones of humanism and equalitarian relationships, we should not lose sight of the fact that the preemptive right to accept or reject proposals remains firmly in the hands of policy elites. For it is the latter who specify degrees of involvement and control strategies of participation. Therefore, since contention is controlled by management in the interest of purposes that they alone specify, the term "democracy" has very limited meaning.

Other models of power equalization at the workplace appear to fall under the general rubric of "industrial democracy."[5] Some goals are:

- democratization of the terms of employment (through collective bargaining and legislation)
- democratization of ownership (through worker profit sharing, buyouts and co-operative arrangements)
- democratization of the government of work (through worker-directors and worker shareholding).

One of the arguments for worker involvement in industrial democracy is that it will generate desires and skills to engage in more generalized political endeavors off the job. The expectation is that, as a result of success at the workplace, lower-level workers will become increasingly educated and knowledgeable about democratic processes in general and therefore more active citizens in the political world. Some have concluded that such expectations are worthy but remain in the realm of conjecture.[6]

Christopher Pollitt in his review of major theories of relationships between bureaucracies and democracy[7] lists various assumptions such as:

- Full participation by workers would greatly reduce the need for bureaucracy (neo-Marxist premises).
- Democracy is a way to curtail the tendency of bureaucracies to oversupply their services (neoclassical economics premises).
- While bureaucracies are essential to democracy, bureaucratic self-interests may concurrently be a threat to democracy.
- Bureaucratic centralization inhibits democratic creativity and participation.

We see, then, that there is a rather wide range of concerns and objectives which appears to cluster around notions of bureaucracy, participation and proactive behavior. An understanding of these existing movements helps to define the model of agency democracy more precisely. In the first place public agency democracy is aimed exclusively at government settings. While the idea of unfavorable balance of power and the need to reduce status differentials is present, a more sophisticated premise than the dichotomy of worker/manager is used. To consider intermediary professionals as mediators and proponents in power relationships enhances the agency's ability to become more specific and inclusive about desirable behaviors and outcomes in a more timely manner.

"Democratic Management" ideas occupy but a small portion of the model of agency democracy in that they seem to apply best to the in-role category under the type of reactive behavior called "Suggest Revisions." There are similarities to borderline-role behavior, but the democratic management movement lacks its independent and spontaneous character. As will be elaborated in chapter 8, when an intermediary professional group takes the initiative and proposes new priorities as well as the nature of problems to be resolved, upper management, at least initially, has less control over outcomes and priorities of action. Out-of-role behavior has no similarity to democratic management since it unilaterally questions and may oppose existing policy elite priorities and/or behaviors.

While the formation of coalitions could appear to be related to collective bargaining, improvement of terms of employment has been deliberately excluded as an aspect of the model. This is because the theory of agency democracy requires a separation between the direct self-interests of professionals and broader public interests. Therefore employee objectives involving pay and working conditions protected by various associations, procedures and laws are outside the purview of this study.

Regarding relationships between bureaucracy and democratic society at large, the assumption of agency democracy is that most dysfunctional agency self-interests are kept in check by the overhead democracy practices described in chapter 3. These controls promote in-role behavior reactive to the authority of policy elites. There are no ideological intentions behind the model of public agency democracy to incrementally change the public ownership control of agencies nor their relationship to existing institutions. Rather, the prevailing desire is to enhance, preserve and stabilize existing political institutions. No doctrine predicting the progressive dissolution of bureaucracy throughout society is espoused. Political efficacy is seen as the primary purpose for all types of behavior in agency democracy, but the goal is not to increase employee efficacy for other types of political activities off the job. These comparisons show that the main thrust of public agency democracy coincides with no other existing models of participation and democracy at the workplace.

GENERAL AGENCY CITIZEN LOYALTIES AND VALUES

While major attention has been given to the citizenship responsibilities of intermediary professionals, the same rights and duties apply to agency policy elites and nonprofessionals. For example, agency policy elites have normal re-active associations with their hierarchical superiors. Their work life is fraught with borderline-role activities as they go about understanding and resolving difficult predicaments incorporating complex relationships between agency and legislative, executive, judicial, other agencies as well as constituency forces.

Out-of-role behavior is at times engaged in by policy elites. On rare occasions the outcome is "resignation in protest." In a study of 34 cases of public-protest resignations and 355 silent resignations by high American administration officials over the period 1900-69, it was found that a tradition of discreet service to the executive encourages silent resignations. When individuals go public, they break a deeply rooted norm against "tattling" or "squealing" which arouses peer pressure, executive rage and an ambivalent reception by voters. Aside from the emotional costs of candor, highly placed dissenters who engage in silent and public contention face an abrupt descent in status and meager prospects for a second chance in top positions. Therefore ethical independence has a steep price, even when the issue is obviously deserving of protest. This encourages intense loyalty to "team play" and careerism.[8] Nonprofessionals also appear in the whistle-blowing literature as initiators of reform. Evidently, out-of-role pro-active behavior at any agency level of responsibility is usually risky and subject to vindictive retaliation.

Yet all employees within agency walls, regardless of position and status, are under citizen obligations to engage in necessary proactive as well as regular reactive behavior. Intermediary professionals are of prime interest because of their underused potential as mediators to discover opportunities for improvement and protect the public interest. Therefore, their relationships with policy elites will continue to be the main concern. At the same time it should be remembered that professionals must put deep thought to specifying desirable relationships with those in nonprofessional positions. The reason is that professionals are in a key position to facilitate proactive behavior on the part of other employees. These matters will be elaborated in the final chapter.

The tendency to engage in proactive efforts is not uniform because family and other interests compete for the time and values associated with employment. It follows that the greater the external claims to one's interests, the less the probability of proactive behavior. On the other hand, professionals normally put a high premium upon their career progress and gratifications because it is of major importance to their self-image as worthy individuals in society. Why are individuals attracted to a profession and its particular activities? Some gravitate toward specializations out of conscious choice, others out of habit, parental or peer influence, but most are inspired by the potential material and psychological gratifications. In any event staying power is required to go through the rigors and sacrifices of getting an advanced education and keeping up with developments in one's field. While commitment is partially derived from other values,

say those related to power and wealth, most who take on professional responsibilities are driven by an emotional attachment to the type of work itself.

Samuel Florman voices these feelings in his treatise on the pleasures of engineering activities and in so doing rejects the idea that scientific dogma only at-
tracts limited personalities. He places "reliance on the passions, urges and in-
tuitions which are the basic ground of our personal existence." He refutes the
arguments of antitechnologists while describing the pleasures of wrestling with
the elements, the yearning for ways to express the immensity of elemental being, all through one's occupation: "Today I will do the work that needs to be
done, the work for which I have been trained, the work which I want to do because in doing it I feel challenged and alive." Then happiness arrives mysteri-
ously as a byproduct of this effort.[9]

Surely similar emotions exist, at least initially, in the minds of most accountants, social workers, foresters, supervisors, managers and other professionals as
they prepare themselves in educational institutions and hone their skills on the
job. It is mainly by adhering to formal role obligations that one has the opportunity to satisfy those needs having to do with the pleasures of the work itself.

At the same time a most vital aspect of career values and loyalties, inade-
quately emphasized in the literature, is the importance to government professionals of the setting within which their work will be done. Many, if not most,
are drawn to government careers because of the power of public ideas; there is
often a willingness to endure lower salaries, less attractive office settings and
more hazardous working environments because public service purposes are of
major value. They give high esteem to improving the health of the populace,
playing a part in protecting natural resources, helping the indigent, protecting
citizens from crime, creating more livable cities, rectifying ethnic discrimination
or any other of the multitude of services performed by government. A profession under these conditions is seen as an instrumental way of making important
and direct contributions to society. This calling helps create loyalty toward an
agency because it permits the use of one's professional knowledge and skills in
a meaningful ultimate manner. Such feelings are a kind of organizational glue
which helps make public agencies work.

Since professionals are drawn to the public service because the pleasures of
exercising their knowledge and skills within public contexts, some will feel
constantly rewarded by their conventional role associations and live out entire
careers of fulfilled expectations, taking pleasure in what they do. Most, however, at crucial times in their working lives, will encounter situations calling for
them to go beyond their formal roles in order to satisfy strong needs to become
socially and ethically responsible. When this is not possible, career deterioration sets in as the demands for organizational loyalty begin to conflict with
loyalty toward the more compelling reasons for one's attachment to agency
work. Several outcomes are then possible. Some competent, energetic people
may leave the public service. Others, equally competent, may remain but be-

come increasingly subject to apathy, cynicism and destructive relationships with co-workers. Yet others will barely tolerate their jobs because it is too late to change their working lives, but this will entail minimal commitment of energy and creativity until retirement. As the number of disaffected professionals grows, the public service suffers a constant depletion of critical resources, of necessary skills. Is this inevitable or will agency democracy help revitalize interest and meaning of work for great numbers of careerists?

A SUMMARY AND PREVIEW

Public agency democracy takes advantage of the necessary tensions between policy elite authority and creative compliance by subordinates. It assumes that reactive and proactive behaviors are essential to democratic relationships. The purpose is not only to reduce the incidence of error but also to bring out and encourage innovative leadership.

A good deal of attention is being given today to various developments at federal, state and local government levels which shows that the right combination of policy elite personality traits and administrative skills can help to overcome traditional bureaucratic roadblocks. The successes of creative leaders who take risks and tolerate the uncertainty and untidiness of change are being reported in increasing numbers. Two major kinds of skills are required, and both can be learned. The first are reasonably well-known management aptitudes such as strategic action, a sense of timing, laying out concrete plans, creating a sense of urgency for change and using political skills to reduce one's exposure to environmental risk.[10] The second set of skills involves mastery of strategies of reform and the aptitude to choose the correct alternative to fit a particular situation. These include reducing management involvement in the direct delivery of services, cutting back rules and regulations, empowering community activists, encouraging competition between prospective deliverers of services, generating special sources of revenue, decentralizing hierarchical relationships, taking on limited market-oriented endeavors and developing customer orientations toward the public.[11]

As of now, however, little mention has been made of reactions on the part of subordinates to these initiatives. Two main advantages of public agency democracy are that it encourages creative in-role responses as well as new entrepreneurial leadership initiatives. Since agency democracy helps professionals to better identify with each other as members of the public service, it serves to extend their interests beyond specialized roles. More will acquire a greater knowledge of the skills and strategies of change and thereby respond more effectively to leadership. Beyond this, proactive efforts involving predicament analysis and change design along with some out-of-role initiatives will draw the attention of the more adventuresome, creative leaders. Since it is evident that all inspiration and creativity does not have to start at higher ranks, agency democracy makes the tensions of the upward influence more acceptable.

These propositions summarize some important themes derived from what has been discussed in this and previous chapters:

1. *While competing schools of thought abound, there is no viable theory of practice for public administration in the United States today.* Therefore government agency employees do not have an agreed-upon, distinctive philosophy to guide their behavior at the workplace.

2. *The void is of increasing importance.* Because agency professionals lack an explicit, encompassing sense of identity and solidarity, (a) the socialization of professionals is not as effective as it should be, (b) political institutional performance suffers, (c) professionals experience unnecessary feelings of career disaffection and (d) public confidence in government continues to decline.

3. *A most salient weakness in both the theory and practice of public administration is that two necessary paths of action have been considered as antithetical and irreconcilable.* The first specifies that those within agencies must *react* in a manner consistent with the desires of the public as expressed through elected and appointed officials in the agency environment. Overhead democracy controls and agency hierarchies are meant to assure such reactive (i.e., objective) performance. The second path specifies that *initiation of action*, called proactive (i.e., subjective) performance, is required on the part of those within agencies to redirect and reform agency activities.

4. *Reconciliation between these points of view becomes more probable if the logic of citizen democratic behavior in society at large is applied to relationships between agency employees and their leaders.* The reasoning is that reactive performance is compliant behavior while proactive performance incorporates the right to initiate changes in the behavior of those who demand compliance. The latitude to use both approaches in appropriate ways is essential to a democratic workplace and, in turn, assures more effective political institutional results.

5. *No theories in use serve the need expressed in proposition 4 above.* Prevailing theories of participation and democracy are either too limited (e.g., management democracy) or inappropriate (e.g., industrial democracy). Efforts by those in the field of public administration to develop an integrated theory may have not gained acceptance because the major interest is in policy elite activities. Inadequate recognition is given by others to the need for and benefits of bureaucratic structure. Much of the existing general policy oriented and deductive discourse is not compatible with practitioner requirements for action-based theory.

6. *The model of agency democracy helps establish a foundation for a more viable theory of professional public administration practice* since it integrates reactive with proactive performance by (a) specifying major categories of acceptable behavior attendant to both approaches, (b) indicating generally desirable frequencies for these behaviors, and (c) broadly predicting the degree of professional risk attendant to each behavior. The logic of the model is consistent with organization design objectives as well as those of political institutions.

7. *Intermediary professionals are the key to creating a demand for and enacting a workable theory of practice.* This is because there are great numbers of these

strategically located and highly skilled citizens in agencies whose combined potential to understand necessary changes and engage in beneficial proactive behavior has been largely untapped.

8. *Acceptance of the above along with the willingness to experiment with proactive behavior on the part of intermediary professionals and policy elites is far from assured.* The training of most experts does not prepare them to deal with ambiguity. Also more must be known about the way that borderline-role and out-of-role behavior works as well as ways to bring about shifts in existing mind-sets that impede progress.

These propositions tell us that it is worthwhile to more closely examine how to make agency democracy a reality in the public service. Recommendations are needed to help activists make certain that their assessments are accurate—that the issues at hand warrant the disruption of change. More must be said about how professionals and influential others could explore existing attitudes and behavior in order to adapt to agency democracy. All of these concerns will be addressed, driven by the conviction that the idea of proactive initiatives is directly in line with the purposes of democratic political institutions. Yet the deeper implications of what is being proposed cannot be ignored. For while these concepts are *politically* conservative, since they reinforce constitutional regime values, they are at the same time *administratively radical*. The reason is that sizable changes are called for in conventional beliefs, which are geared to rationalize reactive, in-role behavior. What is proposed goes counter to the organizational and psychological realities perceived by most practitioners and espoused by management educators.

The conscious insertion of democratic paradoxes into administrative thought produces a degree of disarray in a body of practical and theoretical knowledge that has made its purpose to constantly reduce, if not eliminate, dealing with uncertainty and ambiguity at lower levels. The popular direction is to program decisions and reduce controversy to the greatest possible extent in order to assure proper in-role responses. This makes sense if one assumes that management people are at all times the best endowed to deal with organizational ambiguity; the higher the position, the greater the requisite ability to cope with uncertainty. Such ingrained beliefs tend to undercut exhortations for employees to perform their jobs with zeal, to do the right thing, to live by codes of agency and professional ethics. As long as subordinates are not seen as capable of constructively questioning the right and power of the hierarchy to control the fundamental, essential purposes and values of the workplace, any attempt to instill democratic practices will be perceived as impractical and impossibly utopian.

Given the underlying importance of these matters, there is an immediate priority to examine more detailed aspects of orthodox organizational theory which shape daily thought and action. An exploration of the syntax and logic of administrative power in use will help to better understanding the implications and practicality of proactive behavior. Three areas of inquiry will be of particular interest:

- How should organizational purposes be envisioned and defined?
- What concepts are most appropriate to guide the direction of organizational activities?
- What energizes employees to attain organizational and personal goals?

Each of the next three chapters is devoted to one of the above questions.

The path will not be an easy one; because of applied theoretical inadequacies administrative education and training does not dwell upon the conflicting values that shape management and professional beliefs about their agency rights and duties. Consequently there are sizable deficiencies in the philosophical underpinning, socialization and daily actions which characterize the public service today.

NOTES

1. Daniel Robey, *Designing Organizations* (Homewood, IL: Irwin, 1982), pp. 16-21.

2. Robin M. Williams, Jr., *American Society* (New York: Knopf, 1960), pp. 35-38.

3. Donald A. Schön, *The Reflective Practitioner* (New York: Basic Books, 1983).

4. A classical discussion of power equalization, its advantages and drawbacks is found in George Strauss, "Some Notes on Power Equalization," in *The Social Science of Organizations*, ed. Harold J. Leavitt (Englewood Cliffs, NJ: Prentice-Hall, 1963). For a description of the management style of collaboration-consensus, see William Eddy, *Public Organization Behavior and Development* (Cambridge, MA: Winthrop, 1981), pp. 146-53.

5. Margaret Kiloh, "Industrial Democracy," in *New Forms of Democracy*, eds., David Held and Christopher Pollitt (London: Sage Publishers, 1986), chapter 2.

6. Carole Pateman, *Participation and Democratic Theory* (New York: Cambridge University Press, 1981).

7. Christopher Pollitt, "Democracy and Bureaucracy," in David Held and Christopher Pollitt, chapter 7.

8. Edward Weisband and Thomas Franck, *Resignation in Protest* (New York: Grossman Publishers, 1975).

9. Samuel C. Florman, *The Existential Pleasures of Engineering* (New York: St. Martin's, 1976), p. 148.

10. Russell Linden, *From Vision to Reality* (Charlottesville, VA: LEL Enterprises, 1990).

11. David Osborne and Ted Gaebler, *Reinventing Government* (Reading, MA: Addison-Wesley, 1992).

Chapter 5

Interpreting Effectiveness

. . . effectiveness as a unifying theme has intrinsically or extrinsically underpinned a century of research in organization management and design.

A. Lewin and J. Minton

Effectiveness is a critical concept at this point in our discussion because it is at the heart of beliefs about organizational processes, authority relationships, and employee motivation. Any in-depth understanding will involve paradoxical reasoning, so much so that after noting the vast array of outside constraints upon government bureaucracies along with the conflicting desires of many constituencies, some find it astonishing that they perform as well as they do.[1]

This chapter traces the forces that have shaped contemporary perceptions of organizational effectiveness in government. Business and economic approaches have dominated; the government productivity improvement movement will serve as an illustration. It should then be of interest to see how applied theorists are beginning to recognize and cope with various interpretations of effectiveness. All of these developments have important implications for determining the practicality of agency democracy.

THE ATTRACTION OF GENERIC ADMINISTRATIVE THOUGHT

The goal of administrative self-improvement is intimately associated with organizational efficiency and professional action. Analytical approachs to operations with their emphasis upon work planning, scheduling, work measurement and reporting were slowly adopted by public administration from business. By the beginning of World War II congressional committees and presidential offices had been giving more and more attention to organization and administration issues. In spite of the stimulus from private management, the relatively late start on the part of government in using the methods of scientific management was perhaps due to the "inapplicability of many of the early techniques to governmental functions." Yet it was evident that administrative progress could be made through objective inquiry and analysis by both industry and government.[2]

Benefits of closer ties between students of administration in public and private enterprise were predicted because of the shared emphasis upon structure and other aspects of organization applied theory. The success of the Tennessee Valley Authority project was put forth as a unique public sector application triumph of managerial innovation. The feeling was that public administration had ". . . struggled free from the notion of 'public business' as routine, as primarily negative and restrictive upon personal or private initiative and as an unnatural but necessary evil." Through professional interaction, communication and understanding would continue to increase between public and private organizations so that each would be of mutual support. Differences between business and government organizations were seen as mainly in terms of "ideology." While political office holders must relate to the preferences of constituents, such concerns are in contrast to those of government administrative officers, which are to "get the job done." There are "barriers and resistances imposed by layers above" along with the possibility of conflict between administrators and political office holders; but once policy decisions are made subordinates must be held responsible to comply.[3]

These major orientations in government management prevail to this day, and they are the backbone of the public management movement. At the center is the belief that scientific methods of running organizations will increasingly merge in the public and private sectors. It is paralleled by a feeling that this convergence is at times limited, even obstructed, by the presence of political institutional needs. However, whatever frustrations exist are seen as basically the concerns of higher-level policymakers, for the prime mission of those within public sector organization levels is to follow policy and top management directives in order to "get the job done." These mind-sets which began to crystalize in the mid-1940s include (a) faith in business as the source of generic management theory, (b) recognition that policy elite problems are different in government from those of business (c) belief that many difficulties will be eventually overcome by vigorous initiation of action on the part of higher management aimed at improving agency productivity, and (d) a major preoccupation with the agency unit and its clients, while virtually ignoring political institutional needs and realities.

PRODUCTIVITY AS A GENERIC CONCEPT[4]

It is difficult to think of a more popular definition of organizational effectiveness than productivity. More inclusive than the idea of efficiency, productivity is associated with creating abundance and value. Government productivity is viewed with wide approval, for it promises to get more yield out of scarce resources through technological and other administrative means. It is seen as a direct road to better living standards, associated with traditional values such as hard work, deserved wealth, technological progress and regional or national prominence. Political policy elites find the symbolism of "higher productivity" enormously attractive since it strikes a response in voters because of its businesslike ring. To urge higher productivity implies that efforts are under way to make maximum use of taxes and other public resources by running lean, taut operations. Successful agency, national, even private sector productivity improvement is routinely claimed as the result of political leadership foresight and ability.

The idea of productivity is derived from classical economic thought, in turn borrowed from the physical sciences—to be more precise, from the internal combustion engine. Engineers use the term "thermal efficiency" to describe how well a machine is running. If one considers input into the device as energy contained in fuel and output as the power obtained, then the ratio of output to input is a rating of how well the machine converts energy into work. However, if it is impossible to steer an automobile, then the machine could be highly efficient but quite useless because the output cannot be directed toward a useful purpose. In other words, the quality of output is deficient. Ideas about organizational productivity are drawn from such fundamental machine concepts.

The usual way to think of organizational productivity is as a production process control. In systems terms, inputs are transformed into outputs aimed at meeting desired standards. Each of these elements of the production process can be broken down into specific factors for analytical purposes.

The general production process represented by figure 5-1 shows inputs converted to outputs and compared to standards (i.e., expectations of output characteristics) to determine whether the process should continue "as is" or whether adjustments might be made. If outputs do not meet standards, specific elements of input, throughput, and standards may be changed. The arrows leading from the zone of comparison between output and standards show a variety of alternatives involving changing input, throughput and standard criteria properties. In order to monitor the production process, ratios are used. The best known is the comparison of output to input, known as efficiency. Units produced per employee over time are an example of efficiency ratios.

Quality is a distinct and separate control. This means that a deliberate attempt must be made to relate output to standards as shown in figure 5-1. Technically, ratios of output to standards are called process quality measurements.

Organizational productivity is a closed systems concept because it is a simple input-throughput-output process model independent of other influences that are in the environment. Association between a business corporation's productivity

Figure 5-1
The Production Process and Its Controls

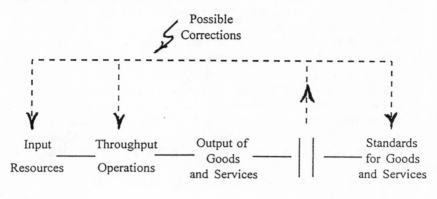

A successful process is one that optimizes efficiency and quality ratios. To put it in basic terms:

$$\text{Productivity} \quad = \quad \text{Efficiency and quality}$$

$$\text{or} \quad = \quad \text{O/I} \quad \& \quad \text{O/S}$$

improvement and favorable economic consequences has persuasive theoretical integrity. More yield from resource inputs at the corporate organizational and suborganizational levels results in greater profits because of an increased capacity to compete for and capture markets. This reasoning is based upon the assumptions that productivity increases result in competitive consumer costs and quality and that consumers are economically rational. Improvement actions depend upon the technical ability of corporate designers to adjust input mixes, revise throughput processes and monitor outputs in order to attain desired results. Increased employee motivation is possible; productivity data enhance the ability to better control employee behavior. All of this is supported by a body of "generic" organizational and behavioral scientific knowledge formulated mainly through studies of private sector enterprises. The basic business productivity construct is depicted in figure 5-2.

This perspective shows the direct effect of organizational action upon resource inputs, guided by a centralized source of policy direction and control. It is a machine metaphor, dependent upon information feedback loops, wherein

Figure 5-2
The Business Productivity Process

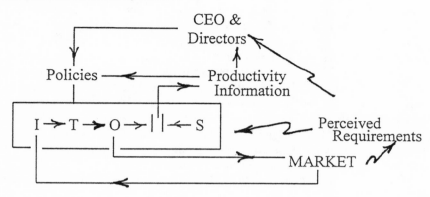

organizations are perceived as engines having direct control over their survival. Efficiency, or the relationship of outputs to inputs, emphasizes cost. Quality, as a systemic variable (i.e., the relationship of outputs to desired standards of shape, function and/or utility), is controlled by line operations and feedback from the marketplace (e.g., poor-quality products are avoided by buyers or returned for rework). Economists aggregate the performance of individual corporations into sectoral and national indicators by relating purchases of goods and services (Domestic National Product) to labor inputs. Thus, productivity trends can be analyzed and policy devised for sectors of or entire large economic systems.

The economic institutional model and its theoretically seamless interaction between organizational micro and macro levels of activities and consequences is, of course, open to serious challenge as the basis for comprehensive social policy. For example, a fundamental tension exists between private sector efficiency and social equity.[5] Yet there is small doubt that productivity improvement theory makes a logically consistent fit between corporate goals and the "good" society as defined by strong economic institutions. To be sure the workings of the marketplace and its associations with production units are infinitely more complex and interactive with other variables than those shown above. Exogenous influences, such as government regulation and other "imperfections" which attend the real-world marketplace, affect the validity of the machine model. Also, services present vexing problems as organizational outputs since they are immediately consumed when produced, thus precluding in-process controls such as inventory buffering. But the appeal of the simple productivity construct is undeniable. It is a major definer of effectiveness for policymakers in business enterprises, less so to those in the public sector.

POLITICAL INSTITUTIONS AND AGENCY PRODUCTIVITY

What happens when we superimpose the machine model of corporate productivity improvement upon public agencies? It is still conceptually sound to perceive a given government agency as an input-throughput-output process. The ethical impetus to strive for more yield from agency resource inputs is that the "savings" can be diverted to other public purposes or used for reduction of taxes. But beyond this, the connection between activities at the micro level and consequences at the macro level, illustrated in figure 5-3, goes far afield from the theoretical simplicity of the business model.

Rather than the "pure" economic-rational processes of the corporate machine model, what occurs is a transformation of public service *outcomes* at the agency level into *political effects*. These take on value-based effectiveness characteristics external to the individual agency.[6] Results are matched with expectations based directly on political systems needs. Evidently only partial aspects of the effects of agency actions can be assessed by rational economic reasoning (e.g., cost/benefit analysis). Policy direction is no longer centralized as in figure 5-2; in fact, the regular activities of the policy-making bodies themselves have a direct impact upon and help shape an agency's political consequences as well as expectations. Thus, the relatively simple theoretical cause-and-effect relationships so sharply visualized in economic institutions are not present in public sector applications.

The conversion from agency activities to political social consequences is only partially affected by the economic productivity perception of agency operations since it deals with but one aspect, *the resource management element*, of the overall purpose of public agencies. As previously mentioned, there are two additional general needs met by government processes aside from resource management: political and judicial responsiveness. Since these three elements are in tension, economic-rational agency management activities are not as centrally controlled nor given as high priority by political policy elites as they are in business.

This comparison between business and political effectiveness shows that it makes little theoretical or pragmatic sense to follow an economic line of reasoning by using raw productivity data for political consequences evaluation. Fundamentally, private sector economists deal with *output goods and services markets* that generate resource inputs to corporations. In the public sector, budgets as resource inputs are generated by *input political bargaining markets*, subject to a wide variety of political/economic needs. Telling support for this argument of limited fit of the generic business productivity theory is reflected by the fact that economists have long ago abandoned approaches to measuring aggregate public sector productivity. Rather "rough and therefore uncertain" estimates are made.[7]

This discussion of the dynamics of government operations shows that agen-

Figure 5-3
The Government Productivity Process

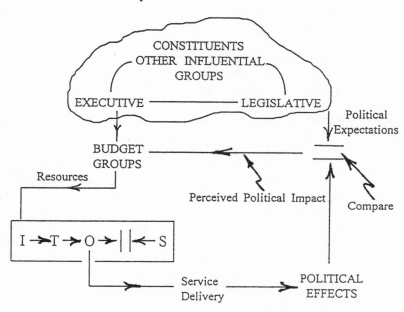

cies have to deal with the fact that they are an integral part of a political institution created to respond to communal needs rather than units created to obtain optimal market yield. Political institutions as systems of social influence and exchange, make dubious assumptions regarding the purposes and control of public agencies. The first is that the process of balancing needs and influence between various centers of government power will result in effective policy. Another is that executives (e.g., presidents, governors, mayors) must exercise control over agencies. Yet another is that all policy elites, after agreement on agency goals and budget formulation, will retain a natural and deep-seated interest in the efficient and effective usage of budgeted resources once these are allocated. This last premise will now be considered in the light of experience.

THE BIRTH OF A MOVEMENT

A good way to understand the rapid emergence of the national government productivity improvement movement is to refer to the *Public Administration Review* symposium issue published in 1972.[8] It begins with an overview by the head of the National Commission on Productivity, established by President Richard Nixon in 1970 to focus on private and public sector problems and make recommendations for improvements. One purpose was to measure the overall productivity of the federal agency workforce. Another was to encourage productivity bargaining experimentation with employees in the public sector.

Since measurement was a central theme in the symposium issue, attention was given to ways to evaluate national labor productivity and their limitations vis-à-vis the public sector. A good deal of enthusiasm was expressed regarding the progress made in measuring the efficiency of federal operations. Preliminary efforts had started in 1962 but had little momentum until 1970 when Senator William Proxmire wrote to the comptroller general that it was "distressing that we have no real measures of the efficiency of the Federal sector."[9] An extensive multi-agency program was then put into motion to inventory existing work, unit cost and efficiency measures. The study came to the technically debatable conclusion that output per employee year had increased at an annual rate of 1.9 percent between fiscal years 1967 and 1971, with plans to formalize and extend the coverage of productivity indices. The general problem of measurement was considered as a central one for federal, state and local government. It was felt that progress was generally inadequate both in the compilation of data and in the state of the art. Of mounting concern was assessing quality of service, for without it "productivity measurement is too likely to be difficult if not actually perverse."[10]

Other major coordinated efforts were described in the 1972 publication. For instance, New York City's productivity program had just been publicized by a 225-page statement of work objectives, units of measures and quarterly performance targets.[11] The governor of Wisconsin got agencies to think about productivity by setting target budget cuts of 2.5 percent per year and having them explain how they would implement the reduction.[12] It was recognized by others that government cost accounting practices, contrary to those of business, do not encourage productivity investments. Methods had to be devised to measure productivity goals and accomplishments in government agencies in an aggregative and cost-rational manner as a fundamental requirement to mount any significant improvement action.[13] All told, the 1972 *Public Administration Review* symposium issue voiced a sense of hope, involvement and progress, tempered by the knowledge that the public sector presented unique problems and that a difficult path lay ahead. Various initiatives taken at city and county levels, reported in a separate publication, showed how a vigorous and mutually supportive productivity improvement effort had started to take root.[14] The federal government played a prominent role, not only in attempts to better its own operations but also to encourage research, to act as an information exchange center and as a funding source for other levels of government.

In the midst of the swelling enthusiasm for government productivity improvement, a voice of pessimism and sharp dissent was raised. Frederick Thayer considered the movement was a management "fad" derived from microeconomic thought. There are basic flaws in the underlying theoretical premises, he reasoned. The problem with productivity thinking is that there must be a very narrow determination of a single objective without regard to the consequences for other agency purposes. Productivity improvement efforts encourage the "cultural isolation" of organizations, interorganizational competition and worker alienation. Also microeconomic axioms "compel those who use its techniques to assume that more of whatever is under study is preferable to less." There are no "tangled assumptions of market economics" that can be operationalized in public policy analysis.[15] Those of us deeply involved at that time in the movement tended to overlook Thayer's words because we put great reliance upon generic (e.g., business) productivity theory. While progress was made, it later became evident that his provocative and important insights had considerable merit.

DECLINE AND EBB

About five years after the appearance of the first *Public Administration Review* edition on government productivity, a second symposium issue asked whether the government productivity improvement effort was "alive and well."[16] The news was disquieting. The National Commission on Productivity, renamed the National Center for Productivity and Quality of Working Life, was barely alive. Federal efforts to measure productivity had increased coverage of the work force but no reports had been issued since 1976. Most of the showcase initiatives of cities, states and counties were rapidly falling apart or had been discontinued or drastically scaled down.

By early 1978 a sharp curtailment of growth and even a reduction of some government employment was well under way. Few in 1972 could have imagined that only three years later New York City, on the brink of financial ruin, would have to reduce its payroll by almost 60,000 employees. Other crucial events were taking place when the second productivity symposium issue appeared. California's Proposition 13 gained nationwide attention as a successful culmination of the taxpayer revolt since it increased "the strength of citizen belief that the public fiscal world was penetrable and perhaps controllable."[17] Similar efforts occurred throughout the nation as the referendum was used to promote drastic taxation and expenditure limitations.

Budget-cutting approaches, spurred on by staggering projected national deficits, were undertaken by the federal government toward the middle 1980s with the impetus of the Gramm-Rudman-Hollings balanced budget act and its repercussions at state and local levels. Throughout the nation grass roots reaction to the size and cost of government intensified as fiscal crises became more visible and threatening. Pent-up frustration and public rage was fed by highly publicized examples of government mismanagement, waste and corruption. The hue and cry was taken up by legislators and executives, all intent upon bashing bureaucratic ineptitude. Symbolic evidence of public anger at government reached new heights. To cite but a few examples, one citizen committee newspaper advertisement pictured garbage cans overflowing with crumpled greenbacks as "federal depositories." Another ad, deploring the Department of Defense purchasing scandals, displayed a picture of a common hammer with a price tag of several hundred dollars. Perhaps the most striking image appeared on the jacket of a book dedicated to reducing the costs of public services. A fist is depicted clenching a legislative building, apparently ready to squeeze the life out of government along with its cost.

The term "cutback management," which became popular during these periods of financial crisis, includes strategies to resist agency decline through external political support, expanding the revenue base, making symbolic responses and improving productivity. Other tactics were to smooth the process of decline by cutting low prestige programs, reducing services to politically weak clients, improving planning techniques, reorganizing, having employees make voluntary sacrifices and deterring maintenance.[18]

In any event almost all the highly publicized productivity improvement programs of the 1970s were discontinued or in final stages of decline early in the 1980s. Fiscal emergencies hastened the end of the coordinated productivity improvement movement. A logical expectation would be for those advocating the movement to redouble their efforts during times of resource shortages; but this was not to occur as short-term overtook long-term concerns. However, some benefits of the national movement are still in evidence.

RESIDUAL EFFECTS

Though integrated action began to draw to a rapid close in 1978, the momentum carried through the early 1980s. The 1970-80 period produced considerable amounts of research, training and publications. Some of the centers for funding and research were the National Science Foundation, the Urban Institute, Public Technology Incorporated and various university research centers and "think tanks" such as the New York City Rand Institute (now defunct). These sources dried up, and by 1981 the U.S. Office of Personnel Management was supporting only five minor productivity improvement projects within four states.

The impetus to systematically turn over more government operations to the private sector, which started during the 1970s, probably helped to dilute interest in government agency workplace productivity. Dubbed "privatization," the intent is to place increasing reliance upon the private sector to improve the effectiveness of government operations. Involved are wholesale transfers of responsibilities to the private sector, contracting out and the use of vouchers for individual citizens to purchase services and franchising. In order to administer privatization prudently, any given transfer of work should have specifiable criteria of performance and multiple sources (to insure continued competition); it must also be constitutionally permissible. While some of the more global claims for the benefits of privatization are open to question, wide-ranging successes have been reported in the transfer of more routine work (e.g., waste management, transportation, grounds work, street cleaning, janitorial services, highway repair and data processing). Surveys show that contracting out public services continues to grow. Reactions have been generally favorable since costs have been cut by one-third and quality has remained satisfactory in some areas. Procedures have been established to foster competition, specify contract terms, denote bidding processes, help compare costs and monitor contract performance.[19] Culturally, any movement that is seen as resulting in smaller numbers of government employees while bolstering the private sector economy is well received.

The impact of privatization has become substantial, especially at local government levels. Public sector unions have attempted to slow down the movement toward outside contracting by using political influence. Some localities have experimented with outside and even reverted back to public provision of services.[20] Intensive privatization will further a progressive decline in government workers employed in the more routine and sharply circumscribed operations. A few professionals will then become redundant, but the effect should be offset by requirements for more government specialists to plan and monitor the performance of outside contractors. Predictably, while the operating core population of agencies will decline, the ratio of intermediary professionals to policy elites and other public agency employees will increase.

Returning to mainstream productivity, the older broad-based program of governmentwide, cooperative self-improvement action has been replaced by Total Quality Management and reinventing government types of efforts. The highwater mark of the past productivity improvement movement left an abundance of applied research literature, much of it directed at local government, originating from and funded by various federal agencies. Measurement has been explored in extensive detail. Professional associations, primarily the International City Management Association, issued excellent "how-to" productivity improvement papers and books. Among the significant publications sparked by the "greening" of the movement are a professional journal and association devoted to public sector productivity, handbooks on state and local government productivity, reviews of state and local government productivity initiatives, manuals on work measurement and studies of the political environment of state government productivity improvement.[21]

In spite of the availability of these references, cooperative and systematic productivity improvement has not ranked very high among government priorities except in the area of TQM and reinventing government. While there has been a sharp reduction of integrated activity among federal, state and other levels, some of the ongoing efforts provide a basis for cautious optimism. As political support is given and professionals become freer to take risks, more innovations and greater benefits should accumulate.[22]

The federal cooperative effort with state and local governments was at a virtual standstill by 1980, along with its own internal efforts to improve productivity. Since then various initiatives have surfaced within the federal sphere that merit comment. The Reagan administration's Reform '88, under the Office of Management and Budgeting (OMB), was initiated to make enduring changes that would survive the next change of administration.[23] The program was energized by heat generated from the Private Sector Survey on Cost Control (Grace Commission) and the Gramm-Rudman-Hollings balanced budget act, both oriented toward budget reduction. Circular A-76, aimed at intensive privatization, enjoined agencies to define their work requirements and compare their costs of operations with private bids. Later on, a comprehensive report on Reform '88 achievements concluded that the federal productivity program prospects are "uncertain" because of staff shortages, burdensome reporting requirements and a lack of integration of productivity improvement activities with other central processes.[24]

Returning to an earlier part of this chapter, Thayer, it will be recalled, faulted "generic" productivity applied theory because it is based upon private sector logic. The recommendation that we examine the social utility of some outputs and question "more of the same" is important. All said, while there is reason to disagree with some of Thayer's arguments, his was a prophetic voice because he reminded us at the onset of the unique political factors and the limitations of business management philosophy. If we had thought through in more depth the nature of political institutional contexts, the level of rhetoric might have been lower and expectations more realistic.

THE TQM MOVEMENT

The best established in the recent succession of performance improvement programs, also adopted from industry, is Total Quality Management along with a number of derivatives. Envisioned as a holistic approach to management/employee cooperation, the focus is upon the agency "customer," better service delivery and continuous agency self-improvement. TQM has an integrative advantage in that it uses existing analytical tools and change techniques in a "team improvement" atmosphere. Major reliance is put upon involvement in the form of joint management/employee planning, shared monitoring of pilot projects and cooperative implementation of change. Among the reputed advantages of TQM programs are that they can deal consistently with improvement initiatives of modest scale, are action, or "hands-on," rather than paperwork-control oriented and seek consciously to reduce employee along with management anxieties over engaging in change.[25]

Proponents of TQM see it as a revolutionary movement because it recognizes the primacy of agency client (customer) satisfaction. This conviction goes back to principles of statistical quality control recast by an American, W. Edwards Deming, enthusiastically elaborated and put into practice by Japanese industrialists. Efforts have been made to accommodate the major principles into government operations by urging clearer mission statements and merging the "voice of the customer with management systems, building quality into process, constant improvement action, better training, improved leadership, creation of trust, encouraging joint action, eliminating quotas and discontinuing the practice of blaming individuals." Managers are urged to create structures and environments which encourage daily efforts to attain TQM principles.

The presence of numerous barriers is recognized; these include the merit system, top-down management styles, overspecialization of skills, restrictive controls, fears of change and budgeting process disincentives. Such obstacles aside, a close to messianic faith promotes hopes that the sheer scope and merit of TQM principles will carry the day. There is some substance to this conviction because advances have been announced since the mid-1980s on a variety of federal operations. Successes have also reported by local and state governments.

While the techniques and philosophy of TQM will undoubtedly continue to have favorable consequences, it is yet an open question whether the programs will achieve the revolutionary expectations of TQM's proponents. Once again, the path follows the dictates of business experience. Successes in government are most probable in the more routine operations that have clearer missions, are able to identify common client needs and produce leaders. Fundamentally, as in other initiatives, an act of volition is expected to overcome what are seen as political institutional deficiencies. Enthusiasm, better human relations, decisions built upon facts, the human need for self-improvement and an identification with customer needs provide the impetus. Whenever a promising approach such as TQM comes on the scene, there is a tendency to forget the institutional realities of government. History shows that ignoring these could have unfavorable consequences.

CYCLES OF FERVOR TO PESSIMISM

The productivity improvement movement is but one of a series of major efforts first taken at the federal level to improve the effectiveness of the public service by concentrating upon decision-making and other processes. The planning-programming-budgeting-system (PPBS), initiated in 1962, was aimed at associating programs, comparing alternatives, integrating changes and intensive progress reporting. It failed. Management by objectives, introduced in 1972, has declined in popularity. Zero-based budgeting, instituted in 1977, lost its impetus. Each was launched with great fanfare, but fell short of publicized expectations because of "analytical idealism, political naiveté and private sector evangelism."[26] George Downs and Patrick Larkey also observe that political and other leaders take a "hubris" approach to reform. In so doing they ignore lessons of past failures that did not take into account the unique aspects of public administration and make overblown promises about the future. Eventually hubris is replaced by an ideology of despair as failures spawn passivity and more exposure to errors.

New approaches to effectiveness in the public sector that are inspired by business experience are always at risk if the realities of agency effectiveness are ignored. For instance corporate top management is moving away from organizational charts, toward redefining key relationships and basic management behaviors. A recent study shows that almost total immersion is required on the part of CEOs to increase organizational creativity, boundary-spanning competence and renew strategies.[27] Many find it distressing that high government officials do not have the same commitment as do business chief executive officers to setting detailed agency policy, closely participating in its installation and making employees accountable. This ignores past experience showing that policy elites have a tendency to become unrealistically enthusiastic over improvement programs and then lose interest over the long haul.

Such lack of persistence can be partially explained by the fact that government bureaucracies operate in a matrix of mandated rules and regulations; at the same time they are burdened with participation demands by outside boards, constituencies, councils, investigators and others. A major requirement of agency policy elites is to survive by not being overpowered by rules, swamped by other outside controls or brought to a halt by citizen participation. These are problems of governance, of broad policy, not those of classical management nor of making the administrative system work better.[28]

Contradictions of this kind help explain inconsistent behavior on the part of those at the top who, after introducing a new approach to effectiveness improvement with great enthusiasm,

- do not give it consistent support (e.g., delegation of responsibility, training, technical support, budgetary resources),
- emphasize short-term goal attainment over steady process improvement,
- use personalized criteria of effectiveness (which best represent their individual values and performances) over more neutral, objective criteria, and then
- lose interest in complex measurement and control systems.

The reasons for such "unbusinesslike" behavior are inherent to the public service. Highly publicized, successful improvement efforts can result in sizable workforce and budget cuts, thus reducing the capacity to respond to emergencies. Data gathered from sophisticated control systems can be used against incumbents as "proof" of their ineptitude to the public at large. Throughout, people in high agency positions try to maintain a posture toward the outside that projects an image of simplicity and comprehensive mastery of operations. Throughout inappropriate comparisons are made with business management because this is the way that the general culture understands administration.

Professionals can respond to agency ineffectiveness by becoming less dependent upon top-level behavior, more understanding of the necessity for their working life contradictions. It is desirable, for instance, to make programs such as TQM work as well as possible within one's realm of responsibility without falling victim to hubris, cynicism or despondency. At the same time it is worth remembering that policy elites may behave in inconsistent ways not because of administrative ineptitude or character defects; but rather because they are attempting to cope with ambiguous political demands.

THE MANY MEANINGS OF EFFECTIVENESS

Conventional assessments of organizational effectiveness have centered upon establishing operational performance standards and defining causes and effects leading to attainment of these standards. As already shown, practitioners tend to gravitate toward norms of microeconomic rationality. The corporate and financial world, for instance, "keeps score" with Return on Investment (ROI) data. Productivity and efficiency-oriented organizational results are used to assess and control operations. The fact that even these private sector data are often murky and based upon incomplete knowledge about cause and effect has been of concern to private sector theorists for some time.[29]

In an effort to connect effectiveness means and ends, John Rohrbaugh and Robert Quinn considered two major polarized dimensions common to all perceptions of effectiveness. Organizational decentralization efforts are in tension with centralization efforts. Paradoxically, a focus upon internal organizational characteristics can detract from a needed emphasis upon external environmental forces. These two dimensions explain why different effectiveness values are logically in competition. For example, the ends of productivity and efficiency are associated with "rational" planning and goal setting. Activities of this nature result in a push for centralization which is then countered by efforts to maintain employee satisfaction and flexibility by developing skills and holding employees in reserve to permit adaptation to change.[30] The history of effectiveness assessment is largely one of trying to adjust to such opposing forces.

Some have rightly suggested that we accept the paradoxical nature of effectiveness as inevitable and learn how to accommodate to the inherent ambiguity and problems of definition. Evaluators of effectiveness often select models, criteria and indicators that are inappropriate to the situation at hand. The reason is that most observers are reluctant to accept the fact that "to be effective, an organization must possess attributes that are simultaneously contrary, even mutually exclusive." Far from despairing at the ubiquitous presence of paradoxical relationships, we should follow three guiding principles: (a) paradoxes are inherent to visualizing effectiveness; (b) paradoxes need not be resolved to take action; and (c) too much emphasis upon any one effectiveness criterion can become dysfunctional.[31] These remarks are particularly salient because, while the idea of public agency democracy is inherently paradoxical, it is quite consistent with the basic nature of effectiveness. On the other hand traditional professional orientations rarely recognize that ambiguity is a normal, even desirable, aspect of problem solving. A knowledge of paradoxical effectiveness relationships helps to realize why experimental, tentative and intuitive approaches are so fruitful. By not immediately imposing order and a technically "rational" problem-solving approach upon agency predicaments, we leave open the exploration of various seemingly conflicting aspects of reality.

Since the nature of government effectiveness is not realistically acknowledged, many are misled. Candidates for office promise to run government operations as in business, but the exigencies of governance do not permit them to give productivity improvement enough attention. Nor are differences in institutional settings acknowledged. Professionals entertain unrealistic, romantic notions about the perfectibility of policy elite guidance instead of adapting to the contradictory realities of political environments. Professionals blame management and political irrationality for errors which they could have helped prevent at formative stages. When asked to join in new approaches to increase effectiveness, given the record of past failures, they often trail along in the glum hope that they will survive the latest improvement fad, that it too will quietly fade away.

Agency democracy provides a rationale to cope with political systems ambiguity by first reaffirming the necessity for reactive, in-role responses. At the same time latitude exists for spontaneous proactive initiatives which do not rely upon management to take the lead. Throughout it is recognized that essential political systems criteria of effectiveness may go counter to and supersede criteria of effectiveness or the interests of agency insiders. While responsive to management leadership, professionals do not expect too much; they understand the necessity for subordinates to initiate action at rare, but crucial times. The reason that paradoxes are inevitable at the workplace is that most organizations have conflicting goals, and therefore different values are in competition, more so, it seems fair to say, in government institutions than in business. Repeated attempts have been made to resolve these paradoxes, but they cannot nor need be resolved. Therefore tentative trust, contingent loyalty and seemingly inconsistent behavior are legitimate means to cope with the exigencies of political environments.

Recognizing and adapting to the ambiguities of government effectiveness puts an additional burden upon intermediary professionals, but what is really at stake for many of these individuals is the meaning of their working lives. Issues involving effectiveness are of high ethical importance because they are so closely associated with ways to define oneself, to find worth in one's occupation such as feelings of being influential and doing things that matter. Untold numbers go to their workplace only to be caught in a vicious circle. Some perform meaningless tasks or have to act busy when there is little to do, all of this because of the enigmatic nature of political institutional processes and the inevitable limitations upon management will and skill. It then becomes important for those in the hierarchy to respond to inside initiatives and accept the stresses involved in meaningful participation on the part of subordinates. As the nature of government agency effectiveness becomes better understood and accepted, then great amounts of innovative energy can be liberated from inside agency walls. Blocking the way, however, are administrative theories and beliefs about authority that are not adequate to the challenge. Some of these will be examined in the next chapter.

NOTES

1. James Q. Wilson, *Bureaucracy* (New York: Basic Books, 1989), pp. 376-78.

2. Donald C. Stone, "Administrative Self Improvement," in *Elements of Public Administration*, ed. Fritz M. Marx (New York: Prentice-Hall, 1946), p. 452.

3. Avery Leiserson, "The Study of Public Administration," in *Elements of Public Administration*, ed. Fritz M. Marx, pp. 47- 50.

4. The development of this section and the next is drawn from two sources by Walter L. Balk, *Improving Government Productivity: Some Policy Perspectives* (Beverly Hills, CA: Sage, 1975), pp. 10-15; and "Productivity Improvement in Government Agencies," in *Policy Studies Review*, vol. 4, no. 3 (Feburary 1985): 475-83.

5. Arthur Okun, *Equality and Efficiency* (Washington: Brookings, 1975).

6. I am indebted to Dr. James Feldt of the University of Georgia and Dr. Alain Belasen of the State University of New York who were instrumental in developing key aspects of this model.

7. Solomon Fabricant, *A Primer on Productivity* (New York: Random House, 1969), pp. 20-21.

8. Chester A. Newland, ed., "Symposium on Productivity in Government," *Public Administration Review*, vol. 32, no. 6 (November/December 1972).

9. Thomas D. Morris et al., "Productivity Measures in the Federal Government," *Public Administration Review*, vol. 32, no. 6, p. 754.

10. Harry Hatry, "Issues in Productivity Measurement for Local Government," *Public Administration Review*, vol. 32, no. 6, p. 778.

11. Edward Hamilton, "Productivity: The New York Approach," *Public Administration Review*, vol. 32, no. 6, p. 284.

12. Patrick J. Lucey, "Wisconsin's Productivity Program," *Public Administration*

Review, vol. 32, no. 6, pp. 795-99. Later, in 1973-75, 7.5 percent of each agency's budget was withheld under the same ground rule. The percentage was dropped back to 3 percent in 1975-77.

13. John W. Kendrick, "Public Capital Expenditures and Budgeting for Productivity Advance," *Public Administration Review*, vol. 32, no. 6, pp. 804-7.

14. Frederick O'R. Hayes, *Productivity in Local Government* (Lexington, MA: Heath, 1977).

15. Frederick C. Thayer, "Productivity: Taylorism Revisited (Round Three)," *Public Administration Review*, vol. 32, no. 6, p. 734. Brief reference is also made in the symposium issue to some of Dwight Waldo's remarks at a conference; one of these was "Why not inquire into delivering more justice and equity, rather than being more productive?" He also questioned the belief that government is highly compatible with private business (p. 844).

16. Walter L. Balk, ed., "Symposium on Productivity in Government," *Public Administration Review*, vol. 38, no. 1 (January/February 1978).

17. Richard A. Eribes and John S. Hall, "Revolt of the Affluent: Local Controls in Three States," *Public Administration Review: The Impact of Resource Scarcity on Urban Public Finance*, vol. 41, special issue (January 1981): 107.

18. Charles H. Levine, "Organizational Decline and Cutback Management," in *Managing with Less*, ed. Elisabeth K. Keller (Washington: International City Management Association, 1979), pp. 28-44.

19. E. S. Savas, "Privatization and Productivity," in *Public Productivity Handbook*, ed. Marc Holzer (New York: Marcel Dekker, 1992), Chapter 5.

20. Timothy Chandler and Peter Feuille, "Municipal Unions and Privatization," *Public Administration Review*, vol. 51, no. 1 (January/February 1991): 15-22.

21. See these publications: Marc Holzer, ed., *Public Productivity and Management Review*; George J. Washnis, ed., *Productivity Handbook for State and Local Government* (New York: John Wiley & Sons, 1980); John M. Grenier, *Productivity and Motivation: A Review of State and Local Government Initiatives* (Washington: Urban Institute, 1981); Edgar G. Crane et al., *State Government Productivity: The Environment for Productivity* (New York: Praeger, 1976); Marc Holzer, ed., *Public Productivity Handbook* (New York: Marcel Dekker, 1992).

22. Holzer, *Public Productivity Handbook*, chapter 1.

23. Executive Order 12552, the White House, February 25, 1986. See also OMB Bulletin 86-8, February 28, 1986.

24. United States General Accounting Office, *Managing the Government*, GAO/GGD-89-65, May 1989, pp. 45-48.

25. Michael E. Milakovich, "Total Quality Management for Public Service Productivity Improvement," *Public Productivity Handbook*, ed. Marc Holzer. See chapter 30 for a review of TQM in government.

26. George W. Downs and Patrick D. Larkey, *The Search for Government Efficiency* (New York: Random House, 1986), p. 179. Without attempting to excuse poor performance, the authors comment upon many of the misperceptions of the public service and the invidious tendency to pit business performance against that of government. The process of going from "hubris to despair" is analyzed and recommendations made for more constructive orientations. See chapter 7.

27. Sumantra Ghosal and Christopher A. Bartlett, "Changing the Role of Top Man-

agement: Beyond Structure and Process," *Harvard Business Review*, vol. 73, no. 1 (1995): 86-96.

28. James Q. Wilson, pp. 113-136 and 375-78.

29. James D. Thompson, *Organizations in Action* (New York: McGraw-Hill, 1967). See chapter 7.

30. Robert E. Quinn and John Rohrbaugh, "A Special Model of Effectiveness Criteria: Towards a Competing Values Approach to Organizational Analysis," *Management Science*, vol. 29 (1983): 363-77.

31. Kim S. Cameron, "Effectiveness as Paradox: Consensus and Conflict in Conceptions of Organizational Effectiveness," *Management Science*, vol. 37, no. 5 (May 1986): 539-53.

Chapter 6

Organizational Authority

It is hard to overestimate the impact of this metaphor of the well-run machine.

Karen Hult and Charles Walcott

The first sections in this chapter discuss some general characteristics of major organizational theories that guide and justify daily action. These are then related to beliefs about the nature of management authority relationships. Concepts involving stress and adaptation are of particular interest because of the constant need to cope with paradox. It is interesting that the more recent innovations in organization thought hold the seeds for the acceptance of the model of agency democracy. Yet existing mind-sets concerning supervisor-subordinate relationships are greatly influenced by traditional corporate management needs and ideologies not receptive to proactive behavior and citizenship values.

ADMINISTRATION AND ORGANIZATIONS

In 1937 a distinguished public administration practitioner and theorist described the principles of a unitary approach to a social science of administration. Recognizing that the science had to be based upon some fundamental purpose, Luther Gulick recommended efficiency as the "single, ultimate test of value in administration." A prime requirement is to make it "possible to approximate more clearly the empirical, valueless world in which exact science has advanced with such success." This requires the use of methods of scientific investigation such as standardizing nomenclature, establishing measurable elements, developing "rational concepts," documenting, generating hypotheses and testing theories.[1] Somewhat ruefully he recognized that there are unique aspects to public administration as compared to business. An important difference is that government organizations are less open to evolutionary changes aimed at "survival of the fittest" since they are not subject to the "purifying influence of competition." Collaterally, Gulick saw the need for public agencies to adapt to an expansion of political bodies and leadership, which would "free the currents of political life" and better assure the survival of democratic political institutions.[2]

Since then a remarkable variety of administrative concepts has been generated providing numerous ways to visualize organizational phenomena. The constant thrust has been toward "generic" theory calculated to serve the needs of all organizations, regardless of their institutional setting. Along these lines it is useful to think of organizations as arrangements of incremental units, as machines arranged to produce major events, called outputs. Departments and other groupings are seen as the counterpart of machine assemblies, useful in designing the technical makeup of each unit and their interactions so as to produce an automatic response to command. To illustrate, a social welfare agency assures that special services are delivered to eligible citizens. Agency members act in their role capacity—which is to say that they work as functionaries whose behavior is routinized by shared impersonal rules and job descriptions. Victor Thompson labels this the *artificial systems* perspective since an organization is seen as an artifact, or tool.

Most government policy elites along with citizens at large share these mechanistic perceptions of public agencies. Unfortunately this point of view leaves little room for social exchanges, for human desires to create and become influential, to adjust and redefine tasks in ways not covered by formal rules. Thompson accounts for these realities by developing a parallel to artificial systems called *natural systems*. He proposes that open, natural systems are essential for members to survive in organizations since "they meet needs that artificial system designers cannot recognize."[3]

While natural systems and artificial systems orientations complement each other, serious psychological paradoxes and dilemmas should not be overlooked. Artificial systems routines can become destructive to the mental stability of workers;[4] it is also true that, at times, bureaucracies may not permit sympathy or compassion on the part of organizational members toward others as they carry out their duties.[5] Clearly, however, contiguous artificial and natural systems are essential for organizations to function. Artificial systems provide the vehicle to implement social purpose with some degree of technical predictability. Natural systems compensate for the imperfections of artificial systems and help organizational members adapt to being governed by impersonal controls.

Two other major general orientations are in evidence—those of prescriptive versus diagnostic approaches. The first is mainly interested in developing ideal arrangements of structure and cooperative behavior. Diagnosticians, on the other hand, explore the details of decisions and processes which make things happen in order to develop more effective action. Those who engage in prescriptive approaches are accused of a nonscientific bias since an emotional attachment to what is "desirable" is seen as contaminating problem-solving logic and reducing the capacity to make logical decisions.[6] Yet the necessity for the more intuitive, prescriptive approaches has not disappeared.

FOUR BROAD CATEGORIES OF APPLIED THEORY

Organizational knowledge can be divided into artificial/natural and prescriptive/diagnostic orientations as shown in figure 6-1. These have evolved so as to accommodate the increasingly sophisticated needs of practitioners.

At the turn of the century quadrant I, organizational structure (e.g., roles, departments, rules), was of major interest. Then worker social perceptions and motivations (quadrant II), starting with the human relations movement in the 1930s, were formally recognized.[7] The content of quadrant III emerged in the 1940s typified by the work of Herbert Simon, who proposed that the analysis of decisions should become the basis for administrative science.[8] Progress in statistical control techniques, operations research and employee testing helped managers and researchers improve the potential of this diagnostic category.

During the 1960s the study of organizational adaptation to a wide variety of external and internal demands gained in importance.[9] By that time social psychologists and other social scientists had made progress in understanding individual, interpersonal and group influences that affect internal as well as external organizational effectiveness. As a result, phenomena of stress and conflict have become incorporated into the body of management knowledge. These are called Systems Influence in figure 6-1. Certainly practitioners have dealt with structure, human factors, decision analysis and systems influence since organizations began, but modern theorists made it more possible to accumulate, sharpen and pass on this knowledge from generation to generation.

Systems Influence introduces a good deal of sophistication into organizational thought. For example, outside organizations and other social forces require coping strategies on the part of any given administrative unit. It is also evident that stress and conflict are normal outcomes of power and dependency. The presence of contradictory and distorted agency goals can be explained as a consequence of external and internal forces attempting to "push" an organization in different directions. To illustrate, public agencies must of necessity adapt to diverging pressures from executive offices, legislators and constituencies. These sometimes present the necessity to make hard choices among competing demands and, as has been noted in the previous chapter, creates difficulties in evaluating effectiveness. The internal makeup of organizations can also be perceived in a unique manner by thinking in systems influence terms. For instance, in mental health centers, three major groups—therapists, clients and administrators—are in evidence. Those within each group have distinctly different, yet overlapping needs, as shown in figure 6-2.

Figure 6-1
Major Categories of Organization Theory

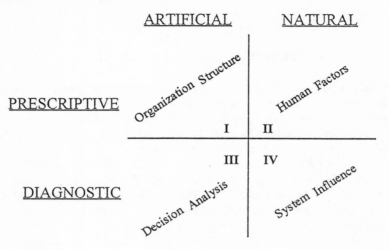

Clients want their problems solved, therapists are keenly interested in exercising their professional skills, and administrators have broad objectives of harboring resources and being accountable to policy elites. The needs of these three sets of actors are divergent but linked at overlaps a, b, c and d. Common organizational goals, values and activities are shown by sector a. Sector b represents therapy services to clients; sector c, administration services to clients; and sector d, administration services to therapists. Exploration of the needs of major actors augmented by the analysis of linkages between sectors can help specify natural and often beneficial stress within organizations.[10] There is an interesting similarity to mechanical structures (such as buildings and bridges) wherein the structural parts are arranged and connected so that advantage can be taken of tensions and pressure. In a similar manner, stressful interplay between organizational functions can be seen as essential to producing organizational form and structure; for without these pressures and tensions, the arrangement would collapse.

Returning to exterior forces, a good deal of progress has been made over the past few years in visualizing how organizations interact with the surrounding environment. There are three major ways for organizations to adapt to their environment. *Constraint responses* assume that a specific organization must make strict accommodations to outside economic, institutional and other surrounding organizational forces. *Strategic choice relationships* focus upon ways that a single organization can alter its environment. One can then proactively

Change responses

Figure 6-2
Organizational Structure and Divergent Needs

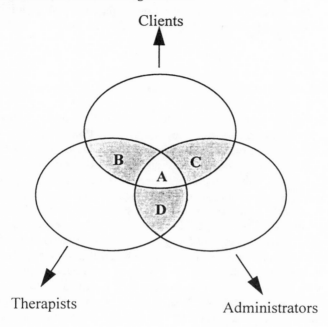

gauge the nature of external challenges through learning, experimentation and making choices. These choices are aimed at increasing organizational legitimacy and advancing its strategic position. The third approach is based upon the idea of *mutual adaptation* through exchanges. Networks of organizational entities and key actors influence one another in dynamic and proactive ways to achieve their goals, gain power and create dependency.[11]

These methods of adaptation should be of interest to the reader since, in the first place, it is likely that any single agency will use a combination of approaches; one may predominate over the other under changing circumstances. The ruling constraint response to overhead democracy provides a strong logic for hierarchical roles and control by policy elites. Legal systems are constraints which define and reinforce in-role behavior on the part of intermediary professionals. Conversely, strategic choice, applied to intermediary professionals, opens the door for lower-level initiation of action aimed at improving organizational effectiveness. The mutual adaptation path appears to fit out-of-role behavior as intermediary professionals become engaged in activities which revise usual patterns of authority.

Clearly, systems influence provides organizational theoretical support for the model of agency democracy. Without an acceptance of stress, tension and adaptation as normal and essential to organizational life, our visualization of the potential for improvement through professionals acting as citizens is shallow and incomplete.

THE DRIVE FOR HARMONY AND LOYALTY

Reconsidering figure 6-1, practitioners and the public appear most comfortable with three of the categories of applied theory. Political leaders and interested constituents are attracted to the simple perception of an agency as a mechanical vehicle for policy implementation. Therefore structure is of major interest along with a limited number of performance indicators, mainly fiscal controls. Intermediary professionals, as problem solvers, are heavily involved in decision analysis. Human factors are also seen as useful because of its seemingly common sense and results-oriented nature. However, in spite of the informal acceptance of everyday bargaining and conflict within and between organizations, systems influence is less of a shared frame of reference between policy elites, agency members and the public. This is because the emphasis of quadrants I, II and III is clearly upon harmony; all fit together to support the bureaucratic machine model. An underlying conviction is that lowering stress through psychological means makes people more contented and therefore more motivated to attain organizational goals. The dubious conclusion is that "high morale"—a very complex and elusive term—is seen as resulting in greater productivity. While these assumptions have not held up very well in even the earlier studies of productivity improvement,[12] many find it appealing since it seems to bring "heart" and human sentiments into organizational life.

At the same time there is small doubt that human factors can become tempting to power holders who want to manipulate employee feelings so as to increase the efficiency of the machine model. This helps explain why the predominant orientation of policy elites in public agencies has historically been toward tight managerial control and smoothing dissension along with demands for subordinate loyalty and trust. Quadrant IV, with its focus upon the realities and dilemmas of divergent power pressures, bargaining and conflict, certainly stands out in stark contrast to the others. It is now possible to visualize a dynamic natural system of individuals and groups expressing dissent as well as forming coalitions in order to gain the social power necessary to accomplish organizational objectives.

Why has applied theory evolved in this manner? Why do the less complex concepts have such enduring utility and durability? Each of the major perspectives in the fourfold table presents unique ways to deal with achieving organizational stability and bringing about change. The first, structure, promotes hierarchical *command* as the key necessity, attained through arrangements of roles, department groupings and formal status relationships. Human factors give primacy to social phenomena in order to *persuade* workers to accomplish organizational goals. Decision analysis follows an analytical view of information flow and controls in order to *program* events so as to decrease uncertainty. The focus of systems influence is situational stresses and constraints, external and internal to one's organization. Since the goal is to produce the right fit between appropriate action and shifting influences, practitioners are urged to *adapt* to situational contingencies.

The range of behaviors found in the model of public agency democracy appear quite consistent with all of the above. Different organizational problems call for the application of different theoretical perspectives. Attachments to harmony and loyalty stem from the relatively straightforward, interconnected and gratifying exercise of power through command, persuasion and programming activities. Adaptation activities are less direct, dependent upon a sophisticated understanding of exchanges, more tentative since they are geared to reconcile paradoxes.

ORGANIZATIONAL CULTURE, METAPHORS AND OTHER APPROACHES

The organizational culture movement emphasizes some of the less tangible, yet important, aspects of organizational life. It is in the tradition of anthropological studies which relate values, beliefs and shared understandings to behavior.[13] Studies of organizational culture incorporate varieties of phenomena such as "war stories," ceremonies, slogans, rites, prevailing myths and even the significance of social space. Attempts are made to understand the values associated with these phenomena so as to understand the assumptions that are behind the observable behavior and perceptions of organizational members. Efforts can then be made to redirect the culture. The appeal of cultural analysis to managers is that it:[14]

- brings the human element into the picture in a global, direct manner while avoiding the complexities of psychological approaches,
- complements technical, impersonal analytical approaches,
- requires "hands-on" understanding of the daily life of organizations and
- is helpful in making comparative studies between organizations.

Studies of organizational culture often call for the intuitive use of metaphors to explain organizational reality, a departure from viewing organizations as variations of bureaucratic structure based upon linear and causal models of inquiry. Changes are needed that accept complexity and diversity, pluralities of hierarchical structures, massive interaction, ambiguity, symbiosis and multiple realities. Termed a "quiet revolution," metaphors encourage more naturalistic, more open inquiry.[15]

Along this vein, several "images of organization" have been proposed,[16] each reflecting a particular view of process and effectiveness. It is instructive for professionals to consider these with respect to the model of public agency democracy. In-role reactive behavior appears to be associated with systemic metaphors of *machines* and *organisms*. Borderline-role behavior depends greatly upon the *brain metaphor* of information processing, learning and innovation. Out-of-role behavior may be also associated with the latter as well as the desire to break out of *psychic prisons* of self-defeating preoccupation and beliefs. The ability to think in terms of the paradoxical relationships and the salience of intermediary professionals depends upon the capacity to envision agencies as *political systems*. Some in the political environment are fearful that agencies will become *instruments of domination* over political processes but the answer to this could be to accept agencies as *systems of flux and transformation* essential to the health of the more-encompassing political institutional system. These examples show how metaphors extend the range of more formal organization theories.

Since individual theorists have a tendency to devalue or attack other perspectives, there are sharp differences as to the cause and control of organizational behavior. Some assume that individuals are the source of organizational change; others see impersonal, external constraints as the major determinants. Individual scholars with antithetical convictions attempt to influence their audience by imposing "their own conceptions of reality upon the practical events of social life." While the theories that have been discussed may appear contradictory, one is not inherently better than the other. Each reflects valid perceptions that can only be reconciled dialectically, which is to say through logical argumentation leading to new insights.[17]

ORTHODOX MANAGEMENT VALUES

Why then is it predictable that public agency democracy, so attuned to what is known about organizations, will encounter resistance? The reason is that common management beliefs and values are fixated upon in-role reactive behavior. This is because outcomes must be planned, controlled and predictable; therefore leaders assume the responsibility to see that action is taken. Since policy elites want to attain organizational goals, they develop convictions about the purpose and rightness of power over subordinates. We should not lose sight of the fact, however, that the main setting for developing justifications for the exercise of this power has been business enterprises.

Corporation policy elites base their needs for organizational control around the workings of market economics. It has already been shown how business organization purposes and processes, contrary to those of public agencies, fit in quite neatly with economic institutions. This frees business managers to represent themselves as custodians of resources in a constant struggle to husband and increase stockholder wealth through corporation performance. Consequently, return on investment is the bottom line, the prime indicator of effectiveness. Success is reflected by favorable quarterly reports, as a result of entrepreneurial vision, talent, courage and charisma. Corporation policy elites take on immense and risky responsibilities; they must see that uncertainty is reduced through logical analysis, energizing others and shrewd intuition. They are expected to be more totally involved in their work than others, more driving, decisive and tough. It follows that these are considered as rare individuals with unique abilities who deserve the best salaries, benefits, office surroundings and other special privileges.

What motivates those in free market enterprises? The winners of competition and strife will survive and be rewarded. This could explain why American orthodox management thought continues to be obsessed with military combat metaphors found early on in the works of popular theorists. The staying power of warlike thought in organizational culture is seen in contemporary management literature which employs terms such as guerrilla warfare, marketing warfare, commando marketing, position defense, frontal attack, principles of the offensive, corporate combat and corporate warrior. With reference to the last, one popular book conjures images of executives, bouncing about on small wiry Mongolian horses, devastating all in their path. The cover of another puts the executive in the garb of a Spanish conquistador.[18] These common business action assumptions call for such combat metaphors:

- Enemies (competitors) must be overcome, or at least kept at bay, before they bring about one's ruin.
- An elite officer corps—management, with its superior training, skills and dedication—has the task of motivating troops (workers) through noncommissioned officers (line supervisors). Officers develop strategies for battles against the competition. Everyone obeys the chief executive officer who reports to a general staff (board of directors).
- Goals are attained through tough leadership, decisive initiatives and the dispensation of appropriate rewards and sanctions.
- If someone within the organization clan reveals secrets, contests orders in public or fails to carry out instructions, then that person deserves to be punished.

While attempts are made to revise and soften this imagery, it is very consistent with the business bureaucratic, artificial systems model. The advantages of the general military metaphor are that it promotes planning, running a "lean and mean" enterprise, group solidarity, loyalty and endurance. The dangers are those of win/lose dichotomies, absence of innovation, an atmosphere of threat, and a devaluation of individuals.[19]

Of course the warlike military comparison has its logical limitations. Among the differences, workers have a full range of constitutional rights, including the right to quit, whereas those in services serve under military government. Differences in interests between workers and managers are often negotiated and institutionalized through labor laws and employee bargaining associations. An equalitarian ethic works toward downplaying the use of formal rituals and encouraging participative subordinate behavior. The presence of movements such as quality circles, quality of work life, organization development, and Total Quality Management may be seen as humanitarian leanings toward affording more employee direction and interest in their jobs. But none of these put into serious question the absolute control of significant organizational events as the cherished "management right" of policy elites.

How can military leadership metaphors be logically applied to the public sector? To begin, who is the enemy? In the case of law enforcement, the dangers of coping with individual and organized criminals provides justification for paramilitary hierarchies. But aside from this where is the foe of, say, mental health, transportation, public works, social welfare? Is it necessary to invent an adversary, a threat in order to manage? This is an age-old question of political power and control, but there are real differences between business corporations and government agencies.

Table 6-1 shows that business organizational purposes vis-à-vis those of civilian government agencies have profound differences in assumptions regarding the desirability and possibility of (a) competition as an organizationally "purifying" process, (b) growth as essential to survival and (c) economic institutional values as the superordinate and primary social purpose. It follows that we must question the appropriateness of orthodox management philosophy for government organizations since the need for authority is based upon such different purposes. Yet most educators, practitioners and the public have accepted orthodox management norms for government agencies in an uncritical manner. The fact that research and the evolution of organization theory has been mostly centered upon attaining the strategic aims of corporate executives is rarely mentioned. It is assumed that the aims of political and business policy elites are quite comparable, so organizations should be managed in the same manner. Consequently the existence of and coping with paradox in government agencies is not recognized as a practical fact. While, the tendency of management orthodoxy is to strive to get rid of equivocality at subordinate levels, in so doing it risks becoming overly rigid and dysfunctional.

Meanwhile, the great majority of organizational theorists, while advocating value-free, scientific analysis, are locked in philosophically with corporate institutional ends and means aimed at the realization of fiscal efficiency. In so doing they reinforce the prevailing tendency to consider employee loyalty toward policy elites and organizational harmony as absolute necessities. The appropriateness of assuming military-like corporate values, mores and structure for any

Table 6-1
Differences Between Corporation and Public Agency Management Assumptions

Corporation Assumptions	Public Agency Assumptions
a • A corporation is considered as an entity with very high control over its own survival.	• An agency's basic mission and purpose must be dictated by external governmental forces.
b • Corporations must grow to survive.	• Public agencies should only grow as a result of public need. Decreases in size may be beneficial when taxes are a burden upon citizens.
c • The freer a corporation is from external restraint, the more effective it will become.	• External regulations are necessary since they force internal responsiveness to political direction.
d • Government's major purpose is to maintain social order, provide services and help create necessary infrastructures so that the market system can flourish.	• The purpose of government is to (a) maintain social order and individual freedoms, (b) promote equity of treatment and opportunity among citizens and (c) support economic institutions.
e • More profitable corporations will shoulder out the less profitable through market competition.	• No agency is entitled to take over the responsibilities of another through competition.
f • Lower cost, higher quality outputs capture consumer markets and generate needed resources.	• Resources are allocated because of political needs and influences.
g • The major gauge of an organization's health is the short-term and long-term profit picture.	• The major gauges of an agency's health are the (a) political impact of its services, (b) ability to follow legislative intent and (c) cost-effective usage of resources.
h • Poor quality of product or service will eventually result in a profit penalty and restriction of resources.	• Poor quality will eventually result in citizen complaints and frequently more restrictive external controls; but rarely fewer budgeted resources.
i • Individuals that rise to become corporate policy elites do so because of their ability to contribute toward a more favorable bottom line.	• Those that rise to become agency policy elites do so because of a combination of "merit," political acumen and the ability to "manage" agency operations.

organization can be debated at length, but this is not the purpose of this book. The main point is that if we are to understand the applicability of conventional management theory to public agencies, then a recognition of the guiding drives behind that body of theory is necessary. Meanwhile, what guides management learning and development?

MANAGEMENT AND BUREAUCRATIC ETHICS

Chester Barnard, one of the most respected classical philosophers in the public management literature,[20] sees organizations as systems of exchange between superiors and subordinates. Thus informal interactions are important so as to maintain communication, cohesion and feelings of integrity. Basically subordinates must have (a) an in-depth understanding of and devotion to their specialized activities and (b) a belief in the higher or ultimate purposes of their organization. People are not objects to be manipulated; rather they must be persuaded to be willing to cooperate through an individual calculus of perceiving that one is receiving more from the organization than one is required to give up. Routines are orders which are automatically obeyed if they do not violate deeply seated individual values ("zone of indifference"). A system of organizational authority is essential because it helps enlarge areas of routine decisionmaking and mediate those that are not routine. Among the major functions of executives are those devising and communicating organizational goals and purposes. Good leaders "inspire cooperative decisions by creating faith"; they grapple with issues of high moral complexity and must create moral codes of conduct. The higher ultimate purposes of organizations are reached this way.

Critics of Barnard's sophisticated, comprehensive and humane view of organizational policy elites have focussed upon five of his major themes: (1) organizational needs and decisions must supersede individual motives and value interpretations; (2) conflict is dysfunctional and irrational; (3) informal groups must always support hierarchical authority; (4) democracy within organizations is expressed by consent and cooperation; and (5) organizations must create their own moral codes and executives are elites charged with this responsibility. Surely the idea of public agency democracy strongly questions these principles.

Barnard concluded that authoritarian management styles are inappropriate. While he was highly aware of the complexities inherent to his theories of executive behavior, less reflective power holders may find in Bernard's works the justification for aspiring to become the highest judges of agency values. Unfortunate consequences can result when elites consider this as a right, especially in the public service. Are there no occasions, no circumstances when subordinates must take the initiative to reshape the behavior and moral direction of those within and those who head the organization? Barnard was aware of such dilemmas, but too many of his successors have ignored the ambiguous aspects of his philosophy.

The problem that subordinates must face is this: When executives depend upon the kind of fealty called for by orthodox management, significant bureaucratic ills can become ingrained and seen as normal. For example, trust on the part of subordinates is deservedly undermined by the behavior of some high level people as they strive to advance. Americans cherish the belief that self-reliance in acquiring skills and devotion to hard work should lead to "just rewards for a job well done," but the dynamics of some bureaucratic hierarchies can undermine this faith. Since hierarchies reward those who claim credit for progress and show visible loyalty to superiors, promotions are at times based upon image, showing self-control, acting like a team player. These surface skills are frequently more valued than objective performance.

The justice of rewards is also put into question when individuals outrun their mistakes by making frequent changes in management positions. "Playing the game" and being adept at covering inadequacies and inconsistencies may contribute toward advancement so that agency conduct "erodes internal and even external standards of morality not only in matters of individual success and failure but also in the issues that managers face in their daily work."[21] Of course, similar conduct occurs in social groups other than bureaucracies, and the real blame lies with exploiters. Bureaucratic environments may accommodate these undesirable behaviors, but structure is not the cause as much as the unethical use of authority. The real problem appears to lie in the reluctance on the part of some policy elites and subordinates to grapple with unethical practices that block operational effectiveness.

In any event such experiences cause professionals to become cynical about their personal ability to influence their destiny or that of their agency. Are these unfavorable manifestations of organizational authority inevitable? The answer could lie with primordial management reasoning. The values of orthodox management are often "subversive to the human spirit" because they assume that people are essentially defective and must be manipulated in order to make their behavior compatible with the goals of organizations. Upper-level managers are seen as endowed with more expertise, objectivity and entrepreneurial ability than "mere human beings." Most directly, the problem with managerial orthodoxy is that it is overwhelmingly market driven, and these preoccupations decrease the ability of humans to experience necessary variations in behavior and thought.[22]

ASPECTS OF AUTHORITY WITHIN GOVERNMENT ORGANIZATIONS

The sharing of authority so essential to public agency democracy is resisted because rigid concepts of organizational effectiveness promote the isolation of agency enclaves and reject paradox. Consequently, agency functionaries are prone to relegate wider political institutional concerns as secondary to their agency responsibilities. The reasons are historical and cultural, since market economies and administrative science values guide theories of effectiveness. This is why agency policy elites develop inappropriate entrepreneurial ambitions as they define, widen and exploit agency "market share." In so doing they can become "as much interested in aggrandizing their share of the public funding as they are in creating rational and just systems of public fulfillment."[23] What encourages such destructive influences is an over-concentration of resource and ethical control at high levels of command.

At the same time it is understandable that most applied organization theories put major priority upon in-role, reactive subordinate behavior. Reduction of uncertainty is necessary in order to turn overall goals into operational reality. Government has, following the lead of business, attempted to turn organizations into scientific instruments dedicated to low-cost, high-quality outputs. Command and programming serve artificial systems needs. Control through persuasion integrates human needs with those of artificial systems. Orthodox management values reinforce these three ways of exercising authority by reserving complex paradoxical organizational concerns for those in higher places. Professionals help to absorb uncertainty by using their skills within well-circumscribed areas of specialized competence. This metaphor of the well-run machine requires a special philosophy of control over subordinates.

I have argued that a warlike, competitive mindset, derived from the needs of market economics, appears to be at the heart of orthodox management thought. Surely most government managers and leaders will deny that outmoded military metaphors and those of the machine consciously guide their interactions at the workplace. Most are sensitive to the paradoxes of internal agency stresses as well as contrary external forces and their leadership is often adaptive to individual differences and concern for others. Much of the popular literature stresses the reduction of formal role differences, decentralization of command and encouraging participation to elicit employee creativity.

Innovative managerial models drive today's government "reinvention" and "reengineering" movements. Adopted from successful business experience, progress is seen as creating a sea change in organizational structure and authority. These new relationships will create learning environments which will expand the powers of employees to create, innovate and share knowledge, all the product of a vast joint improvement momentum. A spirit of entrepreneurship will inspire the shift from conventional, indifferent government bureaucracy to a culture of hope and change. Great faith is put in the ability of leaders to support and protect risk takers.

While successes have been reported, much remains to be done to adapt these movements to the realities of political institutions.[24] What happens when the chips are down, when employees become justifiably proactive beyond their formal roles, even beyond the direct interests of their agencies? It is then that hierarchical incumbents frequently revert to more primitive orthodox management relationships so well supported by major bodies of applied organization theory. How else can we explain the fact that subordinate "transgressors" who press for radical reform, even when fully vindicated, are regularly subjected to harsh career penalties not only regarding advancement, but even continuity of employment? Why are such matters so rarely discussed in the management literature? Why do policy elites and the public permit this undemocratic treatment of their worthy agency citizen activists?

One answer could be that injustices and waste are due to the age-old, unavoidable dysfunctions which occur when some have power over others. Those who have it do not want to share it, want to expand it and so become corrupted in various ways. This explanation is unsatisfactory, certainly an affront to the great majority of decent, sensitive, thoughtful, able policy elites and professionals in government today. A much more likely reason for the tolerance of unjust employee repression is that some sense of order has been violated, that initiating reforms at subordinate levels, that concerning one's self with injustice to others are not really part of one's job. This inadequacy is partially due to the fact that professionals destined to rise to policy elite ranks are by and large trained to become empowered through the development of specialized technical skills. Most see management as a collection of aptitudes emphasizing command, programming, persuasion and limited adaptation. Unfortunately there are few attempts to teach supervisors how to help subordinates become empowered through a better understanding of paradoxical ethical choices.

The case for public agency democracy is that, while congenial to the benefits of various types of administrative machine models, it creates the latitude for subordinates to correct some of the internal and external liabilities of these organizations. In so doing agency members also act as stewards of agency resources and the public interest as well as problem solvers for the powerful few.

The attraction of "generic" orthodox management beliefs is that it reduces uncertainty and is consistent with general cultural expectations. But when inculcated and justified in professional training through the use of organizational theory, it also produces unrealistic and romantic notions. Governmental values and ethics are seen as someone else's concern, and neutral competence becomes the model to conduct a public service career. These idealize the perfectibility of policy elites to defend subordinate interests, agency interests and those of the public. When these beliefs are inadequate, when they fail, subordinates are left with few viable alternatives to bring meaning to their working lives. Rather it should be agreed that some paradoxes are the concern of all within agencies, that attitudes of tentative trust and contingent loyalty increase the capacity to make logical, socially beneficial choices.[25] One of the most disturbing effects of orthodox management beliefs is that it encourages an impoverished view of human potential. Some reasons will be discussed in the next chapter.

NOTES

1. Luther Gulick and Lyndall Urwick, "Some Values in Public Administration," in *Papers on the Science of Administration*, eds. Luther Gulick and Lyndall Urwick (New York: Institute of Public Administration, 1937), pp. 191-95.

2. Luther Gulick, "Notes on the Theory of Organization," in *Papers*, ed. Gulick and Urwick, pp. 43-45.

3. Victor A. Thompson, *Bureaucracy and the Modern World* (Morristown, NJ: General Learning Press, 1976), p. 16. Thompson's work is of special interest because his orientation is derived from a political science disciplinary perspective.

4. Chris Argyris, *Personality and Organization* (New York: Harper, 1957).

5. Victor A. Thompson, *Without Sympathy or Enthusiasm: The Problem of Administrative Compassion* (University, AL: University of Alabama Press, 1973).

6. Herbert A. Simon, *Administrative Behavior* (New York: Free Press, 1965), pp. 20-44.

7. L. J. Henderson et al., "The Effects of Social Environment," in *Papers*, eds. Gulick and Urwick, pp. 145-58.

8. Simon, *Administrative Behavior*, pp. 45-60.

9. James D. Thompson, *Organizations in Action* (New York: McGraw Hill, 1967). See also Jeffrey Pfeffer and Gerald R. Salancik, *The External Control of Organizations* (New York: Harper & Row, 1978).

10. Harold Adams and Walter Balk, *An Analysis of the Division of Vocational Rehabilitation* (Albany, NY: New York State Education Department, 1968), pp. 40-45.

11. Alain Belasen, *Three Patterns of Organizational Adaptation: Constrained, Strategic and Mutual*, Ph.D. thesis, State University of New York at Albany, 1987.

12. Daniel Katz and Robert Kahn, *The Social Psychology of Organizations* (New York: Wiley, 1967), pp. 373-80.

13. William F. Whyte, *Organizational Behavior: Theory and Applications* (Homewood, IL: Irwin, 1969).

14. Daniel Robey, *Designing Organizations*, 2nd ed. (Homewood, IL.: Irwin, 1986), chapter 13.

15. Yvonna S. Lincoln, ed., *Organizational Theory and Inquiry: The Paradigm Revolution* (Beverly Hills: Sage, 1985), pp. 29-40.

16. Gareth Morgan, *Images of Organization* (Beverly Hills: Sage, 1986).

17. W. Graham Astley and Andrew H. Van de Ven, "Central Perspectives and Debates in Organization Theory," *Administrative Science Quarterly*, vol. 28 (1983): 270.

18. Wess Roberts, *Leadership Secrets of Atilla the Hun* (New York: Peregrine, 1987). Also Richard A. Leucke, *Scuttle Your Ships Before Advancing* (New York: Oxford University Press, 1994).

19. Diane J. Garsombke, "Organizational Culture Dons the Mantle of Militarism," *Organizational Dynamics*, vol. 17, no. 2 (Summer 1988): 46-56.

20. Chester Barnard, *The Functions of the Executive* (Cambridge, MA: Harvard University Press, 1968), and Brian R. Fry, *Mastering Public Administration* (Chatham, NJ: Chatham House Publishers, 1989). See chapter 6.

21. Robert Jackall, "Moral Mazes: Bureaucracy and Managerial Work," *Harvard Business Review* (September/October 1983): 118-30.

22. William G. Scott, "Organizational Revolution: An End to Managerial Orthodoxy," *Administration and Society*, vol. 17, no. 2 (1985): 149.

23. Brian Fawcett, *Public Eye* (New York: Grove Weidenfeld, 1990), pp. 152-54.

24. Pan Suk Kim and Lance W. Wolff, "Improving Government Performance: Public Management Reform and the National Performance Review" and Hugh T. Miller, "A Hummelian View of the Gore Report: Toward a Post-Progressive Public Administration." Both articles are in *Public Productivity and Management Review*, vol. 18, no. 1 (Fall 1994): 59-87.

25. Louis B. Barnes, "Managing the Paradox of Organizational Trust," *Harvard Business Review* (March/April 1981).

Chapter 7

Liberating Individual Potential

Everything we do has causes, the causes also have causes, and some are internal, some external.

John Kekes

A major promise of public agency democracy is that it will release creative energy. The first part of this chapter explores relationships between personality and the workplace as well as proactive and reactive aspects of motivation. Discussions of arousal mechanisms, responses to power and ways to judge individual effectiveness follow. All of this should help readers understand how they and others can better engage in paradoxical action. Connections between the mind and action are now the underlying concern.

Representations of the mind range from mechanistic models to opaque clusterings of myths and values.[1] While these renditions are not in short supply, most organizational educators have been drawn to a "behavioral" model which complements in-role, reactive activities. It is assumed that people are similar by nature and driven by observable, external forces. A systematic understanding of these realities helps managers to motivate employees to accomplish organizational goals and ends. Yet humans are not merely passive objects of influence, so a rigid commitment to traditional behavioralism provides an inadequate understanding of why and how people generate desires to affect their individual and community destiny. More specifically, we need to understand proactive behavior in ways that explain why individuals want to become influential regardless of hierarchical position. To go about this employees must be seen as unique beings guided by legitimate sentiments, as self-stimulated and confident of their potential to affect the actions of others. Since this representation of the mind is based upon internal individual cognitions it is called a "phenomenological" approach.

Behavioral psychologists describe humans in terms of their actions and see people as information transmitters, knowable in scientific terms, similar and predictable. Phenomenologists, on the other hand, describe humans in terms of their consciousness and see them as information generators, unique and at times unpredictable, living in a subjective world. In the first orientation humans are considered as observable realities, in the other their potential is emphasized.[2] Behavioralism clearly fits needs to design structure and manage activities. If one wishes to become influential in the "politics" of adaptation to the paradoxical forces of agency democracy, then phenomenological concepts are essential. Each point of view has its merits and practitioners need to feel comfortable with both.

PERSONALITY AND WORK

While different minds handle information in different ways, individuals develop concepts, sentiments and actions that have continuity over time. These cognitions, feelings and behavior are what is called "personality." Why do personalities differ? Heredity accounts for some variations in patterns of thought and behavior. The formation of personality depends upon childhood and family experiences while cultural environments help to ingrain values and rules particular to one's community. The development of personality involves struggles at critical stages as individuals grapple with life's choices and conflicts. Successful outcomes result in capacities to trust maintain autonomy, take the initiative, be industrious, develop a career identity and become intimate with others so as to find an underlying sense of integrity for one's existence. Because these capacities develop over one's lifetime, personalities are not frozen into rigid patterns early on but evolve over time.[3]

Do people change their personalities when they go to work? Is there such a thing as a work personality? Surface impressions would suggest that both things happen: organizational roles set standards for predictable behavior, so individuals may seem to acquire similar personality traits. Yet it is possible to turn on one personality while at work and then switch to a markedly different personality off the job. Role behaviors may serve to cover differences between individual personalities temporarily, but more permanent personality traits become increasingly visible at work over time. Along these lines it has been reasoned that employees have two major objectives. The first is to perform organizational tasks and the second is to develop one's personality. "In addition to its other social functions, the work organization is an arena for the resolution of psychological problems."[4]

Do people strive for similar ends in their professional careers as they do in other aspects of their lives? This is usually so because work is connected with overall life goals having to do with survival, status/power, self-esteem and supporting one's family. The assumption regarding life goals is that they are "essential," which is to say, central to the basic necessities of a satisfactory existence. All share utilitarian characteristics in that they are unavoidable, future oriented, subject to planning and of high personal significance.[5] Organizational activities constrain some and enlarge other ways of satisfying life goals as these overlap and shift in emphasis. For instance, an employee may forego major social and self-esteem goals at the workplace when it is seen as only a means to provide income and benefits that help to meet physiological and family well-being goals.

Self-esteem is enhanced by working conditions that involve freedom from constraint, high responsibility and numerous opportunities to interact with others. Status is related to salary, one's freedom of action and how much social importance others place on the work being done.[6] While we know that work can satisfy needs for creativity and innovation, great numbers of jobs in large organizations are heavily programmed and directed, leaving little room for individual initiative. These feelings of constraint should be markedly less for those in intermediary occupations since professionals normally have more discretion over their activities than do others.

REACTIVE MOTIVATION

Motivation is usually seen as a cluster of attitudes, or predispositions to act. It is a precursor to shifts, initiations and abatements of behavior. Are professionals usually motivated to become high achievers in large organizations? It seems reasonable to think so since they have gone through the rigors of academic qualification. More specifically high achievers (a) like to work on interesting problems, (b) prefer goals that have moderate prospects of being attained rather than ones that are extremely easy or extremely difficult, (c) prefer timely feedback because they want to know how well they are performing, and (d) want to make sure that they get the credit for their achievements.[7]

Some aspects of professional work result in satisfaction; others can only prevent dissatisfaction. Satisfying factors have to do with the stimulation of the work being performed, along with recognition, responsibility and advancement potential. Other influences pertain to the work setting; they include items such as salary, sensitive interpersonal relations, supervisory technical assistance and general working conditions. The latter are external to the work itself in that they prevent dissatisfaction but do not promote high job satisfaction. Distinguishing between the two classes of factors leads to the conclusion that people may have their needs fulfilled in one area but not the other. Logically, satisfying motivators having to do with the intrinsic nature of the job itself are positively related to organizational effectiveness.[8] This is because of deeply ingrained needs for interesting work, autonomy and recognition.

Turning to another aspect of reactive motivation, need primacy is of interest because lower-level needs have to be satiated before one can progress to the next level.[9] For example, social/affiliative needs are directed at exchanges necessary to group interaction. Logically, they are assumed to come *before* needs for esteem and power aimed at feelings of being highly influential. Finally, the notion of self-actualization—that is, a search for development and expression of the "real" self—is compelling because it emphasizes one's achievements along with wide-ranging subjective experiences as a direct source of pleasure.

While this brief discussion has only touched upon the extensive body of motivational needs literature, the works of David McClelland, Frederick Herzberg and Abraham Maslow are among the most commonly discussed in higher education organizational courses. A major advantage of need theory is its simplicity: One can readily visualize individual desires that are important to the attainment of specific accomplishments. This opens prospects for testing and interviewing people to help determine whether they demonstrate individual needs that appear to be associated with organizationally desirable ends. Researchers hold out the hope and present some evidence that once people understand the centrality of a need, it can be developed through training and experience in later life as an integral part of one's personality. However, it is important to remember that supervisors may make the wrong need assumptions when dealing with subordinates. As a case in point, highly considerate supervision will not compensate for inherently unstimulating work provided to a creative subordinate. As another example, a manager at the self-actualization need level may find it quite difficult to understand what motivates an employee at the social/affiliative level.

The concepts in this section have been called "reactive" because they are geared primarily toward understanding and perfecting in-role behavior, behavior responsive to the structure and needs of hierarchical relationships. These provide clues regarding the arousal of employee energy directed toward accepting innovation and change. Even though some employee cognitions are taken into account, the consistent emphasis is upon increasing the performance of responsibilities as defined by policy elites. This is closely tied to generating feelings of employee satisfaction from achievement in and the mastery of organizational roles.[10] Most reactive theories of motivation consider subordinates as potentially passive or malleable agents for the transmission of elite policies and designs. From this point of view, the problem of energizing subordinates is a puzzle to be solved by those in formal positions of power; its resolution revolves around determining what it is that employees want out of their jobs and careers so as to design suitable management stimuli to evoke desired responses. These techniques have been the mainstay of traditional administrative professional training. A good deal less is found in the literature to explain what happens when the stimulation process is reversed so that subordinates motivate their agency leaders.

PROACTIVE MOTIVATION

How we picture the makeup and functioning of the mind controls the way we visualize motivation. The problem is not so much an either/or choice between external reactive stimuli as opposed to internal proactive needs. Rather—accepting the fact that both internal forces as well as external forces control our actions—the real question revolves around how these can best be reconciled for outcomes favorable to oneself and society. Note the parallel to the public agency democracy model; external forces create a predominant need for reactive behavior within agencies, yet internal proactive forces must be accommodated in the interest of greater agency and political systems effectiveness.

Some personality attributes should predispose individual professionals to attempt to motivate their hierarchical superiors and thus change the direction of influence. Logically, the propensity to take risks is associated with proactive behavior.[11] Tolerance of ambiguity is of interest because reactive purposes are often in tension with proactive purposes. Ambiguity is uncertainty of meaning; more specifically it is seen as a condition of admitting one or more possible interpretations of a situation. Personalities differ in their ability to entertain "logically" incompatible beliefs and attitudes so as to better adapt to life's realities and have an influence upon events.[12]

It is intriguing to consider possible connections between organizational imperatives and the predisposition of individuals to engage in proactive behavior. Command, persuasion, programming and adaptation of administrative functions are used respectively to: (a) translate policies into action and control outcomes, (b) persuade others to bring about desired results, (c) program events leading to routines and (d) become involved in the fluid social exchanges essential to adaptation. Skills in persuasion and adaptation on the part of professionals seem essential to successfully motivate policy elites. The extent to which one approach is used vis-à-vis the other could be affected by an individual's attraction to different ways of gathering and evaluating data.[13] Figure 7-1 shows these as two different activities. The gathering axis ranges from preferences for analytically detailed, inductive data to prescriptive, generally deductive data. The evaluation preference axis encompasses ranges from tangible, objective analysis of data to intuitive, subjective means.

There is then a possible association between administrative functions, derived from organization theories, and individual data gathering/evaluating preferences, as shown above. *Commanders* like to associate tangible organizational objectives aimed at implementing policy. *Programmers* are attracted to arranging important detailed procedures into logical, tangible steps. *Persuaders* enjoy interpreting subjective data so as to bring about general changes in the attitudes and dispositions of others. *Adapters* are drawn to exploring subjective data intuitively in order to negotiate detailed changes. Most individuals appear to be more comfortable performing some of these functions over others. This could

Figure 7-1
Information Gathering and Evaluation Predispositions

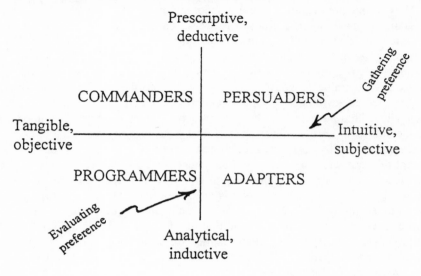

explain why one individual is more predisposed than the other to becoming involved in proactive behavior. Success along these lines depends heavily upon individual capacities to gather and evaluate subjective data about human behavior so as to engage in adaptation and persuasion activities. Variations in predispositions toward information gathering and analyzing interests also may help to explain why some rather than others are attracted to specific professions, prefer certain types of organizational applied theories, and become involved in different types of administrative functions. To be sure, real life does not fall neatly in fourfold categories, so it is important to remember that effective persons develop capacities to gather and evaluate data in appropriate ways to fit various situations. Regardless of one's main preferences, normal agency and other life situations require a modicum of ability to operate in all four quadrants; yet individuals appear to be predisposed to be more effective in some situations rather than others.

AROUSAL AND PROACTIVE BEHAVIOR

Proactive motivation is highly dependent upon timing and energy considerations. This is because borderline-role and out-of-role activities require unusual arousal above and beyond the energy directed at more conventional responsibilities. It has been mentioned that four major purposes, physiological, social, self-esteem and family well-being, are essential to life goals. Michael Apter calls these "telic," a term derived from the ancient Greek for goal or end. When people are in a telic state, activity is focused upon attaining the above purposes. We are also attracted to activities when they are stimulating in their own right and not directly connected with one's necessities of life. Examples include investigating something of personal interest and brainstorming; the "activity itself becomes the goal."[14] These are called "paratelic" states, which is to say, "alongside" the telic. The theory is relevant to agency democracy because it helps envision differences between reactive (telic) states imposed by bodily or social role needs and proactive (paratelic) states occasioned by more personal, global and spontaneous needs. The idea of paratelic activities is an important one because it helps to understand the mental processes required to cope with the ambiguity, risk and general complexity of proactive behavior, all associated with innovation.

Innovation, for our purposes, occurs as something already in existence is reformed, recombined, or reshaped in order to improve its effectiveness. One can readily associate the process of organizational innovation with proactive motivation because both involve changing existing streams of activity as to intensity and direction. Innovation "unfortunately" is not always logical. To ignore sentiments would miss the very essence of innovation. Apparently, success is highly dependent upon ambiguous and uncertain human factors such as feelings, ideals and morals.[15]

Returning to Apter's theory, he considers telic and paratelic activities as mutually exclusive; one has to be in either one state or the other. This premise leads to a theory of reversals of alternate telic/paratelic states. At the risk of oversimplication, I have adapted his ideas to illustrate how switches from reactive to proactive thought might take place.

Figure 7-2 represents the cyclical nature of professional activities. Since telic activities are aimed at establishing routines to attain common goals, major sources of gratification are predictability of results and the reduction of energy-sapping arousals. A high telic state is shown at location 1 on the curve. At this point work activities may appear too constant, too much controlled by others and no longer the source of satisfying outcomes; then feelings of boredom and apathy (location 2) may take over. This starts a search for arousal, involving innovation and attainment to reach a paratelic high state (location 3), quite antithetical to the telic states necessary for in-role requirements. However, high paratelic arousal over protracted periods results in overload, anxiety and stress (location 4). Then efforts to lessen uncertainty and return to the comfort of more routine activities predominate.

Paratelic states require temporary freedom from organizational formal roles.

Figure 7-2
Cycles of Telic & Paratelic Activities

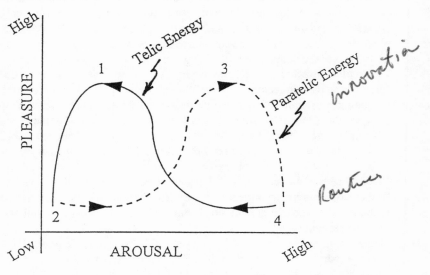

Most professionals can find this kind of latitude since their tasks are usually not rigidly defined. It is interesting that arousal and innovation do not initially start as rational, logical processes; rather the impetus appears to be highly subjective and dependent upon inbuilt emotional stimuli. Therefore different individuals have different thresholds of arousal as well as varying degrees of tolerance of ambiguity toward proactive behavior. Those with a low tolerance for routine activities and a high capacity for subjective reasoning should be more inclined to initiate action than others. Finally, there is an element of chance since paratelic arousal depends upon timing with respect to telic activity satiation and changing role demands.

POWER, EMOTIONS AND FEELING INFLUENTIAL

Tendencies to engage in proactive behavior are dependent upon a sense of optimism regarding one's ability to change the course of events. Many professionals begin their careers with the supposition that once one "makes it," however that is defined in terms of status and salary, then the rest of life will fall neatly into place. As time slips by, career expectations may decrease, or, if initial goals are easily attained, then these are raised along with the exposure to failure. As some realize that their dreams to attain highly ambitious career goals and rewards will probably not come about, the sense of being controlled by organizational and family needs may increase. Alienation and loss of interest in one's work can result along with feelings of being trapped as well as yearnings for a change in life purpose.[16]

Feelings of powerlessness to change one's relationships with others may account for the ineffectiveness of supervisors, the pettiness of staff professionals and leadership crises. They see themselves as at a career dead end with little influence upon policy and "cannot control events; rather they must react to them." These sentiments are compensated for by close supervision, inability to delegate and a reluctance to train others. Staff people show similar inclinations by becoming turf-oriented and distancing themselves from others with different backgrounds and attitudes. Higher-level people compensate for their powerlessness problems by an obsessive preoccupation with routine problems, aiming at short-term results and isolating themselves.[17] We face our most intimate conflicts when troubled by our jobs or those who control us. Some of the more corrosive feelings are inner fears, anxiety, guilt, needs for dependence and aggressive tendencies. "If we can unravel our own paradoxes and balance the requirements of our inner and outer worlds, our reality sense will be strengthened and flexible adaptation might be attainable."[18]

Both policy elites and intermediary professionals should recognize not only the power of behavior-shaping technology to influence others but also its effects upon the users of such powers. To control another is to reduce the amount of free choice available to that person, which also happens to be an express purpose of organizational roles. One of the few who have studied the effects upon the wielders of power warns that there are risks because people who control others may develop undesirable changes in their own values, attitudes and behavior. The successful use of behavioral strategies on the part of managers can cause the power wielder to hold the person influenced in lower esteem because "good" changes in others are seen as the result of the power holder's abilities rather than those of the object of influence. "Hence the target person is not given full credit for anything he or she does." There are deep political implications because "a core assumption of democracy is that people are capable of exercising control over their own lives. Once this assumption is questioned, there is a concurrent reluctance to share power" and "we move away from people who appear passive, subordinate and not in control of their own behavior."[19] These observations apply to intermediary professionals; since they too stand in danger of developing feelings of superiority toward lower-level workers and citizens. Arrogance and oppression are perverse, but unfortunately too common ways to exercise power.

FEELINGS OF SELF-EFFICACY

As they search for constructive ways to cope with powerful others, how do individuals judge their capacity to be effective and its effect upon their behavior? Perceptions of "self-efficacy" are based upon judgments of how well one can take necessary actions in order to deal with prospective situations.[20] More specifically:

- people with confidence in their capabilities develop qualities of self-efficacy.
- a strong sense of self-efficacy helps one withstand experiences involving failure and uncertainty.
- people must constantly test their capacities in order to raise their judgment of self-efficacy. This involves overcoming old fears and gaining new skills.
- mastery of problems increases general efficacy.
- one's sense of self-efficacy is developed by seeing others who have similar competencies perform successfully.
- feelings of self-efficacy do not ordinarily come during states of high arousal since visceral reactions make one vulnerable to stress and tension.
- higher generalized feelings of self-efficacy lead to higher general performance.

Albert Bandura also observes that consistent external incentives for successful performance are not likely to increase perceptions of self-efficacy. This is because the cause for success will not be seen as internally motivated, but rather due to outside reasons. Rather personal standards of performance are required which act as incentives to energize effort. What is also needed is a sense of collective efficacy whereby people feel that they can "solve their problems and improve their lot through concerted effort." They persuade each other that good outcomes are possible. The challenge is to acquire a personal sense of control along with the ability to capitalize upon one's knowledge and skills, all essential to coping with the ambiguity of agency democracy. A common problem is to retain respect for one's self during times of rebuff and rejection.

Assuming that paratelic states are required for unusual arousal of energy in order to break set with routine perceptions of administrative direction and programming, how do professionals "make waves" and engage in the process of innovation? For example, let us say that he or she becomes committed to lowering costs and improving operational effectiveness so as to deliver better services. This might be combined with an empathy toward bored employees and the possibility of increasing the scope of their jobs. Such arousal generates the energy to examine the technical nature of existing routines and the feelings of those who do the job while considering various changes. This appears characteristic of borderline-role behavior.

Some will be able to tolerate high states of arousal while others will be rapidly overtaxed. Most of us have unique styles of gathering and analyzing data, so we must cope with the propensities of others to store, process and retrieve information. Along these lines, a useful notion is that of "schemas" or cognitive structures that help an individual to grapple with complexity by seeking and retaining what appears relevant. Schemas interpret and process data by providing guidance to interpret missing missing and ambiguous information.[21] In detail, they:

- select what will be noticed, processed and stored for subsequent retrieval
- guide the assessment and organization of new material so that it fits into existing schema
- help "fill in the blanks" when information is missing
- provide likely scenarios including outcomes and manners of coping in order to understand and resolve quandaries.

This internal control mechanism filters stimuli, tests information against hypothetical beliefs and selects a manner of behavior to cope with or ignore stimuli. Since dissonance is uncomfortable, individuals attempt to reduce it by avoiding situations and information likely to bring it on. In effect schemas establish limits to the amount of ambiguity that any given individual will tolerate. These limits are affected by the extent of individual knowledge, the threshold of one's ability to endure the stress of ambiguity and the propensity to reduce dissonance through logical thought.

While such constructs of the mind are necessarily speculative, they help us to understand why dealing with ambiguous stimuli is less a fact-oriented, logical process than is commonly thought. When one person's views differ from those of others, they are subject to misinterpretation as irrational, pigheaded, stupid, aggressive and a host of other unfavorable judgments. It stands to reason that the cause for such negative impressions may be that the evaluator's schemas and capacities to entertain dissonance vary from those of the person being evaluated. Effective change agents realize that understanding such differences between themselves and others is a powerful advantage in developing feelings of self-effectiveness.

THE PRACTICALITY OF PUBLIC AGENCY DEMOCRACY

Various aspects of effectiveness, organization theory, management beliefs and motivation were considered in this and the previous two chapters in order to better understand mind-sets which could inhibit proactive behavior. In the discussion of effectiveness it was argued that historical forces have promoted the visualization of agencies as ideally independent enclaves subject to scientific perfection, similar to organizations in the private sector. A review of productivity improvement efforts in government showed that the premises for action are at times inappropriate because upper management attention is unavoidably captured by political concerns and effectiveness criteria are paradoxical.

Organization theories are mainly oriented toward command, programming and persuasion functions, all aimed at reducing uncertainty. The necessity for paradoxical behaviors is explained by theories of adaptation. The use of metaphors provides added insight into proactive initiatives on the part of subordinates. However, orthodox managerial beliefs present real obstacles because they are oriented toward eliciting reactive responses rather than resolving ethical and action paradoxes at subordinate levels. While people in positions of authority may not consciously ascribe to the management combat metaphor, its constant presence appears to reinforce attachments to traditional patterns of authority. Yet, since the purposes and assumptions of public service management differ sharply from those of business, it is essential to tolerate and use the ambiguity of public agency democracy to good advantage.

Discussions of motivation touched upon individuals as objects of influence and generators of change. The organizational behavior literature is primarily geared toward developing strategies to elicit reactive behavior. There is some knowledge, however, about the origins of and needs for proactive behavior as well as conditions which lead to feelings of power over one's environment and to feelings of self-efficacy at work. Yet prevailing mind-sets leave inadequate room for subordinates to express ethical agency values other than those defined by or permitted by hierarchical power holders. As professionals become progressively self-aware, more knowledgeable about the ambiguous nature of agency and political institutional relationships, then they should be increasingly able to express their beliefs in influential ways. Two-way changes are required to liberate individual potential. Power holders will have to resist traditional tendencies to punish constructively proactive subordinates; subordinates will have to become more able to express citizen responsibilities at the workplace.

Learning proactive skills requires an outlook that accepts ethical values and sentiments as key components of effectiveness and self-efficacy at work. The aim should be to integrate reactive and proactive schemas in order to appraise situations and act in the most effective manner. In this way leaders and followers will be better able to cope with the ambiguities of the public service, to moderate unrealistic expectations of and dependence upon authority.[22]

BEYOND TOTAL QUALITY MANAGEMENT

While TQM is less expansive than the "reinvention" and reengineering movements, it includes many of the core ideas that are seen as revolutionizing individual motivation as mentioned in chapter 5. It questions conventional ways of visualizing organizations by stressing customer (or client) satisfaction, shared understandings of agency missions, commitment to quality, constant process improvement, teamwork and the reduction of oppressive controls.

Consistent with the reasoning in this book:

- The emphasis is upon teamwork, delegation and upward communication.
- Employee satisfactions from intuitive and group efforts are considered as natural and essential.
- Employees are encouraged to learn skills which go beyond those required to fulfill their formal roles.
- Conventional approaches to structure, motivation and decision analysis are seen as often problematical, if not dysfunctional.

A most important aspect of TQM is that the needs of customers, outside closed agency systems, are the primary concern. Therefore the major accountability focus is upon responding fluidly to external needs. All of this calls for a organizational cultural revolution in matters of employee empowerment, trust and loyalty. As with other enthusiastic, somewhat breathless ideologies of major management movements the deeper, longer-term implications and realities of TQM have not been adequately explored by activists. In the first place TQM was developed for and by the private sector with its assumptions about the purpose of organizations. For example the emphasis upon "the" customer is to ensure a market niche which, in turn, drives all other ambitions. Yet the public service has many customers and markets which are not necessarily compatible one with the other. Other aspects of TQM do not address the complexities of government service, such as the necessity to focus upon input (e.g., budgets) and legal/mandated procedures. It is also a given that external demands will detract from continuous involvement on the part of policy elites in improving processes and operations.[23]

What has also not been adequately recognized by the TQM literature is that (a) the movement is pushing agencies toward the need to incorporate radically new democratic relationships, (b) successful associations will be dependent upon the ability of professionals to deal with paradox and (c) the resulting tensions will only be resolved in an atmosphere of tentative trust and contingent loyalty toward hierarchical power. It is too simplistic to declare that, following the lead of enthusiastic leaders, employee trust will replace the fear of hierarchical power. The real challenge is to value bureaucratic alongside of democratic initiatives, to generate a "theory and practice of liberating structure, a method of action and direction that integrates freedom and order, empowerment and discipline, inquiry and productivity, transformation and stability."[24]

Expansion of the TQM movement in the public service will increase pressures to resolve the long-standing dilemmas of political/administrative relationships. On the one hand, traditional bureaucratic concerns around matters of economic effectiveness cannot be ignored. On the other hand, democratic values will provide the enduring impetus for professionals to become engaged in complex ethical concerns which drive reform action. Beyond TQM lies the prospect for subordinates to define their accountability in terms of public and political institutional values through borderline-role and out-of-role initiatives. They will then be more free to reduce the impact of waste, malfeasance and policy errors.

The purpose of the previous chapters has been to develop a general understanding of the applied theory and action aspects of public agency democracy as well as some of the difficulties of implementation. It is now time to turn to specifics. The next two chapters examine borderline-role and out-of-role initiatives in considerable detail.

NOTES

1. Charles Hampden-Turner, *Maps of the Mind* (New York: Macmillan, 1982)
2. William D. Hitt, "Two Models of Man," *American Psychologist*, July 1969.
3. Erik Erikson's concepts of personality development are known as "stage theories." For a review and critique of his and other's work in this area, see Dorothy Rogers, *The Adult Years* (Englewood Cliffs, NJ: Prentice-Hall, 1979).
4. Harry Levinson, *Executive* (Cambridge, MA: Harvard Press, 1981), p. 46.
5. Michael J. Apter, *The Experience of Motivation* (London: Academic Press, 1982), pp. 48-49.
6. Walter S. Neff, *Work and Human Behavior* (New York: Atherton, 1968), p. 149.
7. David McClelland, *The Achieving Society* (Princeton, NJ: Van Nostrand, 1961).
8. Frederick Hertzberg et al., *The Motivation to Work* (New York: Wiley, 1959).
9. Abraham H. Maslow, *Motivation and Personality* (New York: Harper, 1970).
10. Joseph Nuttin, *Motivation, Planning and Action* (Hillsdale, NJ: L. Earlbaum Association, 1984), chapter 3.
11. Nathan Kogan and Michael A. Wallach, *Risk Taking* (Westport, CT: Greenwood Press, 1981).
12. Stanley Budner, "Intolerance of Ambiguity as a Personality Variable," *Journal of Personality*, vol. 30 (1962): 29-50.
13. Don Hellreigle et al., *Organizational Behavior* (St. Paul: West, 1986), pp. 118-19. The Jungerian functions are sensation/intuition on the information-gathering axis, thinking/feeling on the information evaluation axis. I have changed these to detailed/general data on the gathering axis and tangible/intuition data on the evaluation axis.
14. Apter, *The Experience of Motivation*, p. 49.
15. Robert K. Muller, *The Innovation Ethic* (New York: American Management Association, 1971).
16. Abraham Korman, *Career Success/Personal Failure* (Englewood Cliffs, NJ: Prentice-Hall, 1980).
17. Rosabeth Moss Kanter, "Power Failure in Management Circuits," *Harvard Business Review* (July/August 1979): 65-79.
18. Manfred F. R. Kets de Vreis, *Organizational Paradoxes* (London: Tavislock, 1980), p. 193.
19. David Kipnis, "The View from the Top," *Psychology Today*, vol. 18, no. 12 (December 1984): 30-37.
20. Albert Bandura, "Self-Efficacy Mechanism in Human Agency," *American Psychologist* (June 1982): 122-45.
21. Doris A. Graber, *Processing the News* (New York: Longman, 1988).
22. James D. Meindl, Sanford B. Ehrilick and Janet M. Dukerich, "The Romance of Leadership," *Administrative Science Quarterly*, vol. 30, vo. 1 (March 1985): 78-102.

23. James E. Swiss, "Adapting Total Quality Management (TQM) to Government,"
Public Administration Review, vol. 52, no. 4 (July/August 1992): 356-61.
24. William Torbert, *The Power of Balance* (Newbury Park, CA: Sage, 1991), p. 6.

Chapter 8

Borderline-Role Performance

My uncertainties may be a source of knowledge for me and for them.

Donald Schön

Borderline-role endeavors are small-scale, spontaneous group initiatives. These have been described as directed toward predicaments, not readily resolved by established in-role relationships. Existing administrative mind-sets promote the belief that predicaments can only be resolved with intensive higher-level management involvement but this chapter discusses a field study that provides evidence to the contrary. Since successful improvement action depends upon developing potential targets of opportunity as well as appropriate motivation, we will first consider some general aspects of reflection, intuition and innovation.

INTUITION AND SELF-RENEWAL

Predicaments were described in chapter 4 as amorphous clusters of intertwined problems that cause agency ineffectiveness. These normally crop up in complex organizational environments and resolutions require unusual approaches. The main reason is that it is necessary to insert oneself psychologically into ambiguous situations rather than play the part of detached, expert observer. What is required is "reflection in action," or the ability to promote inquiry through the exchange of hunches, experience and feelings. Therefore, technical rationality must at first be suspended so as to better understand reasons for tensions, competing ends, power dysfunctions and other sources of ill-defined anxiety. These subjective concerns are the context within which predicaments flourish, and they need to be aired in order to move on to corrective design and change action.

Through reflection in action we discover new ways to frame the understanding of situations and generate innovative strategies to cope with agency pre-dicaments. It entails bringing past experiences to bear upon problematic situa-tions in a tentative, experimental manner. Intuition plays a major role since it sparks creative and innovative remedial action. Successful outcomes satisfy one's curiosity and create feelings of being influential which, in turn, should increase self-esteem and liking for one's career. There is a revitalizing chain of consequences. Intuition leads to creativity, to innovation, to feeling influential, and to more intuition. While individual intuition begins the process of change, successful outcomes are pragmatically bound to a consensual definition, which means that other observers familiar with the task must eventually agree that a response or product is creative.[1] In other words creativity begins with inspira-tion from inside individuals and winds up validated in terms of appropriateness and utility by others.

The product of creativity is an organizational innovation that will correct or reduce the adverse effects of a predicament. Innovations are useful ways of rearranging existing knowledge that result in new ways of doing things. Trans-lating a predicament into something intellectually manageable and then creating an organizational innovation is a difficult activity, filled with the risk of divulg-ing one's feelings as well as exposure to ambiguity and dissonance.

What are the internal rewards? From a cognitive point of view, feelings of mastery over a quandry and the satisfaction of resolving one's curiosity are central. Successful organizational innovations provide feelings of self-efficacy in agency operations and so help to ensure more effective democratic institu-tions. These gratifications provide a special sense of purpose and dignity to one's working life; they renew one's energies and enthusiasm to grapple with other organizational predicaments. The potential rewards are not only intrinsic; repeated successes can draw the favorable attention of management.

Since successful innovations involve individual schema rearrangements, which personality characteristics are helpful? At the onset of the intui-tive/creative process, tolerance of ambiguity seems of central importance along with a willingness to take the risks of reflection in action. Once resolutions are under way, a shift in personality skills is required. Ambiguity must be less tol-erated, skills in command, programming and persuasion are called for as the evolution of change becomes increasingly participative. All of this is intensified by desires to reduce high, sapping levels of paratelic energy. Given these gen-eral processes underlying an applied theory of borderline-role behavior, the problem is how to turn them into reality.

EVOLUTION OF A FIELD STUDY

It is a real challenge to teach organizational behavior and theory in ways that are useful to practitioners. A wide variety of social psychological and sociological concepts must be absorbed and, as previously mentioned, these can appear somewhat abstract and complex to students; therefore applications to actual workplace situations are not always evident. One promising way to make this learning useful is to have students apply it to real problems in the field. We tried various approaches. At first difficulties were experienced in finding adequate sites. Formal entry into agencies was problematical since our students were untested as consultants. Also approval from management upper levels did not come readily because of misgivings over publicizing agency problems and the potentially time-consuming aspects of the projects.

Informal approaches produced the best results. Practical agency productivity issues were emphasized and contacts made at lower agency levels. At the same time confidentiality was assured. The challenges for our students were to (a) acquire the necessary cognitive learning, (b) develop analytical/design skills and (c) make a meaningful field study, all during the course of a regular university term—about fourteen weeks. Various methods were used over the years 1978-91, and procedural improvements were made from year to year. It was only later that we realized that we were experimenting with what were to be called borderline-role activities.

Our researchers were graduate students in public administration who acted as consultants to help design resolutions to more than 200 predicaments in state, local and federal government agencies. About 60 percent were intermediary professionals in continuing education programs, while others were full-time students; most of the latter had held or were holding part-time agency internships. In its final form, the course content included a textbook and other readings on:

- individual psychology and group behavior at the workplace
- communications
- structure and process controls
- organizational power and conflict

Case studies and procedural guides were used to explain principles of organization design, operating controls and change implementation. Role playing proved effective. A major concern was to complete the field study within the limited time available to our student/consultants and agency collaborators. Research sites and projects were mainly developed by individual students who used informal networks to locate agency collaborators; only rarely was outside assistance needed. The initial task was to identify a predicament and form a team with agency "informants" in order to generate a change proposal. Two major papers were required. The first (a) described the agency organizational environment, (b) analyzed the nature of the predicament which required a "need for improvement" and (c) discussed the dynamics between the agency informant and the student consultant. The second paper was a final report which (a) analyzed critical variables, (b) designed a series of change actions and (c) simulated the introduction of change with the agency team.

At the end of the course, students were debriefed in order to determine how to improve future course offerings. The field studies were usually seen as more significant than conventional classroom experiences because they provided opportunities to develop valuable consultant skills.[2] For most participants, the actual process of predicament resolution was more hectic than expected, and unusually long and difficult hours were required to produce satisfactory results.

Over time it became possible to understand in some depth the difficulties of initiating action at lower levels. Most practitioner intermediary professionals who cooperated with our student consultants could identify improvement needs within their part of the agency, but few were able to define these adequately. It was not unusual to confuse an answer with a problem definition. For example, "Our real problem is a lack of trained people" usually indicated an attachment to a solution rather than an understanding of a complex situation. There was a general tendency to rationalize the absence of remedial action because of conditions out of one's control; the most common were (a) "Our budget is inadequate," (b) "The bosses don't know what's going on," (c) "Politics get in our way" and (d) "Civil service practices and employee unions tie our hands." Agency professionals were at first unexpectedly impatient with detailed exploration of the need for improvement. Their reactions were only partially attributable to perceptions that meaningful action was outside their control. As importantly, agency professionals had a good deal of faith in their individual intuition, and this was associated with a tendency to close in rapidly, often incorrectly, with what to them were "obvious" solutions.

The majority of our agency contacts experienced initial difficulties in visualizing or even feeling free to cope with the broad context of their organizational dilemmas. There was a desire to prematurely apply technical rationality to "messy," ill-defined situations. When that didn't work, a series of rationalizations were pursued which created an even lower probability of initiation of action on their part. In other words, few practitioners were able to accurately analyze predicaments and propose adequate corrective action. This seems to support the view that complex improvements require top management motivation and guidance, but our study demonstrated that important initiatives can start at lower levels using rather simple, standardized approaches.

In order to become influential agents of change, we reasoned, a fundamental requirement for professionals was to *first* view themselves as definers of organizational needs for improvement and *then* as comprehensive designers of and planners for innovations, rather than simply specialized problem solvers or reluctant players in agency politics. This called for approaches to design changes in ways that would capture the attention of superiors and influential professional peers. How to operationalize predicament resolution and reflection in action took on increasing importance.

Once analytical guides and methods were provided, professionals became more able to understand agency predicaments. It does not come naturally to most to insert themselves into ambiguous situations and use "reflection in action." While it is necessary to promote inquiry through the exchange of hunches, experiences and feelings, the approach often goes counter to established norms. This is because professionals are trained to maintain a psychological distance from the object being studied. Consequently they do not readily explore the feelings that surround ambiguity and uncertainty in order to understand why a situation exists, but leave it to others in higher positions to present them with reasonably well-defined problems. It is difficult for specialists to suspend technical rationality by initially putting aside these skills so as not to compete with other orientations. Also predicament discussions lead to exploring reasons for feelings of anxiety and tension; these can be seen as risky and sensitive matters that are better avoided.

All of these factors—the complexity of predicaments, the necessity to voice subjective interpretations, the possibility of being seen as meddling with what top managers are supposed to, and the potential for inadvertently stepping into political difficulties—are significant obstacles to initiation of action. Therefore it was necessary to develop ways to help predicament analysis teams visualize situations before taking concrete improvement design steps.

THE GENERAL APPROACH

A framework for connecting intuitively grounded data was needed. The first requirement is for the interested group to see itself as composed of comprehensive analysts, planners and designers of innovations aimed at meeting a specific agency need for self-improvement. Three major steps are essential:

1. Elements at the heart of a need for improvement (e.g., the predicament) must be visualized in terms of their cause and effect upon agency purposes.
2. The understanding from step 1 has to be converted into a review of possible actions to change the dynamics of the predicament.
3. An action strategy must be designed that will (a) overcome or lessen the undesired effects of the situation while (b) specifying needs for change in the status quo.

Since the group must visualize cause-and-effect relationships without inhibiting the range of intuitive thought, we settled upon recording the results of a free-flowing exchange of views into a tentative cause-and-effect diagram. This served as a stimulus to add new elements and arrive at a preliminary consensus as to the definition of the predicament. The second step was aimed at identifying discrete elements subject to change action so as to generate an agreed-upon visualization of causes and effects. This provides a picture of small-scale political dynamics that reflect the conflicting perceptions and interests of participants.

Gaps of knowledge, oversights and variations in terminology exist which must be compensated for in order to engage in change analysis and implementation design.

To recap, it was necessary to overlay, integrate and elaborate the *predicament scan* generated by step 1. A construct of agency processes, called an *action scan*, was used to fulfill these needs at step 2 above. The final step involved selecting and sequencing the best and most appropriate change actions. Many of these actions, usually more than expected, were under at least partial control of the group and their supervisors. A list of priorities of action in order to help policy elites and others to engage in operational change was the main goal. This *action strategy*, a culmination of the three steps, is a planned innovation that can be submitted by intermediary professionals for management consideration. The expectation is that policy elites will then be motivated to join in the process of change.

The purpose of our research was to see whether intermediary professionals could define organizational predicaments and propose logical resolutions. The literature is replete with calls for action on the part of top management for subordinates to do just this, implying that highly motivated employees only have to become creative. We found that this is indeed possible, but it does not come easily or naturally. The next three sections discuss details of the general approach.

PREDICAMENT SCANS

When a need for improvement is agreed upon, professionals must interact in order to better understand the situation. Straightforward, simple cause-and-effect problems are best handled by in-role relationships as defined in the agency democracy model. Predicaments, however, call for tentative, explanatory approaches. At the onset, professionals strive to understand why the need for improvement exists. Intuitive exchanges are required, and as these occur "we find that practical activity is confusing, ambiguous and contradictory; it requires some kind of work to be understood, some kind of clarification and elucidation."[3] Stress and low-level contention often attend free-flowing exchanges aimed at capturing the benefits of reflection in action because team members are trying to put aside vested interests while refraining from imposing resolutions. Since it is necessary to clarify what is being said in a manner that the group will agree to, a diagram helps summarize the free flow of ideas.

An organizational predicament can be conceived of as a sequence of causal events which cascade into a core or "focal problem," defined as the central undesired outcome of causes. It is then possible to think of events, radiating out from the core problem, which are its effects. Visualizing a predicament in such a manner helps to communicate and reach agreement as to its makeup. Three types of core problems are logically at the heart of organizational predicaments:

- Costs are too high.
- Quality of services is inadequate.
- Response to policy directives is not adequate.

Knowing the origins or causes of core problems provides clues for corrective action. Then an understanding of consequences or effects helps define the importance of the core problem as well as who and what might be affected by corrective action. Identifying which of the above core problems appeared to be at the center of a predicament's cause-and-effect chain was not always easy since recollections are ill-defined, fragmentary and nonlinear. Team members are often attempted to describe events that are not part of their formal role responsibility. Therefore our consultants elicited connections in nondirective ways by asking, "Why does this happen?" "What happens next?" "Why is this important?" Eventually the trail of events defined a network entering and exiting one or a combination of the three core problems above. As teams of students and practitioners charted networks of events, rough sequences were diagrammed with more distant causes converging upon and effects radiating further away from the core problem(s). As these interactions were reviewed and revised, some effects were observed to loop back to causes which seemed to keep the predicament alive, in a kind of balance.[4]

An example of the cause-and-effect analysis, called a "predicament scan," pertaining to a transportation agency is shown in figure 8-1. The Focal Problem (FP) has been identified as a combination of high costs and low quality; the chain of events starts with budgetary, management support and external cooperation problems; it ends with disapproval on the part of legislators and the budget office. These linkages help professionals to visualize: (a) what produced the FP, (b) what occurs as a reaction to the FP and (c) the feedback loops which could be associated with the persistence of the FP (e.g., connections between budget warnings and shortages, links between service delays and lack of cooperation by an external organization). The diagram, subject to ongoing reanalysis and revision, serves as a common reference. It is essentially a political statement showing the need for corrective action on the part of various people in positions of power. Corrections cannot always and often should not be made sequentially from right to left because some conditions may be impossible to change (e.g., budget shortages). On the other hand, intervening in the middle of a network may serve to bring about change in more remote causes (e.g., improved cooperation by an outside agency). Another experience with a predicament scan follows:

Figure 8-1
A Predicament Scan

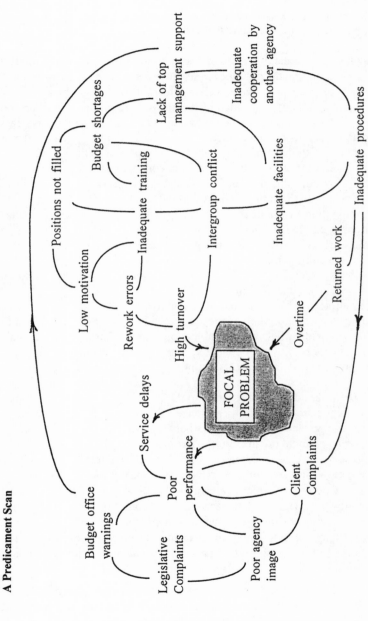

The City Maintenance Crew

This unit is part of a public health care facility consisting of thirty-four members headed by a supervisor. Their skills include cleaning, plumbing, carpentry, refrigeration repairs, painting, motor vehicle maintenance and electrical systems upkeep. Little turnover in employment exists. The recently appointed supervisor reports to a plant manager who, in turn, is accountable to a deputy director for administration. The supervisor, his accounting department colleague and our student consultant explored an improvement predicament.

Focal problems centered on issues of cost and quality of services. Remote causes were perceived as having to do with insufficient budgeted resources and a lack of higher management interest in the unit. An intermediate cause was an abnormal incidence of absenteeism and low work motivations, possibly related to the fact that many employees held other jobs to supplement their income. Intergroup conflict was in evidence as well as theft of supplies. There was little training or employee counseling. This combination led to various tangible events involving unattended maintenance needs, reworking poorly done repairs, materials shortages and attending the "squeaky wheel" at the expense of more logical, systematic coverage.

Some immediate effects of the focal problem were inadequate, poor-quality services and frequent complaints. An interesting consequence was that maintenance backlogs had to be reduced by expensive subcontracting costs. More remote effects were facility deterioration and a poor image of the maintenance operation. All of these appeared to contribute to chronic resource shortages and poor scheduling. Less clear was the reason for the apparent lack of higher administrative interest in maintenance operations. The supervisor agreed with the predicament scan but felt that higher management would "continue to allow the situation to exist" since the real priorities were "political."

This common first-line supervisory attitude is interesting since it illustrates a sense of frustration at the perceived inability to get the sustained attention of organizational superiors. It was evident that the supervisor felt incapable of taking independent action without concrete higher-level support, yet he did not recognize that his lack of initiative was a significant reason that the situation continued to exist. Several attempts were made by our researcher to convey this, but it was not accepted by the supervisor until the action scan stage. Only then did the need for better standards of performance and control data, along with the necessity to restructure roles, became apparent. These became the basis for specific plans to improve communications, take internal action and gain outside support.

The case shows that while a Predicament Network Analysis diagram may provide important clues for remedial action, it is usually not sufficient for remedial action. Relationships between the intuitive language of cause/effect and a more precise language of organization action are needed.

ACTION SCANNING TECHNIQUES

Since the major challenge is to move toward defining specific improvement actions, it then becomes necessary to understand how a predicament is related to existing organizational events and what might have been overlooked in the original predicament scan. The first part of this section, describing a general action scan device and intervention techniques, will be followed by a summary of a field study.

A construct[5] was devised to represent major categories of events within agencies as well as between agencies and their environment. These are the main features:

- The impetus for the resolution of a predicament usually comes from a central source—an agency or a department from within that agency, labeled a *focal organization*.
- The major categories of events within organizations are *goal-setting*, service-producing *operations* and *controls* (to see that operational outputs meet goals).
- Each focal organization interacts with *other organizations* and *other groups*.
- All of the above can be seen as artificial systems events involving command and programming functions. These are energized by people also engaged in natural systems activities.

Figure 8-2 shows how these features are related one to the other.

The focal organization is shown as interacting with other organizations within the parent agency, as well as other external organizations and groups. To simplify the illustration only one of the interconnected organizations is shown in the figure, but usually there are many interactions. Each of these organizations, like the Focal Organization, also engages in interacting events involving goals, controls and operations. Controls, as shown by the flow of arrows, provide performance information and help determine the need for goal revisions and/or operations adjustments.

All relationships depicted by boxes and straight lines in figure 8-2 represent *artificial systems* elements which can be revised and redeployed in a relatively technical manner. It is from this point of view a mechanism, subject to impersonal analysis and change. People energize, shape and adjust their environment, so their *natural systems* inputs are represented by free-flowing, interconnected curves. Separating artificial and natural systems encourages a design mood that heightens awareness of the need to adapt technical reasoning to human needs. All told, the figure shows (a) how focal organizations are in a matrix of surrounding organizational and social influences, (b) that changes usually involve internal revisions of focal organization goals, controls and processes and (c) that

Figure 8-2
An Organizational Construct

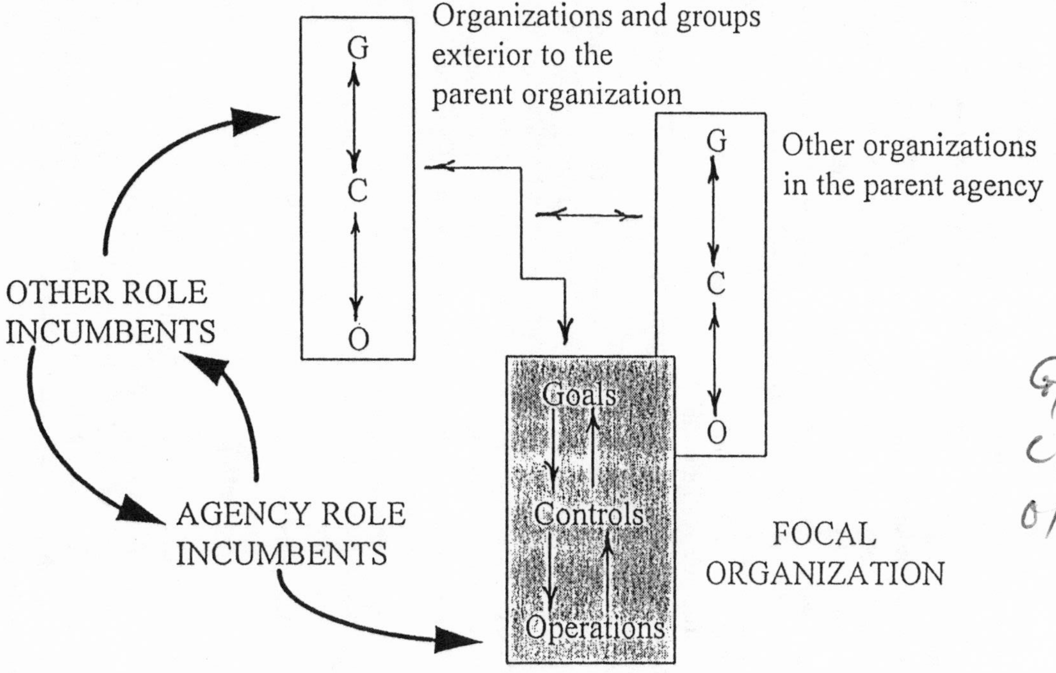

Organizations and groups
exterior to the
parent organization

Other organizations
in the parent agency

FOCAL
ORGANIZATION

Goals

Controls

Operations

G ← → C ← → O

G ← → C ← → O

OTHER ROLE
INCUMBENTS

AGENCY ROLE
INCUMBENTS

G/Goals
c/Controls
o/Operations

changes within the focal organization may require compensatory adjustments in artificial and natural systems environments. These considerations help define ways to channel the stresses and conflicts that attend changing seemingly stable relationships to a new configuration.

The construct is useful because its features are consistent with the organizational theory and behavior literature on intervention techniques. As the team transfers its knowledge of a particular predicament scan to specific areas of the construct, certain intervention techniques become appropriate. Table 8-1 lists some possibilities.

Some interventions on the left-hand side of table 8-1 affect goals, and others, operations; consequently controls usually have to be revised to accommodate these changes. Note that potential artificial systems interventions seem to significantly outnumber those of natural systems. Interventions are highly interactive since artificial systems changes frequently require associated natural systems counterparts. For example, assume that job redesign is contemplated; training is likely to be an important element in the planned change. When goals and controls are realigned in a focal organization, compensating adjustments may be necessary in other parent agency organizations or other structures in the environment. This ability to blend interventions is a major design skill.

To recapitulate, a construct was discussed depicting major categories of artificial and natural systems events. These events are associated with interventions so that change actions can be contemplated. The first step in analyzing a complex change is to relate the specific predicament scan to the construct so as to determine where revisions are required. Then the construct is used to determine which intervention techniques appear best suited. The outcome of these two steps is called an *action scan*, which serves three major purposes: A predicament is put into manageable organizational change terms. The *action scan* also serves as a checking device to make certain that the *predicament scan* did not overlook important events. The result is a list of potential change actions and their locations. A summary of a study made in the field follows:

The State Coordination Group (SCG)

This unit of twenty-two professionals and clerks coordinates grant funds designated for social service agencies throughout a northern state. The SCG also provides technical assistance and various types of training to their agencies. Most professional responsibilities are allocated according to geographical area. An SCG has considerable autonomy, but it utilizes the functional services of and is responsible to the state social services hierarchy. The structure of SCG is rigid and rule driven. Participation in internal decision making is rare.

Two intermediary-level professionals and our researcher generated a predicament scan around the core problem of adaptability. Major causes centered upon inconsistent application of policies and procedures to different localities.

Table 8-1
Some Common Intervention Techniques

INTERNAL ORGANIZATION INTERVENTION	JOINT INTERVENTIONS BETWEEN FOCAL ORGANIZATION AND OTHER ORGANIZATIONS AND GROUPS

Goals (G) - Controls (C)

- Realign management priorities
- Specify new goals

- Make control information consistent with goals and priorities

Controls (C) - Operations (O)

- Realign performance controls (cost, quality)

- Restructure operations
    - Processes
    - Functions, responsibilities
    - Rules and procedures
    - Groups (size, physical arrangements)

- Introduce new technology
    - Equipment
    - Communications systems
    - Materials
    - Job and work design (task, layout, flow)

- Increase compatibility of G, C and O between organizations and groups

- Examine consequences of transfers of load and responsibilities from one site to another

- Form new technical coalitions (e.g., information-pooling and inter-organizational committees)

NATURAL SYSTEMS INTERVENTIONS

- Engage in organizational development exercises (includes survey research, conflict resolution)

- Change rewards and reinforcements

- Develop new skills (Training)

- Shift individuals between roles

- Develop new informal coalitions

These were traced back to other causes involving uncoordinated reporting systems, lack of peer consultation and the lack of participative management styles. More remote causes were an autocratic head of SCG, the relative isolation of higher-level state social service executives and coordination as well as incentive problems with federal agencies. Some effects of the focal problem of adaptability were unequal level of services to citizens in different regions, recriminations on the part of local social service agencies and complaints by township council members and state legislators. The action scan resulted in a number of possible interventions, as shown in table 8-2.

The next step was to develop an action strategy from the above scan, but it was evident that, in order to discuss strategy, a major priority was to get the attention of the director who was reputedly disinterested in details. How to beard the lion took on major proportions, so the group considered using the services of an outside consultant who would then try to bring the director to support the change. She had to be convinced that (a) complaints about unequal treatment were not inevitable, (b) there was a need to restructure some roles and develop controls and (c) leadership was needed to resolve internal and external ambiguities.

This case is illustrative of speculations that emerge at the action scan stage. The perceived management style of someone in charge can become a predominant concern. Subordinates may hesitate to take the risk of proposing an extensive change and prefer to leave this to an outsider. Such "solutions" are questionable, of course, because consultants have to be invited in, either by the unit head or that manager's superior. The group eventually considered forming a delegation to meet with the unit director after a specific action strategy was devised. Before that, however, it seemed necessary to find out if unequal treatment of counties was not a deliberate political policy. If so, the issue would become much more complex; well beyond the realm of borderline-role activities or even out-of-role initiatives.

As illustrated, an action scan usually presents many choices for intervention. Some may be more or less practical; others can only occur if preceeded by another intervention. Therefore a strategy to bring about change is required as a final step.

ACTION STRATEGIES

Organizational change is commonly defined as a continuous problem-solving exercise. Predicament and action scanning are analytical steps which identify change variables. A strategy of what to do sequentially involves simulation and leaving open the necessity to change these sequences as experience is gained. Simulation is a matter of "trying on" various action alternatives. During this

Table 8-2
SCG Action Scan

SCG AGENCY	OTHER AGENCIES (INTERORGANIZATIONAL)

Goals - Controls

- Increase Focal Organization (SCG) goal compatibility with goals of state, county and federal agencies

- Clarify goals to include better equality of service delivery

- Develop consistency checks

- Standardize feedback controls from other agencies and townships to the Focal Organization

Controls - Operations

NATURAL SYSTEMS

- Assign internal coordination functions

- Schedule internal coordination meetings

- Engage in a survey to better understand "client" perceptions

- Release coordination information to other agencies

- Encourage coordination conferences between SCG and county counterparts

- Generate a policy and performance update bulletin

phase team members use their intuition to test various scenarios so as to gauge the agency's, along with their personal, costs and rewards of engaging in the change. Discussions are often fraught with subtle bargaining and value overtones.[6] Designers help those affected to simulate the future and adjust action strategies to accommodate the needs of participants. The compatibility of goals between organizations is a major consideration in the exploration/ simulation phase. When there is agreement regarding goals and priorities, it then becomes possible to investigate the future impact of the change on controls and operations as well as their integration with natural systems.

Another consideration in action strategy is the timing involved in putting a change design into effect. Not all interventions can be introduced at the same time, nor is it usually advisable to attempt to solve all the identified causes. Sometimes changes have to occur concurrently. Throughout, intuition plays a major role as the design group determines what interventions are necessary and recommends the most logical sequence. The *action scan* along with the *action strategy*, are planned responses to an agency predicament that will then be presented by intermediary professionals to policy elites for their evaluation and follow-through. At some point higher management discussions could result in revision of the *predicament scan, action scan* and *action strategy*. As the circle of participation and discussion widens, new input often results in changes. Later, when implementation action begins, new facts come to life; thus the possibility of reiteration is ever present.

This overall approach to predicament resolution clearly differs from conventional problem orientations. While most professionals are trained to solve technically rational puzzles wherein pieces fit into a reasonably well-defined framework, action scanning and strategy approaches encourage trial and error. It is normal for partial answers to evolve in shifting and often unforeseen manners. The pulsing, reiterative process continues as networks of organizations and groups become more aware of the mutual need to define what needs fixing, generate alternatives and take change action. An example of an *action strategy*, originating during a field study, follows:

The County Mental Health Organization (CMHO)

This clinic delivers direct services so as to help clients remain in community settings. It also serves in a consulting capacity to local mental health service providers. The agency is subordinate to board and state regulatory bodies; other influential policy groups are the county executive office and county legislature.

An executive director directs the agency's work force of over forty employees. Her immediate subordinate is a medical director in charge of specialized adult, children and crisis teams. There are necessary interactions between CMHO and other public agencies involved in educational, social services, probation and detention activities. Since patient populations are mobile, clinical teams are interdependent. Intuitive clinical judgments are the norm, thus limiting the consistency of rules, regulations and procedures.

The executive director had reorganized the agency in order to increase quality of services and lower costs, but subordinates were having difficulties in redefining functions, methods and operating responsibilities. Our researcher collaborated with a team leader, a procedures specialist and a team professional.

The *predicament scan* identified remote causes for the focal problems of quality and cost which included budgetary constraints and an increasing client load. Other causes were inexperienced employees, inadequate facilities, disruption caused by the recent reorganization and job dissatisfaction while more immediate causes centered on lack of team cohesiveness, interteam tensions, client overload, inadequate understanding of client needs and procedural confusion. Immediate effects were faulty services and delays. These were associated with client complaints and poor liaison with other agencies. More remote effects included poor community image, legislative complaints and certification problems.

The *action scan* showed a need for closer compatibility between the goals and controls of the agency and those of external organizations. New needs to exchange data, coordinate planning and analyze client loads came to the surface. Focal organization action items involved the restructuring of teams, redesigning workflow and improved computer usage to analyze and coordinate performance. Natural systems change possibilities were training, client surveys, employee surveys and media coalitions.

Our researcher noted that one member of his group was fixated upon organization development techniques in order to increase team motivation. The second was especially interested in better role and goal specification, while the third person seemed to lose interest as more detailed actions were discussed. An action strategy proposal was presented to upper management consisting of five roughly sequential steps:

1. Increase the general compatibility of goals and controls between CMHO and key surrounding agencies.
2. Increase the compatibility of goals and controls between CMHO teams; of special interest was greater standardization of case records.
3. Develop improved intake and discharge procedures.
4. Decentralize some control operations and rearrange data workflow so as to improve flexibility and productivity.
5. Increase communication with board, state and county officials by initiating progress reports regarding CMHO's performance.

The strategy was then discussed in detail with the executive director of CMHO, who was interested in the specifics of each phase. She was especially attuned to the tentative, reiterative nature of action and saw possibilities for rearranging and paralleling sequences. Of major concern to the executive was the overcoming resistance to change by key people within the agency. An outside consultant was seen as a possible resource to increase communications flow and participation. As a matter of interest, the researcher (an intern at CMHO) was later hired as a permanent employee and assigned to the executive director's staff to help expedite the action strategy.

The case is representative of successful outcomes in influencing higher management behavior. A major reason for the rapid acceptance was that the thrust of change coincided with a prevailing executive priority. At the same time it was instructive to note that when a team agrees upon the nature of a predicament and its resolution, interest may flag on the part of some members when specifics require intensive consideration and effort.

EVALUATION OF THE FIELD PROJECTS

The studies were undertaken to (a) enable graduate students to use their learning in a direct, practical manner and (b) see whether it was possible to generate effectiveness improvements from within agencies in a spontaneous manner without initial direction on the part of policy elites and upper agency management. It was not possible to engage in a classical longitudinal evaluation of the project since analytical methods changed over time, new researchers took over every term, and there was considerable variation in sites and environments. Debriefing procedures were updated to adapt to course program revisions and, while anonymous questionnaires along with interviews were intermittently used to determine course effectiveness, the drawbacks that attend these methodologies could have distorted responses. Studies were made under a good deal of time pressure and there was no way to verify the accuracy of the reports without breaking confidentiality ground rules.

Over 85 percent of 180 students who responded to various questionnaires over an eight-year period rated the experience favorably. The remainder was indifferent or discontented because of the workload, an inability to relate to constructs, feelings of being confined by the consultant methodology and difficulties in maintaining adequate site contacts. Some felt that the course should have been extended to two academic semesters. There were consistently high ratings in periodic department student course evaluations and expressions of enthusiasm during and after the course. Only two higher-level agency executives contacted me over the twelve-year period in order to verify the intent and legitimacy of the project. Eight studies had to be discontinued because agency participants dropped out. On one memorable occasion a student intern engaged in a predicament scan within his municipal agency was summarily fired, probably because further exploration of the need for improvement could have surfaced some questionable practices. Another internship was provided, and the student joined an ongoing study in order to complete the course.

As mentioned, while the field studies were initially undertaken for other purposes, it became clear that the activities produced significant results regarding ways to enhance borderline-role relationships. Unfortunately we were not able to track each of the initiatives so as to determine the rate of successful application. This would have required additional surveys in order to understand the reasons that *action strategies* were accepted, rejected or left fallow. Not only were time and resources limited, but follow-up activities could have been perceived as threatening and access to future sites cut off.

Considering the studies as a whole, it was proven that intermediary professionals are capable of analyzing complex predicaments and designing resolutions without hierarchical motivation or higher-level guidance. This has interesting implications regarding agency democracy.

SOME GENERAL ASPECTS OF BORDERLINE-ROLE INITIATIVES

Normally, failures in agency effectiveness should be corrected by in-role re-lationships. Problems are identified through monitoring devices; employee in-put is encouraged; corrective technical designs are made along with adjustments in command, programming, persuasion and adaptation. Total Quality Manage-ment programs can make substantial contributions. While this can be very de-manding and complex, some situations are not subject to conventional rational analysis because they consist of intertwined problems and feelings called pre-dicaments.

Borderline-role behavior is a temporary distortion of power relationships which goes counter to administrative mind-sets about specialists confining their activities to formal roles within a specific area of technical expertise through the exercise of neutral competences. It is assumed rather that subordinates are on occasion as capable, if not more capable, of understanding power and technical relationships than the usual "management team." They are seen as having an increased capacity to design resolutions when temporarily liberated from in-role tensions as well as conventional institutionalized contention.[7]

There is a logical sequence to borderline-role analysis and action.

- The initial predicament analysis helps to untangle emotional as well as technical aspects of situations. This is a highly intuitive phase calling for paratelic activi-ties and interpersonal skills. The analytical mode is mainly political since it permits explorations among peers of tensions, competing ends, power games and other anxieties.
- Once that a predicament is understood, then it is necessary to discover its dis-tinct organizational attributes. This is an essential design phase, creative from the point of view that the predicament is converted into manageable variables, subject to revision.
- In the final design phase intuition and creativity are used to rearrange the knowledge gained in the previous phases. The product is an action plan de-signed to integrate change into regular bureaucratic routines. The results of the team's work are turned over to management for implementation consideration.

There are two levels to organizational transitions, the first is "inquiry from the inside," wherein the actors are immersed in the situation, express particular, idiographic thoughts, validate data experimentally and interpret data contextu-ally. The second level is a shift to "inquiry from the outside," in which actors strive for detachment, language generalizable to others along with factual vali-dation/interpretation of data.[8] While the process has been put forth as a steady transition in this discussion, there is often a need to shift back to previous levels as new information comes to light.

According to conventional lore, accepting proactive subordinate initiatives should be an easy matter. Traditional management rhetoric claims that policy elites welcome creative efforts from subordinates and respect their special insight. But this may be less so when initiators of action have more control over defining situations and want a positive outcome. Policy elites, on the other hand, are used to a multiplicity of requests from various sources and may not see internally generated ideas in the same significant and positive manner as do their subordinates. Traditional superiors tend to value actions they initiate more highly than proposals initiated for them.[9] Executives in the public service are sensitive over matters of turf, taking risks and the sanctity of "management rights." Changes could involve matters which may be seen as the exclusive domain of policy elites. Less enlightened executives may then doubt the creative capacity of professionals and question their motives rather than the feasibility of a proposal.

In order to build a more favorable change environment, executives should see themselves as mentors, or teachers of others, and this involves a willingness to share power. The essence of their task is to enhance the capacity of subordinates to accomplish mutual goals and fulfill joint needs. Clinical analytical skills can help locate the sources of potential pain and consider mutual patterns of affection, aggression and dependency.[10] This is difficult for many policy elites because mentoring involves reflection in action with subordinates along with its attendant time and risks.

There are other reasons that policy elites will vary in their capacity to respond positively to initiation of action involving borderline-role innovations. Research shows that most have little time to interact in painstaking exploratory and tentative ways. They react to events and do not plan ahead in a textbook manner. Their activities tend to be brief, varied and discontinuous. They prefer face-to-face, informal contacts, and many are not normally reflective.[11] This seems especially probable for less experienced political appointees and some lower-level managers who are prone to exercise raw power in order to get things done. Many have risen to their positions by acting in highly directive ways, so they are not likely to make sudden changes of managerial style. While it is commonly observed but rarely studied, the acquisition of power can breed a high degree of insensitivity and arrogance toward subordinates even at the very highest executive levels.[12] Finally, when paths for upward mobility appear blocked, some managers guard their power and perogatives in an obsessive manner. For all these reasons intermediary professionals are often pessimistic regarding the degree of enthusiasm their proposals may engender.

Successful change design and implementation requires the capacity to arrive at mutual understandings in the face of the external organizational constraints that typify government agencies. Even in today's climate of great concern over scarce resources, other priorities can take logical precedence. A proposal could force confrontations between an agency and other influential groups at politically inappropriate times. It could detract from more important political priorities. Intractable positions on the part of other agencies may prevent enactment of essential elements of the change process. Intermediary professionals must be prepared for such eventualities and remain open to the realities of logical priorities that could inhibit predicament resolution at a given time.

Usually professionals will not take naturally to borderline-role behavior. They have to overcome the limitations conditioned by experience in formal role relationships and reliance upon specialized knowledge. Not the least of these is the need to become more sensitive to common interests with other intermediary professionals within and beyond one's direct chain of command. Most must learn to surmount the mind-sets pertaining to effectiveness, organizational, managerial and motivation that were acquired as part of their professional training. Over the long run no one will do this for them until they take a hand in revising their training and education.

In spite of these difficulties, experience in the field leaves room for optimism that fertile fields for self-improvement in public agencies exist. The research also shows that there is a high probability that important organizational changes are abandoned, stalled or unnecessarily costly because of an incomplete knowledge of predicament analysis, remedial design and implementation techniques.

NOTES

1. Teresa M. Amabile, *The Social Psychology of Creativity* (New York: Springer-Verlag, 1983).

2. Some of these aspects are discussed in Walter L. Balk, "Coping with Organizational Predicaments: A Structured Intuitive Approach," *Industrial Engineer*, vol. 17, no. 7, (August 1985): 64-71.

3. Martin J. Packer, "Hermeneutic Inquiry in the Study of Human Conduct" *American Psychologist*, vol. 40, no. 10 (1985): 1081-93.

4. The convention for flow and sequence of causes in this construct runs generally from right to left, but reverse interactions can occur within clusters of causes from left to right as well as vertically. The technique is derived from an approach described in Stephan Konz, "Quality Circles: A Japanese Success Story," *Industrial Engineering*, vol. 2, no. 9 (October 1979): 25.

5. "Construct" is defined as a representation of reality that refers to relationships between things and/or events and their various properties. See Melvin Herman, *The General Nature of Theory Construction* (New York: Wiley 1969), p. 10.

6. The concerns of Chris Argyris are germane. See "Theories of Action That Inhibit Individual Learning," *American Psychologist*, vol. 31, no. 9 (September 1976): 638-54, and "Making the Undiscussable and Its Undiscussability Discussable," *Public Administration Review*, vol. 3 (May/June 1980): 205-13.

7. Donald A. Schön, *The Reflective Practitioner* (New York: Basic Books, 1983), p. 348-50.

8. Roger Evered and Meryl Louis, "Alternative Perspectives in the Organizational Sciences: Inquiry from the Inside and Inquiry from the Outside," *Academy of Management Review*, vol. 6, no. 3 (1981): 385-95.

9. Edward R. Lawler et al., "Managers' Attitudes Toward Interaction Episodes,"

Journal of Applied Psychology, vol. 52, no. 6 (1968): 432-39.

   10. Harry Levinson, *Executive: The Guide to Responsive Management* (Cambridge, MA: Harvard University Press, 1981).

   11. Henry Mintzberg, *The Nature of Managerial Work* (New York: Harper & Row, 1973).

   12. Peter Nulty, "America's Toughest Bosses," *Fortune*, vol. 119, no. 5 (February 27, 1989).

Chapter 9

Out-of-Role Performance

The fundamental difficulty is to combine the efficacy of a social system with consciousness of what it involves.

Bernard Williams

Borderline-role activists increase their agency's effectiveness by designing predicament resolutions for management consideration. In contrast, out-of-role behaviors require pronounced breaks from conventional agency hierarchical relationships. Confrontations occur which more often than not include the discomfort and pain of vigorous reform efforts. The model of agency democracy helps to think through tensions and pitfalls by specifying three distinct types of logically legitimate out-of-role initiatives. The purpose is to have public employees "share visions of what is desirable," based upon a self-image that enables them to legitimately engage in reform activities at crucial times.[1] To go about this professionals must see themselves as singularly well equipped not only to identify a wide variety of errors of omission and commission but also to take action as moral agents in support of political institutional purposes and values. Important principles have been put forth regarding out-of-role initiatives. The first is that these will logically be of low frequency, clearly aimed at very significant issues. The second is that stressful relationships are legitimate when they can clearly help correct policy inadequacies and dysfunctional behaviors that harm the public. Yet there is no guarantee that professionals will never be motivated by destructive intentions such as revenge or sabotage, nor is it assumed that they are not prone to erroneous judgment or myopic arrogance. Democratic relationships within agencies do not give subordinates license to destroy the overall stability of in-role relationships, to go counter to regime values. How to control such potentially dysfunctional initiatives will be an ongoing concern. Since these are dangerous waters, uncharted by prevailing administrative beliefs, this chapter is oriented toward making out-of-role action more understandable and operational.

We begin by discussing ethical reasoning in a democratic institutional environment and ways to envision specific agency issues. Guides for action are suggested which can serve to reduce the incidence of ill-conceived efforts while increasing beneficial outcomes. Then various aspects of coalition formation, internal solitary opposition and whistle-blowing are examined. The discussions return to the importance of tentative trust and contingent loyalty as a necessary foundation for democratic action. All of this leads to considering some necessary changes in awareness and behavior that will be discussed in the final chapters of this book.

THE SEARCH FOR ETHICAL MEANING

"Ethics refers to the study of the good and bad, the theory and system of moral values defining duties or responsibilities governing human conduct." While legal and moral responsibilities may overlap, they are not identical since many moral matters cannot be mandated.[2] Communication difficulties are foreseeable when ethical reasoning is used to initiate action. This is because moral stances are inescapably subjective, determined by emotional and intellectual commitments to what should be. On the other hand individuals will vary in their perceptions of moral values dependent upon their personality, aspirations and past experiences. In spite of the difficulties of interpreting and communicating ethical matters, it is vital to be able to express these concerns because our feelings of personal worth depend upon following social values which guide us as we strive to develop feelings of optimism and purpose about our individual lives. Maintaining a faith in the integrity of our careers is essential to meeting these needs. For these reasons, ethical issues are not just the concern of "management"; they are the responsibility by all agency members.

How can the ethical purposes of public administrators be better understood? To begin, professionals, as members of a political system, have the power to do good for or help inflict harm upon others. Therefore they are necessarily accountable to the community at large as well as agency to management. Their predominant and necessary concern is with authoritative and legal collective decision making within structured settings bound by rules dedicated to conflict resolution,[3] all built upon ethical foundations.

Dwight Waldo once mapped a "rough terrain" of ethical responsibilities for public administrators with the caution that "the list is capable of indefinite expansion and does not lend itself to logical ordering." There are obligations to:

- The constitution and the upholding of regimes, its values and its laws
- The nation, country and its people
- Democracy as an expression of the will of the people
- Professional values

- The public interest or general welfare
- Family and friends
- Self
- Humanity and the world
- Religion or God.

Other necessities are to serve "middle range collectivities" such as party, race, class, union and church, all imbued with conflict, lack of clarity, unanswered questions, ambiguities and contradictions. Therefore it is difficult to clearly specify obligations to the public interest or general welfare since moral obligations are "notoriously difficult to operationalize."[4] While this is of small comfort to prospective reformers it is interesting to note that agency democracy centers upon the first four items in the list as a way of defining the fifth item relating to aspects of the public interest.

The American Society for Public Administration has brought some order to ethical considerations by stipulating codes and implementation guidelines. These emphasize personal integrity, service to the public, striving for professional excellence, positive attitudes, dedication and compassion. To be avoided are undue personal gain, conflicts of interest, the divulging of privileged information, illegal discrimination and fraud. To be supported are the use of discretionary authority to promote the public interest, merit employment, equal opportunity, constitutional knowledge. Colleagues, in difficulty because of responsible efforts to correct discrimination, fraud, mismanagement or abuse, should be defended. Professionals are urged to show a sense of solidarity with reformers in difficulty. Yet there is little recognition of the complexities and contradictions involved. The codes have been criticized because of their ambiguity and lack of specificity; also if ethics rather than external controls are used as a basis for action, then bureaucrats could conceivably become responsive only to themselves and their particular concepts of morality.[5] Again the specter of professional power over that of democratic institutions is raised.

Meanwhile it is worth remembering that, even with their limitations, ASPA's codes of ethics will not be familiar to many public service professionals because so small a percentage has had formal public administration training or other exposure to these rules of conduct. On the other hand various kinds of specialized professional ethical training, for instance that of the legal profession, could coincide with agency needs. In general, existing professional ethics seem to emphasize desirable character attributes and keeping out of trouble; but little attention is given to a more relevant self-image based upon the "grand principles of the Republic" which takes the high road of constitutionally based "regime values." In this manner professionals would be looked upon "not as neutral instruments of management, but as a mighty institution of government." By reflecting upon the meaning of the constitution they have sworn to support, agency employees can develop a self-perception consistent with the public interest and general welfare, for they are part of the governing process of democracy. John Rohr also notes that there is wide discretionary latitude for bureau-crats to "advise, respond, initiate, inform, question, caution, complain, applaud, encourage, rebuke, promote, retard and mediate" so as to impact "agency pol-icy."[6]   While agency democracy seems consistent with such reasoning, ethical analytical and action problems remain. How wide should this latitude be? How can the ethics of public interest best be incorporated into one's job?

Out-of-role initiatives are based upon individual value judgments and intui-tions regarding the public good. While laws and codes are necessary to guide one's actions, all significant moral matters cannot be predicted, mandated or prescribed. Therefore ethical obligations may involve the stresses of uncertainty and acting as agents of disclosure. The key is to expand permissible discretion beyond the confines of established roles, to empower professionals to express valid ethical concerns. Generalized reasoning about these matters can only set the stage for the necessary understanding of ethical meaning and action must relate to specific issues.

MORAL REASONING AND APPROPRIATE ISSUES

As individual moral agents, professionals take on the obligation to recognize and reduce the incidence of evil, which has been defined as "undeserved harm inflicted on human beings."[7]   While most of us have aspirations to lead a good life, we are frequently blinded by expediency, or the commitment to achieving success-oriented goals. Also, individual inadequacies such as dogmatic stances and insensitivity diminish our capacity to take appropriate action. Finally, we are all subject to feelings of malevolence including envy, vindictiveness and cynicism. What is needed is a "reflective temper" that can help strengthen ana-lytical powers and overcome common ill-suited responses to vital issues, re-sponses such as (a) pragmatic actions which ignore needs to question basic pur-poses of policies, (b) ironic attitudes that make moral commitments appear ab-surd and (c) romantic attachments which result in a kind of carelessness toward the existence of evil. Since it is necessary to lead an examined working life in order to decrease ethical inhibitions and inappropriate responses, how can the range and certainty of the need for moral action be better understood?

It is instructive to think of all ethical issues in the public service on two di-mensions, social effect and lawfulness.[8]   Figure 9-1 describes some essential relationships. When issues revolve around actions that are perceived as lawful and good (quadrant I), questions of morality and appropriate action are rea-sonably straightforward. Laws tend to confirm the "goodness" of actions, though there are differences in opinion as to their meaning and resolution. Ob-versely, quadrant III actions that are transparently unlawful and harmful are most liable to be perceived by the majority as morally "evil" because they do injury to others while violating community standards which exist to protect

Figure 9-1
Categories of Ethical Issues

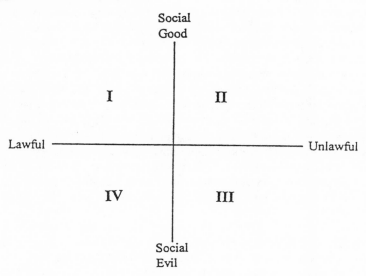

society. Again, laws undergird these judgments.

Issues falling within the other quadrants require very careful examination since they are less clear-cut. It is possible to enhance the social good by unlawful actions as implied by quadrant II. For example, the public has only recently become acquainted with the perils of radioactive waste dumping at the Hanford nuclear missile production site in Washington state. These practices began in the 1950s, and major hazards of leakage of radioactive materials into the Columbia River and other parts of the environment were recognized early on, before 1960. Over thirty years passed before the general public became fully aware of the ongoing need to radically revise dumping and storage procedures. At present it is not known whether concentrations of plutonium along with isotopes of immense longevity can be effectively contained.[9] If a group of concerned and knowledgeable government professionals had alerted the public to the perils of dumping radioactive waste thirty years ago, steps might have been taken to limit the damage, expense and unprecedented danger that is still being experienced today. Ironically, individual career concerns aside, such actions could have violated national defense security mandates, making those who sounded the alert liable to prosecution. This supports the notion that there are complex instances wherein breaking laws and rules can be beneficial to the public good.

Quadrant IV has equally troublesome implications. Lawful behavior can result in social evil. The painfully slow emergence of automobile seat-belt regulations are a good example. Consider the generations of local and county professionals who knew of the potential for these devices to save lives and the inadequacies of existing laws. Many had intimate knowledge of the pain and suffering involved in automobile disasters as they brought aid to the wounded, notified the families of the killed and gathered the grim statistics. Since the effectiveness of seat-belt technology was not precisely known and extra cost was involved,, automobile manufacturers mounted vast lobbying forces to prevent changes. Without going into the history of seat-belt and other passenger protective devices, it seems evident that, if public service professionals had united early on by forming interagency coalitions to press for legal reform, they could have become a powerful voice in acquainting the public with the need for changes in the law. More pressure might have been put upon policy elites, and thousands of lives could have been saved. To be sure, small enclaves of dedicated professionals were eventually instrumental in bringing about change, but why were they not joined decades ago by great numbers of public service professionals?

It is easy to look at past events and deplore the lack of initiative on the part of knowledgeable inside professionals at crucial times. There is also a potential downside to reform-minded activists, and that is zealotry, which ignores crucial aspects of situations. Nevertheless not enough thought has been or is being put to the essential and complex nature of action motivated by moral purposes in the public service. Consequently, there are insufficient efforts to learn from our failures how change might be brought about in a more timely manner by intermediary professionals. We also need to better understand why the resolution of some major issues involving unlawful practices and social evil will at times not be consonant with in-role responsibilities. For example, out-of-role attempts to correct quadrant III events may be necessary to fulfill in-role accountability. Issues pertaining to quadrants II and IV are usually more difficult to analyze and justifications for action will usually be rooted in broader regime values.

These general aspects of ethical judgments appear important:

- *Salience*—How essential is progress toward resolution in the eyes of the public at large, policy elites and other agency members?
- *Ethical Agreement*—Will those involved agree upon the moral imperatives that create the need for action?
- *Resolution Path*—What are the complexities of resolution? These include technical factors, the existence of entrenched opposing interests and pressures to resist resolution.

Case studies of major successes and failures in resolving critical ethical issues could help to better understand where active involvement of intermediary professionals could have expedited the process of change, when the use of agency democracy would be proper and beneficial. At the same time, it is worth restating that large numbers of issues dealt with by policy elites are not appropriate for intermediary professional involvement. As one instance, while most agree that abortion laws are of salient general concern, there is great public disagreement regarding ethical premises and path for resolution is unclear. Whenever the understanding of what is to the public good is not clear to the majority, involvement of intermediary professionals is inappropriate.

The resolution of ethical issues produces struggles among major actors because of self-centered instrumental interests. Reform is not an easy matter for agency policy elites since, unfortunately, any salient issue that is correctable by lower-level initiatives is often seem as a failure of management to predict the consequences and take action before the situation becomes problematical. Also, since agency public image is very important, defenses are easily raised along hierarchical lines. The simplistic assumptions regarding agency higher-level accountability for failures are frequently not rational ones because in-role relationships cannot control all that can go wrong. In any event, when subordinates raise ethical issues they frequently question or appear to question accepted top level policies, priorities and competence, thereby arousing resistance.

A GUIDE TO PROACTIVE ETHICAL ENGAGEMENT

Issues appear quite straightforward when they involve malfeasance, or illegal, willful wrongdoing and misconduct; these are clearly quadrant III occurrences as defined in figure 9-1. Normally, malfeasance will be corrected by the in-role initiative called "suggesting revisions." For example, person A, a private contractor, offers a bribe to agency professional B. The matter is then reported by B to his/her immediate supervisor, C, who then takes steps to see that justice is done. In practice, of course, such matters are far from simple. Evidence has to be provided and a legal case made while protecting the rights of the accused. Beyond these normal complexities, what can B do if C is nonresponsive or attempts to intimidate B in order to protect A? To pursue the matter, B could then consider acting out of role by attempting to form a coalition of peers, engaging in internal opposition or whistle-blowing. Many difficulties are imaginable, but the ethical premises of issues involving malfeasance are more widely supported because taking action is justified by laws. The reason is that these are community agreements about what is morally prohibited and established procedures usually exist to enforce desired rules of conduct.

Given the problematical aspects of attempts to bring about reform, some subordinates make anonymous contacts through unsigned letters or other covert means. Unless the issue is of extremely high salience to policy elites and the evidence overwhelming, the contact is liable to be seen as that work of a crank and not taken seriously. Sometimes anonymous tips are formally encouraged by establishing hot-lines in order to root out malfeasance. These channels tend to become overloaded with unsuitable complaints often intent upon justifying hallucinations, exercising revenge or deliberately creating unnecessary disarray. While such hot-line messages are disregarded, others require investigatory resources.   Processes of gathering evidence to correct situations are time-consuming, and corrections are very difficult to put in effect when the originators of complaints are not known.   At times the investigation may inadvertently disclose the name of the informer when anonymity is necessary to shield that person from harm.   As a dramatic example, consider the danger to an individual who exposes a drug-running operation at the workplace.

Most importantly, few are comfortable playing the furtive part of informant. It goes counter to the frank, open contention that is characteristic of democratic exchanges.   Secretive contacts tend not only to restrict the range of change, they also reduce the ability to jointly examine and learn from important ethical issues.   They encourage an atmosphere of mistrust and suspicion that stifles creativity.   They lessen the prospects for revising orthodox management/subordinate relationships toward more candid interactions.

Intermediary professionals who are considering acting on ethical issues need to develop strategies in order to maximize beneficial impact.   Ralph Nader gives advice to prospective whistle-blowers that, slightly modified, appear pertinent to all out-of-role behavior:[10]

- Identify the objectionable situation or practice with precision as well as the public interests at stake and the potential harm.
- Verify with others the accuracy of your knowledge and back it up with documentation where possible.
- Identify laws, rules, regulations and ethical standards that support initiation of action.
- Consider the probable response of likely supporters and opponents as well as the personal costs of taking action.
- Get help from outside sources when possible and necessary.

These commonsense ideas may be elaborated into more precise considerations for engagement:

1. *The justification for the inevitable agency disruption resulting from proactive behavior must be based upon the values of democratic political institutions.* Even borderline-role behavior turned toward increasing agency productivity has a legitimate political purpose, usually aimed at getting more yield out of tax-payer dollars.
2. *Defensive responses on the part of supervisors are predictable.* Their first impulse will be to center upon aspects of the case that are ill conceived and excessively disruptive.   This makes sense but a well-taken issue is too often seen as an implied criticism of hierarchical control and thus an implicit threat to those in positions of authority.   At other times hierarchical superiors may be put in a difficult position because it may not be right or prudent to divulge confidential plans or formative policies.

3. *Issues should be resolved at the least possible disruptive level of proactive be-havior.* Agency disturbance and individual career risks usually increase as the arena escalates from in-role initiatives to borderline-role to internal agency coalition, to internal individual action to whistle-blowing.

4. *The lower the level of escalation, the higher the probability of power sharing and negotiation between initiators of action and upper management.* Border-line-role predicament resolution processes, for example, are by design open to change and compromise. Coalition formation and internal opposition are basi-cally attempts to find mutually acceptable resolutions to issues within agency walls. At the whistle-blowing stage, however, action is forced, usually with zero-sum outcomes. For these reasons attempts to bring about reform should decline in incidence as escalation increases.

5. *The higher the level of escalation, the greater the need to clearly define the ethi-cal and moral content of issues.* Borderline-role resolutions, for instance, are eventually played out within conventional rational/technical contexts; usually these are easier to cope with than moral/ethical standoffs having to do with less systematic aspects of political systems effectiveness.

6. *Borderline-role, internal coalition and urgent individual representation activi-ties should be considered by those involved as natural, potentially beneficial re-sponses to public agency social and technical complexity.* It stands to reason that hierarchical structures will be increasingly limited in their ability to predict and act upon all important needs for change and reform. Systems complexity magnifies the potential for agency goal conflicts and unforeseeable paradoxes along with errors of omission and commission. These conditions produce or-ganizational frailities that at crucial times require citizen corrective action.

7. *Resistance to employee proactive behavior on any other basis than the immedi-ate or eventual benefit to the public good is a sign of hierarchical inadequacy.* Reasonable people, as previously noted, may differ regarding ethical criteria. But two types of behavior on the part of policy elites should be unacceptable. One is fueled by grossly self-serving interests that appear to be at the heart of many acts of revenge and oppression against agency employee proactivists. The other is a shortsighted and immutable attachment to existing power relationships and policy and playing the "good soldier" in the face of patently detrimental consequences for citizens at large.

The first five of the above are essential strategic considerations. The last two describe necessary attitudes which increase the stability and evolution of politi-cal democratic institutions. Various categories of out-of-role behavior will now be discussed.

COALITION FORMATION

A coalition is a temporary alliance of individuals around a common purpose. The group is held together by common values and shared understandings of desired results over a period of time. The intent is to resolve the issue and re-sume full-time in-role activities. Coalition formation has great advantages as a means of engaging in proactive ventures. In the first place intermediary professionals can first test, elaborate and communicate ideas with peers in order to better assure that issues are pertinent and that specific action strategies will be effective. Many minds directed toward joint purposes contribute toward a better product; groups expressing a common ethical concern usually attract more attention and so become more influential than do individuals. The possibility of building effective coalitions is enhanced when:

- Salience of the issue is very high. Also helpful are low ethical complexity and high explicitness regarding the nature of resolution.
- Other groups external to the agency have the potential to act as allies to increase pressures for change.
- There are low expectations for hierarchical resistance, thus decreasing the prospects for retaliation.

Yet coalition formation appears to be a rare occurrence. In the first place it is not easy to get rapid agreement among peers regarding the salience of a particular issue, especially when various kinds of professions are involved. The more obvious matters involving low complexity, high explicitness and common ethical concern should normally be handled by in-role action through established, normal legal, legislative and executive channels. It is interesting that initiators of coalitional activities in over-rigid bureaucracies may be faced with dilemmas not unlike those experienced by members of totalitarian societies. In such surroundings reform initiatives are apt to be seen as a threat to hierarchical control unless the goals of the "agitators" happen to coincide with the purposes and priorities of the ruling elite. As activists persist in the face of elite disapproval, they are considered as obstructionists, a menace to stability and order. During the time that coalitions take shape, other peers not part of the initiative could tip off higher authorities that trouble is brewing, thus increasing the prospects for preemptive, intimidating action against the reform minded. As already mentioned, the precise sources of and exact reasons for retaliation, either before or after initiation of action are often difficult to pinpoint. On the other hand coalition formation fits in with the values of a democratic society because there exists the potential for citizen activists to escalate issues to wider, more inclusive arenas of public awareness.

Given the fear of retaliation, the need for group self-sufficiency, the painstaking requirements for factual evidence and convincing logic as well as the necessity for tactical judgment, it is understandable why coalition formation is such a difficult endeavor. Trust in the fairness of the overall system is required as well as confidence in the other members of the coalition so as to press ahead. The main faith is that there is justice in democratic institutions and this justice will prevail. Another necessary belief is that policy elites at higher levels are motivated by public ideas and not only responsive to narrow self-interests.[11] The third belief is that initiators of justifiable action will, at best, be favorably viewed and, at worst, not punished for their activities. Therefore it is not only the rationality of the argument for reform that reigns; as importantly a prevailing confidence is required that agency and power elites can, when faced by exceptional requirements, transcend their needs for power and subordinate compliance, all in the public interest. This is easier said than done because people of good will may disagree, but dilemmas such as these are part of the price that is paid for any democratic society.

URGENT INDIVIDUAL REPRESENTATIONS

This type of out-of-role behavior involves individual attempts to ignore, question, block or distort desired role responses while appealing to higher authority to change the situation. A possible advantage of the approach in the eyes of upper management is that it does not make the issue as visible as coalition formation, thus providing hierarchical authorities the opportunity to investigate and quietly correct, or at least control the manner of correcting undesirable situations. Activists should be extended opportunities to discuss, think through, acquire more information and reevaluate initial positions in a collegial manner. Successful outcomes are enhanced when:

- The salience of the issue is high to agency policy elites.
- Ethical agreement is complex and resolution paths are open to question. Under ideal conditions discussions will help better define the issues and develop more effective corrective actions.
- Expectations for highly adverse reactions, pressures to desist and retaliation by agency policy elites are not high.

There are several drawbacks to these individual initiatives. First, intermediary professionals often enter unknown territory when they assume that those in hierarchical capacities will forthrightly and rationally explore ethical situations with subordinates. Already mentioned is the fact that managers may not be in a position to be frank and outgoing because involvement in discussions could call for divulging confidential information. Another is that when subordinates short-circuit immediate supervisory levels and go to higher authority, potential problems regarding command integrity and lower management morale can emerge. Finally higher-level executives rarely know whether the professional's motives can be accepted at face value.

Traditional lore tells us that a "good" higher executive will listen to the concerns of anyone at lower levels, jointly explore alternatives and then take the necessary corrective action. Such beneficial outcomes are not readily predictable since intermediary professionals are in less powerful positions. Higher-level people have a great capacity to absorb information provided by subordinates while divulging little regarding sensitive matters. They are usually very skilled at listening, enduring silences and prompting others to express themselves. Such caution is understandable because frank exchanges may be relayed to others and used in ways to, for example, strengthen union bargaining positions, discredit the public image of the agency or even provide evidence in litigation. Nevertheless, the implacable reserve of many in upper management roles has intimidating potential. Professionals, anxious to present a rational, succinct position, less used to conversational nuances, can be at a severe tactical disadvantage because their counterpart is usually more skilled at withholding reactions, exploiting unforeseen weaknesses and using persuasive techniques. This one-way information flow can result in resentment on the part of the professional when outcomes are not satisfactory.

Normally, policy elites have a strong team loyalty that, at times, can run counter to ethical necessity and the public interest. Thomas Franck and Edward Weisband, in their study of relationships between the nation's president and senior staff, were hoping to better understand disturbing events such as those that occurred during the Vietnam and Watergate eras. The researchers found that there is a compulsion to go along with the top leaders "hardly anyone says 'no' very forcefully in private and just about no one says it in public." They see the origins of this behavior as occurring in childhood since "tattlers" are regarded with scorn. Most importantly, the costs to policy elites of being regarded as non-team players by colleagues are extraordinarily high in professional and private life.[12]

Surely an organizational tolerance of thoughtful, justifiable internal individual deviation from established power relationships is a necessary element of public agency democracy, essential to the public good; but there are strong traditions against this ideal. At the same time little is known about out-of-role behavior within agencies because favorable outcomes often occur precisely because of the confidential nature of corrective action. Evidently we need to better understand organizational and motivational variables that would predict success.

WHISTLE-BLOWING

The term "whistle-blower" has been reserved in this study for solitary individual public efforts by professionals to press for reform. This is the ultimate escalation of disruptive contention because the protagonist does not benefit from the safety in numbers of coalitional activity nor the possible quiet protection afforded by inside efforts to bring about change. Whistle-blowing is characterized by strenuous agitation for reform and high public visibility. It represents the most extreme level of commitment to citizen opposition and agency democracy because of its spectacular, dramatic nature. For this reason, whistle-blowing has received sporadic media attention. Simply put, whistle-blowing is a last resort on the part of professionals to alert as many people as possible about a condition that is judged detrimental to the general welfare. The field of reform action usually extends beyond the whistle-blower's individual department or agency. Logically one would expect more successful efforts to (a) have very high and explicit public salience, (b) be of very low ethical complexity and (c) have great appeal to public interest groups.

There is little question here regarding the immense pressures to desist and the high probability of reprisal. One of the most instructive cases is that of a professional by the name of Ernest Fitzgerald who, at the beginning of his career in the Department of Defense, received outstanding performance ratings for successes in cost reduction and containment. Consequently he was rapidly promoted by the Air Force, but then he decided to take on his agency higher management along with that of the Pentagon for their lack of action in controlling defense equipment expenses.[13] Although he was tolerated initially as a gadfly, management attitudes hardened as Fitzgerald prepared to give public testimony regarding cost overruns. Pressures were applied to "soften" and revise his public stance since agency policy elites were concerned that his actions would be highly embarrassing and involve very time-consuming congressional inquiries, which came to pass. As he persisted he was demoted, given uninteresting work and told that he had no future in the Air Force; efforts were also made to dismiss him on trumped-up charges.

The initial outcome was better than for most activists because he was then asked to become a adviser to the federal Joint Economic Commission, and so he continued to be influential. Yet when he attempted to establish himself as an independent consultant, he was blacklisted by the defense industries. Later, exonerated from all charges brought against him because of his unusual devotion to the public interest, Fitzgerald was reemployed in a carefully controlled Pentagon position.

Endeavors of this type take on heroic and frequently tragic proportions. In an effort to discover what becomes of whistle-blowers, their motivations and the severity of retaliation more than 150 involved and committed federal employees were studied.[14] There was "overwhelming personal and professional hardship" involving loss of job, salary reduction and harassment. Congressional committees, professional organizations and the Merit System Protection Board were of little help to activists. Lengthy legal battles had to be engaged in at heavy personal expense. More than half found the stresses so great that they required medical consultation. Over three-quarters of the sample population of whistle-blowers were managers or employed in other professional capacities; as a group they were highly educated, intensely attached to organizational goals, politically conservative, low on cynicism and, at least initially, "too trusting of their organization's willingness to respond to their concerns." They were extraordinarily committed to ethical behavior and practically impervious to social pressures to conform. The authors conclude that these highly vulnerable, "difficult people" are an important check on the abuse of the public interest because they have the capacity to impact government performance at close range.

Whistle-blowing cases are interesting because, as in the case of Fitzgerald, most are preceded by efforts on the part of activists to get the attention of their agency superiors. When rebuffed, they persist in spite of extreme pressures and are seemingly irrational in their obsession to right a wrong—irrational, that is, in terms of personal and family costs. One can but wonder how many essential reforms have dropped by the wayside as less tenacious, less intensively committed individuals have succumbed to coercion to stop their efforts. Surely these travails do not go unnoticed by others who are inclined to become proactive; the hardships experienced by whistle-blowers adversely condition others to remain quiescent. It follows that many professionals are regularly co-opted into joining practices destructive to self and society.

TOLERATING CONFLICTING LOYALTIES AND VALUES

A central theme throughout this book is that feelings about loyalty and trust are at the heart of acceptance or rejection of proactive behavior. When absolute faith in policy elite judgment, decisions and goals is demanded, this requires absolute trust in the chain of command. Management's motivations are thus assumed to be representative of society's values and needs. Arguably, on occasion (a) hierarchical values will not represent those of society at large, (b) individuals and groups may use their power for selfish, nonethical purposes and (c) hierarchical errors in decisions to attain agency and political institutional purposes are inevitable. If this is so, then conditional or tentative trust in hierarchical incumbents on the part of subordinates is necessary so that they can, when necessary, resist the demands for bureaucratic loyalty so as to protect the public good. There is a compelling sense of balance in such reasoning because managers reserve the right to withdraw trust in and loyalty toward subordinates when their performance is grossly unsatisfactory. Why then is the reverse not an acceptable, logical administrative belief? It stands to reason then that effective, democratic, hierarchical relationships must incorporate two-way feelings of *tentative* trust and *contingent* loyalty. This is essential condition for a truly effective, creative public service.

In cases involving clear-cut violations of legal and ethical standards by direct managers and/or fellow employees, there should be no doubt that an activist's loyalty and trust may be shifted to some other set of persons inside or outside the agency. Complexities emerge when employees no longer accept organizationally derived values and change their allegiance to the values of government institutions that legitimate their agencies. Organizational benefits may be in conflict with political systems effectiveness, but there should be no doubt as to which should be subordinate to the other.

Management has the right to demand in-role loyalty and trust so long as its behavior and values coincide with the demands of democratic political institutions. At the same time subordinates must have the right to question their conventional obligations if institutional necessities are not being met. When tentative trust and contingent loyalty is seen by all as the normal and logical basis for hierarchical relationships, then agency democracy becomes possible. It has been reasoned that this is not an impractical concept as long as we accept the fact that ethical quandaries and tensions are normal to human existence in and out of agencies. The problem is to make certain that the resolution of issues is consistently in the direction of higher order political institutional imperatives. To do this requires the firm conviction that intermediary professionals are in a unique position to understand matters critical to the common good. It is their legitimate responsibility to press for necessary reform.

Without question out-of-role initiatives are difficult to analyze systematically since they involve coping with paradox and making critical subjective judgments around specific issues. Yet the potential benefits of this type of reasoning should prompt public administrators to face and grapple with administrative mind-sets which are major reasons for important agency and political institutional failures. As things stand today neither professionals, policy elites nor other key actors appear adequately prepared to engage in proactive thought and action. Reasonable transitions in awareness, aspirations and behavior are required. The next two chapters explore some possibilities and continue integrating major themes.

NOTES

1. Barry R. Hammond, "The Enacted Image of Public Administrators: Challenge to the Traditional Truths," *Dialogue*, vol. 11, no. 1 (Fall 1988): 45-77.

2. Kenneth D. Walters, "Ethics and Responsibility," in *Papers on the Ethics of Administration*, ed. Dale N. Wright (Provo, UT: Brigham Young University, 1988), p. 126.

3. Karen M. Hult and Charles Walcott, *Governing Public Organizations* (Pacific Grove, CA: Brooks/Cole, 1990), pp. 27-32.

4. Dwight Waldo, *The Enterprise of Public Administration* (Novato, CA: Chandler and Sharp, 1980), p. 184.

5. Kenneth J. Meier, *Politics and the Bureaucracy* (Monterey, CA: Brooks/Cole, 1987), pp. 171-75.

6. John Rohr, *Ethics for Bureaucrats* (New York: Marcel Dekker, 1978), pp. 59-78.

7. John Kekes, *Facing Evil* (Princeton, NJ: Princeton University Press, 1990), pp. 4, 203-22.

8. Verne E. Henerson, "The Ethical Side of Enterprise," *Sloan Management Review*, vol. 23, no. 3 (Spring 1982): 37-48.

9. Keith Schneider, "In the Trail of The Nuclear Arms Industry," *New York Times*, August 26, 1990, section E, p. 5, and Michael D'Antonio, *Atomic Harvest* (New York: Crown Publishers, 1993).

10. Ralph Nader, *Whistle-Blowing, The Report of the Conference on Professional Re-*

sponsibility (New York: Grossman, 1972), pp. 225-43.

11. Robert B. Reich, "Policy Making in a Democracy," in *The Power of Public Ideas*, ed. Robert B. Reich (Cambridge, MA: Balinger, 1988), chapter 2.

12. Thomas M. Franck and Edward Weisband, *Resignation in Protest* (New York: Grossman, 1975), chapter 7.

13. Myron Glazer and Penina Glazer, *The Whistleblowers* (New York: Basic Books, 1989), pp. 21-24.

14. Philip H. Jos, Mark E. Thompkins and Steven W. Hays, "In Praise of Difficult People: A Portrait of the Committed Whistleblower," *Public Administration Review*, vol. 49, no. 6 (November/December 1989): 552-61.

Chapter 10

Professional Transitions

They knock on silence for an answering music; they pursue meaninglessness until they can force it to mean.

Rollo May

It is up to professionals to to break the silence as they seek to realize their yearnings for more meaningful careers. Bureaucratic structure and conventional roles normally provide the opportunity and latitude to exercise their talents, to fulfill major purposes of their life's work. However, beyond the usual, ongoing problems of fitting in with and surmounting frustrating aspects of bureaucratic life, major career crises can occur which put in jeopardy the individual integrity of professional careers and aspirations. These emerge when members experience palpable threats to the operational effectiveness and moral meaning of their workplace. They perceive power directed toward unacceptable ends, the waste of resources passively accepted, insensitivity to public needs tolerated and other major errors, all running counter to the public good. They cannot in good conscience retreat to the safe haven of their official, isolated responsibilities because they know that uncorrected, such widespread ills undermine and diminish the dignity and meaning of their life's work.

Much of the responsibility to make agency democracy a reality is in the hands of intermediary professionals. Yet proactive behavior may be judged as unacceptably disruptive, if not suspect, by defensive administrators who see these initiatives as reducing stability, as questioning the actions, motives and competence of powerful groups and individuals. Therefore reformers are subject to rebuff and retaliation. Cynicism and a lack of faith in agency management and political institutions are common responses. Not only do these decrease motivation and creativity; they make some professionals vulnerable to corruptive influences.

Surely adjustments have to occur in policy elite responses to public agency democracy, but powerful demands for change will have to come directly from intermediary ranks. The difficulty is that many will lack the patience and imagination to press on. They reason that if people at higher levels would only become more "rational," less "political," then all would be well. Let us assume then, for purposes of discussion, that a magical transformation has suddenly come over policy elites. All of those at upper reaches have become eminently reasonable, no longer intolerant of the difficulties of dealing with proactive behavior. In this imaginary world management is very willing to jointly consider sensitive matters of authority relationships and quite ready to cope with the stresses of change initiated from within agencies. One reasonable stipulation for such an accommodation would be that change must not disrupt necessary agency operations so as to seriously impede regular service delivery. Another sensible premise would be that essential public interest priorities and needs could at times delay or supercede subordinate recommendations. Under these conditions, in an agency world no longer encumbered by concerns over upper management resistance, how well prepared are most professionals to engage in proactive change?

ACTIVIST INHIBITIONS AND CONCERNS

To the unsophisticated, agency reform will simply be a question of doing the right thing at the right time and place. Already mentioned were a naive faith in simple, direct action, an impatience with understanding the knotty nature of and the necessity to cope with the dilemmas attendant to ethical action in public life. Because of inadequate political and organizational insight, some professionals will find it difficult to envision the problems and complications of readjustment. Others will not be predisposed to engage in the emotional discomfort and costs of change since reform is seen as a simple matter of righting obvious wrongs. Why this lack of sophistication?

We have seen that the training and socialization of most experts employed in the public service gives scant attention to paradox as a necessary aspect of action. Even the minority educated in public administration appears to reject "theoretical" and seemingly abstract ethical matters soon after or well before they encounter the daily demands of the workplace. Such concerns are often dropped in the face of having to get things done under pressures of time and meeting specific objectives. We know that effective change initiators are highly aware of complex interrelationships; inclined to examine matters of moral accountability.

Most, however, tend to avoid such complexities not only because of the press for daily action, but more fundamentally because:

- American cultural influences centered upon the virtues of individualism, special interest politics and consumer gratification have gained increasing ascendancy over civic virtue, community feelings and governance as a way to reach moral consensus.[1]
- The obligation to strive to understand the public good as high-minded necessity is not clearly seen as part of the formulation for individual success. Thus the motivation to learn is highly focused upon role activities as externally defined responsibilities. The gratification for professional work is seen as revolving around more tangible purposes such as the pleasure of exercising skills and the rewards of salary and status mobility.
- Professional administrative education assumes a management-worker dichotomy within which most professionals are perceived as naturally part of the management team. Little, if any, attention is given to the special interests and promise of professional enclaves which mediate between policymakers, other workers and extra-agency forces. Therefore, the concerns, perceptions, attitudes, and objectives of policy elites dominate preparation for the public service.
- Most professional education is aimed at specific areas of specialized knowledge. Categorical, technical, scientific, neutral competence is prized. Each specialized body of knowledge promotes singular ways to perceive, analyze and act upon data. Since the professions are isolated one from the other, expressing widely held subjective feelings and commonality of purpose must be consciously planned and nurtured.

Given this array of dampening influences, the impetus for reform is not easy to generate. Some have fire in their bellies about the mission of their agency and the need to resolve specific issues, but most leave it to the more powerful to develop tactics and strategies and to promote collegial efforts to maintain agency integrity. It is common, then, for professionals to blame others for what is not right, to see themselves as unfairly oppressed, as victims of higher level managerial forces which result in passivity, career disaffection, and the tendency to endure a wide variety of affronts to their agencies integrity. Feelings of powerlessness multiply as the discouraged seek out like-minded acquaintances who agree that indeed, the world is unfair, that most politicians and upper management are driven by only the basest motives.

What I have described is a kind of neurotic behavior which occurs when groups develop paralyzing anxieties over events and conditions that they should be able to control.[2] In order to break these reinforcing feelings of inadequacy and despondency, those affected need to engage in an active search for insight into the forces that shape their careers. An inclusive theory of professional action is required, involving reflection and self-awareness, combined with the desire to strive for responsible empowerment. One step toward becoming more adequately proactive is for professionals to understand how prevailing organizational, cultural and educational influences can blur their ethical vision and judgment. Since personality and situational differences between peers affect the disposition to engage in proactive efforts, many gradations of motivation for involvement on the part of intermediary professionals must be accommodated. Rarely are these conditions stable.

The public agency democracy model requires appropriate "selves" or aggregations of individual cognitions and sentiments that fit different needs for action. There is a strong connection between feelings of personal worth and the motivation to engage in reform action. In effect, the self must be protected since it becomes empty when it cannot fulfill its need for integrity.[3]

Role-centered selves gain their feelings of worth through the exercise of professional craft in the service of agency management goals. As change agents, they are adjusters rather than reformers to what is already in place. *Predicament-centered selves* become involved with complex situations that eventually should be resolvable through conventional channels. *Reform-centered selves*, driven by a passion to correct something patently wrong, strive to mobilize influential forces through unconventional means. Professionals must understand the potential for and limitations of these three states, always gravitating toward normal, role-centered selves. During times of transition from one type of self to the other, subordinates should support each other in order to arrive at outcomes beneficial to the public. Yet, there is no escaping the fact that proactive behavior is paratelic involvement requiring unusually high levels of exertion. Since individual levels of energy vary, some individuals will be less able than others to endure the temporary disruption of role-centered activities with their familiar, gratifying rewards.

A major deterrent to unity of purpose among intermediary professionals is judgment error. Ill-conceived, rash, illogical, emotionally distorted attempts to bring about reform carry justifiably heavy penalties. They harden the attitudes of management traditionalists and discourage future proactive efforts by others. Also, it would be a mistake to confuse necessary agency reform, directed toward the interests of the public, with material self-interests. For example, it is not consistent with the logic of agency democracy to rationalize that a strike action will eventually serve the public good because higher pay and benefits will bring about better employee motivation. Such reasoning may have a legitimacy of its own, but borderline and out-of-role proactive initiatives must be evaluated on their direct public interest merits alone, independent of material self-interest. It is instructive to return now to the saga of one of the legendary proactive professionals in the United States.

LESSONS FROM THE CAREER OF ERNEST FITZGERALD[4]

Already mentioned in the previous chapter, Fitzgerald, an industrial engineer expert in cost control, was appointed as a deputy for systems management in the office of the assistant secretary of the U.S. Air Force in 1965. Upon discovering that serious cost overruns were illegally built into contracts, he repeatedly cautioned his superiors. These initiatives were rejected by his immediate management but he did not desist. Consequently, despite his excellent record, he no longer received favorable evaluations. Undaunted, Ernest Fitzgerald alerted the Office of the Secretary of Defense to make top policy makers aware of many ongoing irregularities. He then testified before Congress, thereby arousing more wrath on the part of his supervisors. Against many odds, Fitzgerald fought to keep his Pentagon job and eventually prevailed with outside help from Congress and the American Civil Liberties Union. He has since persisted in his efforts to expose cost problems in military procurement, to increase public awareness, and he has persuaded legislators to pass laws to protect other whistle-blowers. Because of his endeavors much has been learned about collusion between government officials and business to violate the public trust. Ernest Fitzgerald is a prime example of ethical steadfastness in the face of seemingly unsurmountable difficulties.

Still it is interesting that more powerful forces favoring agency integrity were not present at lower levels. Fitzgerald at first took the reactive route of the role-centered self by counting upon the integrity of his peers and management to bring about change, but his associates did not respond well. It could be that some were active participants in wrongdoing, while others were surely already defeated by what they saw as the "politics" of the situation; certainly many feared for their jobs. Fitzgerald then resorted to out-of-role behavior by circumventing normal channels and going to the highest authority in the Department of Defense. When unsuccessful, he eventually voiced his concerns in public and had to overcome great difficulties before arriving at an eventual accommodation.

The reasons for whistle-blower hardship and oppression are regularly attributed to vengeful, misdirected power holders; yet it is revealing that the Fitzgeralds of the world are considered so unique and extraordinarily courageous—as somewhat eccentric. By concentrating upon individual heroism in the face of adversity we forget that the odds are not only created by regressive political and hierarchical forces. We ignore the fact that systemic agency corruption usually can only take place because large numbers of subordinates routinely tolerate it. We excuse passivity at lower levels in the face of wrongdoing as natural because powerful people might identify the reform minded, remove them or make them toe the line. As a result, restoring the integrity of public agencies is seen as a responsibility of lawmakers and other policy elites. This approach has serious limitations since hopes for major reform often appear to hinge upon the random emergence of self-sacrificing subordinates who will take action at the proper time. Each upheaval purportedly teaches us what new laws and top-down controls are needed, but no one seems to ask why ethical violations are so passively accepted by subordinates. Surely the tendency for supervisors to punish those who get out of line is not the only reason, for it stands to reason that when public servants present a more unified front, oppressive power can be counterbalanced.

Another lesson of the case is how unusual it is for tough-minded reformers to continue to lead fulfilling careers similar to that of Ernest Fitzgerald. Whistle-blowing studies show that society rarely values or protects its reformers, in spite of codes, laws and institutionalized methods of assistance. While the public becomes sporadically indignant over ethical failures, it soon forgets those with the courage to initiate reform. So it stands to reason that intermediary professionals as a group must become more active in seeing that the reform minded become less vulnerable.

The process and consequences of demoralization among subordinates require serious study and better understanding. For each misguided leader there are usually many more followers who share in the returns of agency improbity or observe it passively. It is but a small step from observer to exploiter. How then can waste and other errors be curtailed from deep within agencies? In the first place it is apparent that reform-minded professionals are often stymied because they cannot make the conversion from role-centered to predicament-solving selves. The reasons for these inhibitions include (a) being too easily intimidated, (b) leading insular working lives, (c) the fear of making mistakes and (d) the lack of internal and external support for advice and encouragement. When these inhibitions are reduced, then it should become more possible for professionals to create a more proactive momentum. If Fitzgerald could have at the onset joined hundreds at his own and lower ranks in demanding reform, changes would have taken place much more rapidly and permanently. Clearly policy elites must become increasingly receptive to determined efforts from those within agencies bent on acquiring more intrinsic meaning to their working lives. While the idea of spontaneous solidarity on the part of professionals from within agencies to become liberated from ineffectiveness and wrongdoing could appear visionary to some, it is at heart no more so than the most fundamental tenant of democracy, the right to promote the common good and oppose its detractors.

WHEN ARE INITIATIVES TIMELY AND APPROPRIATE?

Most professionals will be drawn to consider proactive behavior at some time in their careers. How can borderline-role and out-of-role initiatives become less risky, uncertain and isolated? Since the extent of difficulties will vary according to the type of intervention, it will be necessary for activists to assess the salience of issues, validate intuitive judgments and plan viable strategies. In so doing it is worth remembering that administrative processes are necessarily geared to satisfice rather than optimize. Consequently many deviances from rationally ideal standards of effectiveness are not worth the expenditure of time and effort to correct. Organizational relationships require considerable leeway because too much rigidity can lead to an unacceptably high incidence of breakdown. Therefore what are judged as less important errors of omission and commission are tolerated so long as these do not appear to seriously detract from desired results. Evidently judgment enters the picture, but how is one to determine routinely what deviances are "small," what leeway is required so that agency interests are not "seriously" affected? Since not only technical ethical matters are involved, the problem is that subjective judgments will vary according to personality. For instance, person A could see a great moral transgression if an employee brings a single agency-owned pencil home for personal use. Person B could tolerate the disappearance of thousands of pencils without considering the costs or illegalities. Therefore individual assessments of issues require some kind of external discussion and validation before engaging in borderline or out-of-role behavior.

When they experience the need to become proactive, professionals must be sure of their assessments and comfortable with paradoxical relationships. A variety of stresses could come into play including (a) cultural norms against "tattling" on others, (b) inadequate understanding as to what is in the public good, (c) lack of insight into organizational dynamics and (d) romantic expectations for policy elites to act in flawless ways. All of these underscore how important it is to check out, modify and/or reaffirm one's judgments, to gather facts and formulate a corrective strategy. Knowledgeable advisers can help one to better determine, for example, whether an undesirable situation is unlawful. Codes of professional ethical conduct are useful, but these are usually vague and passive, oriented toward in-role compliance. Understanding what to do has many complex ramifications since other actors within one's network of influence may be initially disinterested in or even hostile toward reform action. So it will not be unusual to feel lonely and ambivalent when trying to think through the strategy and consequences of proactive involvement.

Plainly, the requirements for borderline-role self-awareness are less demanding and complex than those needed for out-of-role behavior. In the first instance, improvements are undertaken with the expectation that once resolutions are designed, then it is a question of following well-established professional and hierarchical in-role approaches to bring about change. To be sure reflection in action and input from other colleagues are necessary when engaged in predicament scanning and action design. However, once that the design is submitted, activists expect "rational" managers to approve and join in efforts to reduce costs, increase quality or other ways to improve agency effectiveness. If this does not occur, then the would-be reformers have to make a judgment. Should they desist or press on, using out-of-role initiatives, to get the change made? It is then that greater necessities for information and advice emerge.

Who might be of assistance to potential out-of-role activists, who might they rely for suggestions to think through the strategies and consequences of proactive behavior? Knowledgeable friends, family and reliable associates could be helpful, but members of professional associations and educators might also provide insight and guidance.

PROFESSIONAL ASSOCIATIONS

Employee associations such as unions exist in order to protect member rights and to improve their renumeration and working conditions. While they could seem to be a promising source for help there are foreseeable drawbacks. The major reason is that unions are in a traditional, arguably necessary, adversary stance vis-à-vis management. They are concerned with well-defined issues that can be bargained for with improvements extended to all members. Initially, out-of-role action require confidential, exploratory, objective analysis. Unions may not inclined to extend such a service because regular involvement of this sort has little payoff to the association. When advice is provided, then there is a possibility that the issue could be used in order to serve other union purposes. Finally, agency policy elites are not normally inclined to view employee-union cooperation in understanding and resolving agency reform needs as objective or even directed primarily toward the public interest.

Other professional associations, dedicated to supporting the interests of members, should have a moral responsibility to help explore the feasibility of out-of-role action. In spite of the great differences between say, the American Institute of Industrial Engineers and the National Association of Social Workers, each has codes of service ethics and access to knowledgeable specialists who could assist the individual practitioner faced with the dilemma of taking reform initiatives. However, most professional associations are interested in one particular type of occupational specialization. Theirs is usually a limited view of the ethics and workings of the public interest, so a comprehensive knowledge of government administrative matters is rare. It is probable that the major purposes of the majority are too distant from the practical needs of the would-be activist to provide adequate assistance. Rather most associations are interested in (a) lobbying for changes which will benefit the status and renumeration of its membership, (b) maintaining and developing criteria for admittance to the profession, (c) providing professional training programs, (d) engaging in public relations emphasizing favorable aspects of the profession and (e) publishing specialized journals devoted to keeping their membership updated as to new research and developments in the profession. In addition, what have been called the "bureaucratic" professions tend toward a policy elite, orthodox management bias. Therefore raising possibilities of systemic organizational error or hierarchical fallibility could appear too radical or anti-management.

Professionals in search of advice need to find an association with broad public interests and enough expertise to understand a broad spectrum of government issues. The American Society for Public Administration may seem, at first glance, to be a logical choice. It is intended to encompass many diverse professional specializations engaged in government and membership is open to all. Its journal, the _Public Administration Review_ covers an extensive range of public interest perceptions and problems. Its code of ethics is tailored to guide professionals in the public service. In spite of the fact that ASPA is primarily policy elite and upper management-oriented, it does not avoid controversy. For example, the association presented an award to Ernest Fitzgerald for his contributions to the public service. While ASPA comes closest to a professional group capable of supporting individuals seeking consultation regarding out-of-role initiatives, it will find it difficult to use its very scarce resources to advise individual practitioners. However, the association could help to direct potential activists toward sources which could, for example, provide assistance in interpreting the ASPA Code of Ethics. National headquarters or chapters might direct professionals to a specific person for consultation, say a retiree or someone in academia. At the local chapter level, the ability to be of help will depend upon membership composition, strength and proximity to appropriate sources of information.

Turning now to issue-oriented public interest groups (e.g., environmental protection associations), an ideal relationship for proactive-minded professionals would seem to be one that first considers the effects of possible change upon the public good and then, in a reasonably detached and analytical manner, helps to examine various alternative choices. The major drawback is that most interest groups have already taken public positions against existing government shortcomings and directions already established by policy elites. Others may be seen as politically too doctrinaire.[5] Policy elites could then become suspicious of an alliance on the part of a professional with a "radical" group biased toward a controversial cause.

Would it be feasible, given the inadequacies of other existing groups, for intermediary professionals to form their own public interest group; one that would seek the intrinsic rewards of membership rather than material self-interests? The probability of a massive, spontaneous coalition is low since it would require at the onset a firm conviction on the part of many professionals that they (a) will on occasion have to make transitions from role- to reform-centered selves, (b) can subordinate individual professional identities to that of the public service and (c) are willing to give the time, effort and money essential toward creating and maintaining the new association. While these sentiments will ideally grow over time, most employees will probably not be initially attracted toward forming a new association of this type.

The most viable, admittedly difficult, accommodation would be for ASPA to enlarge its scope and mission to nuture the proactive needs of intermediary level professionals. This would require an open acceptance of the need for members at times to confront policy elites so as to protect the public interest. For ASPA to expand its services in this direction could significantly increase membership as it becomes involved in more direct and meaningful membership service activities. The transition would not be easy, but it remains one of the more promising long-term ways to increase professional public service solidarity.

As matters now stand, professionals will find but very limited support among their existing associations to think through the accuracy of their perceptions and assist in the development of plans for action. The main reasons are that most potential sources of help will usually have limited missions and unsuitable leanings. Others may simply perceive out-of-role behavior as a contaminating influence upon rational professional reasoning and therefore suspect. This leads us to another possibility: some response to the need for advice and support for reform action could be found in higher educational circles.

COLLEGES AND UNIVERSITIES

In searching for assistance, one might contact a faculty member with whom one has been associated in the past. The value of the contact depends upon the adviser's knowledge of matters pertinent to the issue at hand. As a first step, the concerned professional could approach school deans or department chairs. If receptive, these administrators will probably refer the professional to specific faculty members. While some may take an interest in the issue at hand and find it fruitful to engage in consultation, most are quite preoccupied with their regular duties. Others may have difficulty in relating to proactive behavior because, they too, have been conditioned by orthodox management beliefs.

Public administration schools and departments present fairly good possibilities for helping the professional think through the potential effects of and strategy for out-of-role action. There is an understanding here of public service dilemmas and knowledge of specific activities since faculty members are normally engaged in research with government agencies. Faculty with a political science background are likely to be sympathetic to the idea of citizen action from within an agency. Those with expertise in law could provide advice regarding issues of malfeasance and/or special procedural aspects of a contemplated action. At times experts in functional areas (e.g., budgeting, personnel, policy analysis) may be too much oriented toward orthodox management practices to relate to proactive initiatives.

Long-term solutions lie in finding ways for students to gain more adequate self-awareness and knowledge during their training and preparation. This calls for changes in the educational environment. Public administration departments and schools should lead the way to increase the capacity of professionals not only to generate proactive strategy but to also press for employee citizen rights to initiate beneficial reforms at the workplace. I will center on public administration for the remainder of this discussion in the hope that other professional schools will find similar revisions to the advantage of their students. How can educators introduce the necessary proactive orientations and self-awareness directly into their teaching practice? As discussed, there has to be a better understanding of the mind-sets and limitations that go with conventional concepts of agency effectiveness, orthodox management and supervisory motivation of employees. This should lead to consideration of issues of loyalty and trust as well as the different conditions under which role-centered, predicament-centered and reform-centered selves are most appropriate. As shifts in educational content occurs, faculty members and students may be drawn toward examining their own interactions.

Professional school faculty and student relationships are usually in close accord with conventional administrative practice. While student initiatives aimed at improving their educational environment are generally encouraged, most faculty members insist upon tight control over the content and nature of learning as well as methods of evaluation. They see themselves as responsible to define educational problems and strategies for their resolution. Bureaucratic logic is used to promote equity in the evaluation of student performance. Consequently teacher-student relationships are highly structured, at times more so than those in public agencies.

Clearly, conventional in-role student-faculty relationships help to efficiently deliver services. At the same time these bureaucratic means free up teachers to pursue very important personal professional needs and avenues of advancement such as research, consulting and professional association networking. However, it should come as a disturbing realization that, as they employ conventional hierarchical practices, teachers serve as authority referrents to students. The extensive use of orthodox administrative techniques and practices causes most teachers to become authority role models. Because of their exposure to highly regulated, at times paternalistic treatment in educational environments, students may develop rigid professional and organizational attitudes that carry forth in their careers. Certainly, the more proactive democratic visions of subordinate empowerment, participation in decisions, group endeavors and reform initiatives are not consistent with the realities that shape most contemporary educational teaching and administrative environments.

Since students have had a lifetime of cultural conditioning in grade and high schools to respond to authority, they do not readily question the effects upon their own attitudes and predispositions. Those that seek changes are liable to be seen as misfits by their peers as well as faculty. This is not to say that higher education should abandon structure, rules and authority relationships, but the situation is akin to that of agencies. Like other large organizational endeavors, educational systems are also subject to systemic errors of omission and commission which "subordinates" can help correct. In order to learn how to become proactive, student inclinations to engage in predicament resolving within and reform of the educational environment should be better accommodated by the faculty.

To facilitate proactive behavior on the part of students in higher education endeavors, various approaches merit consideration such as:[6]

- encouraging students to explore and recommend well-considered changes to reduce their feelings of frustration and impotence in educational environments.
- the formation of student governance groups that will create reasonable pressures for change.
- encouraging group assignments and projects whenever possible so as to increase reflection in action and predicament-solving skills.
- balancing policy elite perspectives in course work with action-oriented intermediary professional concerns and perspectives.
- opening the design of courses, exercises and examinations to appropriate student input.

Major reorientations will not come about easily because faculty people, like their agency management counterparts, will understandably be concerned about loss of efficiency and potential chaos. Also, students who are empowered can be impetuous and impatient, intolerant of ambiguity and prone to striving for unrealistic goals; past excesses on campuses across the land show that such outcomes are possible. Today, in spite of increased representation on governance groups and other accommodations to participation, students do not take easily to proactive initiatives vis-à-vis faculty. A major reason is that potential student activists may fear being labeled as troublemakers and open to retaliation such as low grades. Throughout pedagogical and equity difficulties resulting from student input and group projects cannot be ignored.

Several other sources of resistance to educational change should be kept in mind. The first is that most faculty people have themselves been educated and shaped in traditional ways, so the risks of encouraging student proactive behavior could be seen as highly problematical. The second concern is that nurturing student proactive skills requires more faculty time and effort to be spent on institution building and improving student interactions. These can compete with traditional paths of upward faculty mobility. It is also probable that many students will not take easily to transitions aimed at developing citizen responsibilities as part of their educational experience. The more "pragmatic" ones prefer to manipulate objects, use technical competence for problem resolution and emphasize specialization values over wider goals.[7] Highly tractable, their major goal is to gain unambiguous knowledge that will enable them to gain autonomy, power and prestige. Others may resent putting time into improving the educational process because it detracts from direct course-related efforts and, after all, since the school environment is only temporary, it could appear to have little long-term personal significance. All of these are powerful forces that work against the evolution of agency democracy learning and practice in universities and colleges. However, if the hold of orthodox administration at large is to undergo change, then resolute attention must be given to revising the educational setting of future wielders of policy elite and intermediary power.

A POSSIBLE PROFESSION

We have examined some practical aspects of transitions on the part of professionals toward the exercise of citizen rights at the workplace. While difficulties in making the adjustments are predictable, progress begins with greater awareness regarding the forces that predispose agency members toward passivity in the face of major agency shortcomings. Inadequate attention has been given to internal personal responsibilities to protect the public interests. Little will change in the long run if professionals do not become better aware of how cultural and educational influences have conditioned them to toe the line within bureaucratic environments. Little will change if professionals do not learn how to support one another during difficult transitions of selves. Finally, little will change if professionals do not take action to revise their associations and educational institutions so as to satisfy their ethical needs. All said, the future of agency democracy is heavily contingent upon the capacity of intermediary professionals to influence those who shape their ideas and actions. Much depends upon their ability to generate a collectivity of common interests and solidarity in the face of the many odds. These include understanding:

- their exposure to incompatibilities between political institutional values and agency behavior
- the dysfunctional effectiveness, management and motivational beliefs that work against proactive behavior
- the reasons that gaps exist between public administration philosophy, organization applied theory and practitioner needs.

The new orientations should recognize the unrealistic dependence upon notions of leadership that tend to make subordinates blind to their personal potential for democratic action. By not accepting the necessity for tentative trust in and contingent loyalty toward policy elites, subordinates live in the hope that more-than-human chiefs and commanders will emerge; they become despondent when these leaders do not meet unrealizable expectations. When no one fits this quest for someone in real charge, someone in whom to invest unbounded trust and loyalty, then passivity and melancholy are common outcomes. These feelings are usually magnified as individual hopes for the highest status and material gains are not attained.

A new sense of public service professionalism, while respecting the value of leadership and in-role authority, will also encourage developing the capacity for all to express vital democratic responsibilities toward society at large. It will be less fixated upon classical economic institutional values centered primarily upon material self-gratification.[8] The attraction of efficiency will not squeeze out considerations of quality; organizational goals will be more open to question; political leaders will become more responsive toward the need for ethical expression at the agency workplace and these concerns will be more extensively integrated into career preparation. This grass-roots revisionist movement will go well beyond the present fixation upon individualism and neutral competence. The "new professional" will become more reflective, more self-aware and supportive of colleagues. A critical mass will then coalesce to press for changes in professional associations and educational practices so as to make agency democracy a reality.

Throughout a deeply ingrained sense of value and responsibility will remain toward (a) the rational merits of bureaucratic structure and process and (b) the need to work out proactive initiatives in ways least disruptive to agency and political purposes. It will be recognized that normally, trust and loyalty toward agency management and goals are desirable. Alongside the need to respect existing practice it is essential to actively cope with the ambiguities of the public service so as to more effectively advance public interests and provide more meaning to the lifework of government employees. This new resolve can become a powerful force to revitalize the public service, but it will also require appropriate responses on the part of others. Some of these are addressed in the next, final chapter.

NOTES

1. R. N. Bellah et al., *Habits of the Heart* (Berkeley: University of California Press, 1985), chapter 8.

2. Jerry B. Harvey and D. Richard Alberston, "Neurotic Organizations: Symptoms, Causes and Treatment," in *The Dynamics of Organization Theory*, ed. John F. Veigas and John N. Yanouzas (St. Paul, MN: West, 1984), pp. 349-58.

3. Philip Cushman, "Why the Self Is Empty," *American Psychologist*, vol. 45, no. 5, (May 1990): 599-611.

4. Myron Peretez Glazer and Penia Migdal Glazer, *Whistle Blowers* (New York: Basic Books, 1989), pp. 21-25, 37-38.

5. Andrew McFarland, "Public Interest Lobbies Versus Minority Faction," in *Interest Group Politics*, eds. Allan J. Cigler and Burdett B. Loomis (Washington, D.C.: Congressional Quarterly Press, 1983), pp. 346-47.

6. Walter L. Balk and Burton Gummer, "Career Dissatisfaction Among Public Service Professionals: Analysis and Recommendations," in *Bureaucratic and Governmental Reform*, ed. Donald J. Calista (Greenwich, CT: JAI Press, 1986).

7. Morgan W. McCall, Jr., "Leadership and the Professional" in *Managing Professionals in Innovative Organization*, ed. Ralph Katz (Cambridge, MA: Ballinger, 1988), pp. 148-61.

8. Amitai Etzioni, *The Moral Dimension: Toward a New Economics* (New York: Free Press, 1988), chapter 14.

Chapter 11

Stakeholders in the Future

Fragile as our existence may be, however ineffectual our interrogation of the world, there is nevertheless some thing that has more meaning than the rest.

Umberto Eco

What are the probable impacts of public agency democracy upon the wide variety of people who interact with intermediary professionals? Given its potential to increase the effectiveness of government, how can those in surrounding activities encourage proactive initiatives from within agencies? A reasonable starting point is to agree that government agencies will be under ever greater pressures to improve their performance and adaptability. At the same time that public demand for less government waste and higher effectiveness rises, the sheer intricacy and size of operations increases agency exposure to unforeseen errors of omission and commission. Inevitably, modern organizational systems will continue to generate opportunities to undermine their fundamental purpose and integrity.[1]

Information technology and better management are seen as the major means to meet today's challenges. The first promises more accurate, rapid, flexible and less costly transactions. The second promises greater innovation and motivation. Proponents for change decry bureaucracies as old-fashioned and see a need for smaller, more adaptable organizational structures. To be sure, some restructuring is occurring and will continue, but it would be wrong to hope that bureaucracies will disappear. They are, after all, the major organizational invention that assures appropriate responses to most legislative, judicial and executive needs such as predictability, economics of scale and equitable treatment of citizens. It is becoming increasingly evident, however, that technology and management are not sufficient to meet contemporary needs. People from deep within bureaucracies must have more freedom to propose innovations, call attention to unfavorable developments and press for change. As discussed, this calls for a revision of authority relationships, a small revolution in orthodox administrative beliefs and practices.

The next section summarizes what it is that stakeholders around intermediary professionals should react to; it is a brief summary of the major action aspects of agency democracy. Various types of adaptation are then considered in four sections which discuss the dynamics of stakeholder relationships, effects upon line authority relationships, impacts upon other stakeholders and approaches to coping with change. Together, these call for a unique government ethos. A proposal is then outlined that transcends orthodox business beliefs. The final sections explore new directions for reseach and consider the potential for agency democracy to help revitalize the public service.

AN ACTION OVERVIEW

Intermediary professionals, normally located in strategic agency positions, have important insights and skills which can be better turned to the benefit of the public (chapter 1). Their potential has not been realized because contemporary public administration thought and practice do not adequately encourage professionals to use their knowledge and judgment to initiate reforms (chapter 2). Meanwhile, the literature has long recognized that there exist serious inconsistencies between democratic political purposes and bureaucratic operations (chapter 3).

The promise of public agency democracy is that it will promote better utilization of professional talent. To do this, initiatives on the part of subordinates in the form of borderline-role and out-of-role proactive behavior, must become more acceptable. Both forms of behavior are entirely consistent with democratic political institutions (chapter 4). Ethically inspired proactive citizen behavior is a logical, viable way of tempering a wide variety of emerging errors before they get out of hand. At present too many in the public service experience confusion and remain passive in the face of wasteful and corrupt practices. Such feelings of powerlessness generate identity crises and neurotic behaviors which contribute to the waste of public resources and career despair.

The applied theory of public agency democracy is difficult to envision because proactive behavior goes counter to ingrained bureaucratic theories and beliefs primarily geared toward the reduction of uncertainty and ambiguity. While proactive efforts are adaptive behaviors, directed at the need to cope with paradox, these are liable to be seen as a threat to essential order. Yet an examination of organizational effectiveness, management control and motivation provides clear evidence that there is a need to recognize and deal with the inevitability of organizational authority paradoxes in a more conscious and shared manner (chapters 5, 6, and 7).

Professionals must act responsibly when undertaking proactive initiatives.

Research has shown that borderline-role behavior can be engaged in without major disruption to regular, ongoing agency activities. Effective out-of-role initiatives will depend upon the capacity of professionals to consult with others in order to correctly interpret issues and develop viable strategies for action. Throughout professionals will have to become prime movers in expressing the need for agency democracy and pressing for changes aimed at enhancing their educational environment (chapters 8, 9, and 10).

While some proactive behavior occurs today in the public service, it must become more acceptable and normal. If not, government agencies will continue to experience unnecessary productivity problems and other damaging crises that adversely affect political institutions. There is no logical reason, in terms of the public interest, that agencies should not realign their purposes, norms and attitudes to the dynamics of public agency democracy; but this involves thoughtful readjustments by key people who influence the aspirations and behavior of professionals.

A STAKEHOLDER PERSPECTIVE

To clarify the meaning of "stakeholders," think of the major actors within and around agencies.[2] All of those involved with governmental institutions and their agencies have interests in diverse as well as common outcomes. For example, society at large wants order, equity along with economic promise and stability. Political policy elites seek to satisfy particular constituency and community interests. Judiciary experts strive to interpret and enforce a body of law. Within agencies, policy elites want to implement and guide public policy. Professionals and other employees aspire to exercise their skills and become influential. In the orbit of political institutions, educators strive to prepare competent and innovative members of society. Professional associations aim to serve the interests of their constituencies. The media report events and act as advocates of change. This immense, complex network becomes operational when the material and emotional needs of the participants (e.g., salary, status, friendships, feelings of purpose and other rewards) seem reasonably consistent and fair compared to other actors.

There are inevitable conflicts of interest among stakeholders and differences in desired outcomes, but the expectation is that adjustments can be made to satisfy the needs of various actors. This dynamic balance, the major requirement for network cohesion, is threatened when single or groups of stakeholders begin to exploit the system unfairly. Then the common good, or what is considered as right and just regarding the general expectations of members, is violated. Simply put, threats to network integrity crop up when some appear to receive benefits that unjustly work to the detriment of others. Errors of commission cause significantly less satisfying outcomes for some stakeholders than legitimately expected. For instance corruption results when laws are violated or other major agreed-upon norms of desirable behavior are intentionally broken. Failures also happen because of the tendency for networks to undergo deterioration because of unforeseen causes; also decision errors are inevitable. When not recognized over time or ignored, these can be seen as errors of omission.

The map of stakeholder interactions illustrates some patterns of mutual dependence and support. Professionals are envisioned as surrounded by groups of influential others, each with its own interests and concerns. Changes in power relationships urged by those in professional positions will at times require compensating adjustments by others in the network. Figure 11-1 illustrates thirteen categories of actors ensconced in a matrix of other interacting groups, organizations and social institutions. Path 1 has been of prime interest in this book since it represents the major conduit for policy implementation and resource allocation, consistent with in-role professional reactive behavior. The reader should ask why these patterns are presently in some kind of dynamic balance. How might the advantages and disadvantages of agency democracy be perceived by different actors? Which actors will be most profoundly affected? How can a new balance be reached with the least disruption?

Returning to the major in-role relationships, five types of policy elites are found in figure 11-1.

- Political Executives (PE) and Legislators (L) are elected to represent "the" public and in this capacity, aided by staff, formulate overall political policy and determine action priorities.
- Judiciary (J) actors interpret legal issues and enforce compliance. Many of their major concerns center upon individual rights and due process.
- Top agency executives are Political Managers (PMs) appointed by PEs; therefore their time in office is usually of shorter duration compared to that of other managers and professionals. The attention of PMs is mainly upon the issue and constituency interests of the PE. Similar to their elected superiors they must often use qualitative, fragmented, informal, unsystematic modes of communication.[3] Since their direct superiors react to a wide range of external forces, PM priorities are often subject to rapid change.
- Civil Service executives are usually technical managers (TMs) more oriented inward to the agency and interested in clarifying, generating and implementing operational goals and controls. Emphasis is upon predictable, in-role behavior of subordinates as an essential requirement for systematic communications and performance controls.

The path for policy implementation and the orderly flow of resources, PE - PM - TM - IP, is also the major influence upon professional careers. Civil Service executives (TMs) are normally the most immediately significant actors to professionals. The sequence of associations implies that a series of accommodations have to be reached between political managers who interpret the needs of political executives, the technical managers who direct systematic ways

Figure 11-1
Some Stakeholder Interaction

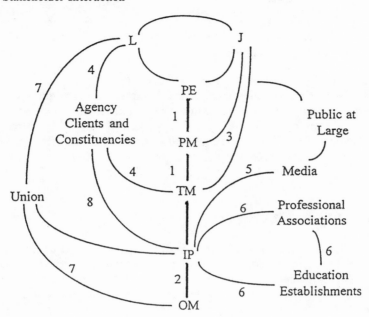

to implement policy and professionals who exercise their specialized craft. Another important influence between professionals and other agency members (OMs) is depicted by path 2. Since professionals mediate between the interests of policy elites and other agency members, they should normally experience a sense of gratification when their plans, suggestions and instructions are implemented by OMs; but this raises other problems which will be addressed later.

Returning now to the overall stakeholder system, channels of influence between key actors help account for a dynamic equilibrium. At the heart of the entire system is the power balance between judicial, elected political executive and legislative bodies established through constitutional authority.

Path 3 indicates the potential for judiciary actors to intercede at various agency levels.

Path 4 depicts possible "iron triangle" relationships between constituency, civil service executive and legislative member interests[4] that tend to bypass Path 1.

Path 5 depicts rare direct interactions between intermediary professionals and the media which may advocate change to the public at large.

Path 6 is a socializing, accreditation and guidance set of influences between professionals, their professional associations and educational establishments.

Path 7 traces how employee unions regularly lobby legislative members in the interests of their constituencies.

Path 8 shows how agency clients and constituencies are systematically influenced by the direct actions of professionals and other agency members. Impressions of and reactions to these influences are on occasion passed on to the media and general public.

While figure 11-1 does not represent all interactions, the major ones are present. Even this primitive rendition is a picture of great intricacy and movement, portraying how major areas of government and the environment normally interrelate and accommodate in shifting, often paradoxical ways. The introduction of public agency democracy practices into this pattern of influence must fully recognize the need for agency stability, dependent primarily upon reactive behavior.

PATH 2 AND PATH 1 EFFECTS

While agency democracy has been considered mainly from an intermediary professional perspective, citizen rights to initiate action must exist for all agency members. This means that other agency members (OMs) in operating line, support and service functions can also engage in borderline role and out-of-role behavior. Since their discretion to perform in-role activities is more limited, the opportunities to perceive and experience potentially proactive events will usually be lower than those afforded to individuals in intermediary professional positions (IPs). On the other hand there are usually much larger numbers of OMs, compared to IPs, so the potential for proactive initiatives on their part should be significant.

Role borderline activities by OMs requiring accommodations on the part of IPs can create tensions along path 1. For example, it has been observed that many-lower level managers perform unneeded routine functions that can be assimilated by line workers. The reasons for this kind of agency ineffectiveness are attributed to grade escalation and the misapplication of standard ratios of supervisors to subordinates. Employees are often capable of discovering ways to redesign their tasks and, as they become more influential, may find a greater sense of value and interest in their jobs.[5] Since the trend is for larger numbers of college-educated people to become employed in operational line jobs, the prospects for such initiatives should increase as higher levels of analytical skills are brought to the workplace. Some IPs could then become redundant since their subordinates would, in effect, absorb supervisory planning and coordination functions. Rather than resisting such efforts, IPs should help to deal creatively with the impact by helping to find resolutions to the redeployment of supervisory and coordinating positions.

Turning to another possible problem area, out-of-role action by OMs through whistle-blowing can have an impact upon IPs. For instance, suppose that a custodial employee (OM) observes government employees filling their privately owned cars with gasoline paid for by county taxpayers. The OM then decides to go up the ladder of command and requests the assistance of his/her direct supervisor (IP) to stop the practice. Once the claim is verified, the IP would then have an ethical obligation to help the OM and "make waves" with those at higher levels. Suppose, then, that no satisfactory explanations come forth and no corrective action is taken. The IPs then have to choose between retreating to the sidelines or joining forces with the OM, to the extreme of becoming partners in whistle-blowing. Even if the OM contacts the media and engages directly in responsible whistle-blowing, IPs as agency citizens may have an ethical obligation to support and help protect these initiatives. This shows why acceptance of the principles of agency democracy does not mean that IPs can limit the initiation and implementation of proactive behavior only to their peers and hierarchical superiors. At times they may have to decide how and when they should become involved in the concerns of people at lower organizational levels.

Along with IPs, career executives called Technical Managers should feel the greatest direct impact of shifts toward agency democracy, for their relationship with IPs is similar to that of IPs to OMs, with added complexities. As discussed in chapter 8, sensitive relationships on the part of TMs with politically appointed superiors (PMs) are involved which may require giving thought to changing established operational and policy priorities. When hierarchical interests and perceptions diverge, it will at times be difficult for TMs to influence PMs.

Other Connections

The introduction of proactive behavior into the stakeholder influence networks will be initially and predominantly felt in path 1, followed by other effects:

Path 3—Communications on the part of IPs regarding malfeasance could increase activities along path 3, but no great change in the behavior of Js appears to be involved, since their responses will be in-role.

Path 4—Initiatives along path 1 or direct action between IPs and other actors might jeopardize informal arrangements and priorities of existing "iron triangles."[6]

Path 5—As out-of-role initiatives become more common, IPs are liable to feel extra pressure by the media to provide insight and elaborate upon specific issues. This, of course, would cause grave concern to the path 1 hierarchy. The IPs should only resort to the media path when the issue is appropriate and after other alternatives have proven fruitless.

Path 6—The effects, discussed in the previous chapter, call for changes in educational processes and the policies of some professional associations.

Path 7—Some unions and employee associations might, at times, take up causes of IPs and OMs through lobbying for action on the part of Ls. As noted, this could present dangers since it is at times difficult to separate the narrow interests of actors from public interests.

Path 8—As out-of-role initiatives become more visible to agency clients and constituencies, it is possible that some of these will be taken up by public special interest groups, but these may or may not represent what is in the general public interest.

Table 11-1 is a summary of the major impacts of introducing the concept of agency democracy into existing paths of influence. The major actors are listed along with the advantages and disadvantages of involvement in borderline-role and out-of-role initiatives.

The table serves as a point of departure to better understand what concerns over the introduction of agency democracy may be experienced throughout the stakeholder network. It is a striking reminder of fundamental differences between public and private organizational environments. While techniques and processes commonly employed in business administration are essential to public administration, a very special vision of government administration and management is required for agency employees to exercise their citizen rights. As they experience the benefits of proactive engagement from within agencies, stakeholders will support whatever is required to orient, protect, and help public servants make accurate ethical assessments.

COPING WITH CHANGE

The importance of education and association organizations for intermediary professionals was discussed in chapter 10. An increased self-awareness on the part of professionals is needed along with a readiness to consult with others. Mention was made of the American Society for Public Administration Code of Ethics and Implementation Guidelines of 1984 which specify some necessary commitments on the part of professionals. These call for performing one's function with personal integrity, serving the public, striving for professional excellence, having a "positive" attitude, not realizing undue personal gain, keeping up to date on issues and administering in a "competent" manner.[7]

Agency democracy holds good potential for enhancing many of these purposes, but consideration should be given to changing the existing codes of conduct. These observations could lead to revisions of these ASPA guidelines at a future time:

- *Avoid any interest or activity which is in conflict with the conduct of official duties.* The problem here is that "official duties" could be limited to in-role, reac-

Table 11-1
A Summary of the Impacts of Proactive Behavior

STAKEHOLDERS	PATH	MAJOR POTENTIAL ADVANTAGES	MAJOR CONCERNS
Intermediary professionals and other agency members (OMs)	1	Increased agency and political effectiveness	Initial disinterest
Technical managers (career executives)	1	Increased long-term agency effectiveness	Possible distraction from existing short term priorities
Political managers and political executives	1	Increased implementation effectiveness for some policies	Possible distraction from other political objectives
Judiciary	3	Increased awareness of malfeasance; more equity	None
Iron triangles	4	None	Could disrupt tacit arrangements
Media	5	More meaningful "news"	Possible damage to agency image through inaccurate, uncoordinated premature release of information
Higher educational and professional associations	6	More effective and influential professional socialization	Necessity to make difficult adaptations within schools and associations
Unions and other employee associations	2 & 7	New constituency causes	Not directly compatible with current association goals and member self-interests
Clients and constituencies	8	More overall political institutional effectiveness. More confidence in "open" government	Possible distraction from specific special interest political action priorities

tive behavior. A wider meaning is required whereby professionals have a more comprehensive sense of duty, a higher loyalty toward what have been called regime, or constitutionally based values.

- *Respect and protect the privileged information we have access to in the course of our official duties.* On rare occasions, knowledge considered as "privileged" by policy elites must be divulged in the public interest. Since most successful cases of whistle blowing involve the airing of such information, this item should be worded so to make such exceptions more permissible.
- *Exercise whatever discretionary authority we have under law to promote the public interest.* Again, the present emphasis is upon in-role relationships. Agency democracy specifies two new classes of discretionary authority; borderline-role and out-of-role behavior which should also be recognized.
- *Eliminate all forms of illegal discrimination, fraud and mismanagement of public funds and support colleagues if they are in difficulty because of responsible efforts to correct such discrimination, fraud, mismanagement or abuse.* Because public agency democracy helps to give more legitimacy to these initiatives it should be seen as essential to fulfilling their basic purposes.

At present the 1984 Code of Ethics (adopted by the ASPA National Council in 1985) is a statement of laudable intentions that does not squarely face the complexities of initiating reform. Therefore regressive managers could even use the existing code as a rationale to punish the "untrusting" and "disloyal." Agency democracy clarifies matters of employee control since it recognizes ambivalences and provides explicit ways for subordinates to, at important times, take internal agency initiatives involving controversial citizen behavior. Recognizing this, making it part of the ethos of public administration, is a high priority.

The policy elites called *Technical Managers* need to better articulate their inevitable tensions with political managers[8] so as to better understand the impact of agency democracy. It will then be possible to envision intermediary professionals as a group confronted with similar problems of adaptation as technical managers have to political managers. All need to recognize the nature of the cultural and socialization influences that make proactive behavior difficult to accept. Progress begins with understanding the gap between contemporary applied theory in public administration and effective practitioner action. Then it is important to comprehend how "generic" administrative theories have predisposed most government administrators to value approaches aimed at the shaping of subordinate attitudes and behavior that are at times inappropriate to political institutional purposes.

A most important area of self-awareness is for TMs to recognize how feelings of futility in subordinate managers and professionals reduce their capacity to take beneficial action. Chapter 8 mentioned how superiors may pass on their sense of powerlessness by (a) an overemphasis upon short-term goals, (b) overcontrolling routine decisions, (c) sealing themselves off from information at lower levels, (d) becoming overconcerned with the need for secrecy and (e) overzealous protection of turf.[9] These practices encourage passivity and corruption; they repress the thoughtful airing of issues that require borderline-role and out-of-role initiatives. Agency democracy is based upon the conviction that power can often be put to best use by sharing it with those lower in the hierarchy so as to encourage reasoned proactive initiatives. As successful instances of borderline-role and out-of-role behavior occur, some can be reviewed with employees as examples of how proactive initiatives works to the benefit of agency and political institutional purposes. Not only would knowledge of these cases be motivating, it would help define the general characteristics of well-considered initiatives. *Political Manager appointees* are major mediators between the desires of political executives and the activities of agency implementation, at times involving inevitable, stressful relationships with immediate subordinates. These frustrations can be also transmitted in the form of inappropriate authoritarian behavior, isolation and destructive desires to control turf. Political manager support, given the management ambiguities and difficulties of political appointees, is important to the success of agency democracy.

Turning to the major balancing powers and their involvement with agency democracy, *Judiciary and legislative bodies* have at times taken the lead as they attempted to devise ways to protect whistle-blowers. *Political executives* do not appear to have been active sources of innovation nor inspiration along these lines, possibly because proactive behavior is seen as a threat to short-term control. Prompted ideally by political managers and technical managers, they should give thoughtful consideration to political factors which work against an ethic of proactive employee behavior. Executive and legislative political agreements often depend upon interpersonal trust and loyalty and what are seen as violations of these norms usually are followed by retaliatory action. But it is neither rational nor beneficial to extend these political deal-making mind sets to agencies where the prime needs for agency democracy are tentative trust and conditional loyalty.

Public statements supporting agency democracy are needed. These could be promoted by *public interest groups* (e.g., the League of Women Voters) and the *media*. The potential beneficial effects should be emphasized while recognizing that relationships between hierarchical levels within agencies and outside forces are complex and necessarily fraught with the ambiguities, inconsistencies and countervailing stresses that typify democratic processes of governance. All said, the potential for laws and regulations to protect initiators of out-of-role initiatives is limited. So there is a need for agency democracy to become a cultural value incorporated into the system of public beliefs and political institutions that the media should support.

While some effects are predictable, it is not possible to account for all possible aspects of readjustment to accommodate agency democracy. Any applied theory is incomplete until put into effect, experimented with and evolutionary adjustments made through what is learned in daily practice.

TOWARD A UNIQUE GOVERNMENT MANAGEMENT ETHOS

As discussed in chapters 3 and 6, practitioners, researchers and educators have tried over the span of many years to fit a business-inspired, management philosophy to agency operations. Nevertheless, throughout the history of public administration it has been recognized that something is wrong, that there is a lack of fit between political and administrative purposes. The major focus has been upon outside citizen participation in bureaucratic decisions, emphasizing the need for change in policy elite attitudes and behavior.

Practitioners have traditionally concerned themselves with making bureaucracies more effective through research in areas of structure, process of motivation. While techniques developed in the private sector have been adjusted to the special needs of public agencies, orthodox management philosophy has retained its prominence. As a result, when agency environments are compared to those of business, it is common to say that public sector endeavors do not lend themselves to "good" management practices. On rare occasions the nature of action from the unique perspective of public employees has been examined in order to improve organizational effectiveness. Some have already seen the problem as a moral one which, once addressed, will free up commitment to tasks. Consequently, as values become integral to the structure of work, employees will participate in change, managers will become less autocratic, knowledge of transitional process will increase, and organizational goals will be enhanced.[10] These are praiseworthy objectives, but little is said about the heart of ethical action, that is, the need for subordinates to go at crucial times, beyond narrow agency objectives or initiate internal action to resolve complex predicaments.

Important applied theoretical matters necessary to adapt to the unique nature of public service management have been, by and large, ignored by practitioners. Most go into government with little exposure to public administration knowledge, and the pertinent literature has limited circulation. Even those who have learned specialized public administration theoretical knowledge seem to lose interest, arguably because of the disarray of the field and its distance from activist concerns. Consequently policy elites and professionals are drawn to what appear to be universal management principles centering upon command, persuade and program actions, all aimed at reducing uncertainty at the expense of coping with equivocality.

These management orientations are essential to in-role activities, but they do not take into account other crucial aspects of agency existence which are unique to effective government operations. Since the realities of governance, allegiance to regime values and public ownership are not deliberately incorporated into management philosophy, proactive initiatives are liable to be seen as aberrations, as deviances from the ideal way to run things. Consequently, the failure is not placed where it belongs, on the inadequacies of orthodox management thought; rather political institutions are seen as barriers to sound management.

This encourages inappropriate exercise of authority at higher agency levels. Some managers, for example, copy the tough, cynical behavior of their entrepreneurial counterparts in order to force the system into line. At times neurotic supervisory reactions, similar to those of intermediary professionals, emerge. Blame is externalized to the machinations of politics and some retreat to the temporary consolidations of protection of turf, self-agrandizement and intensive control over subordinates. Others decry the adverse impact of civil service rules and regulations upon employee motivation, the inability to hire and fire as in private enterprise. Many of these common complaints can be seen as symptomatic of the inadequacies of management philosophies that do not fit the public sector.

Public agency democracy has been proposed as a way to overcome major shortcomings of the public service but, given the state of management beliefs, there is little assurance that those in authority will immediately see its potential. To accept, even encourage, paradoxical activities may be seen as inviting "irrational" behavior on the part of subordinates. However, if the aims of public agency democracy are clearly to the benefit of political institutions, then the real problem is less with political environments than it is with the way that management is envisioned in the public sector. Suppose that these principles took the place of existing orientations:

1. The primary mission of any government agency is to make political institutions work in the most effective way.
2. When interests and activities of those within agencies are in conflict with the above (e.g., curtailment of flagrant waste and abuses of power), then *all* agency members have a duty to take corrective action in favor of the primary mission.
3. Subordinates, because of their agency position and training, will at times possess superior evaluation and design skills which must be turned toward resolving problems of agency and political effectiveness.
   3a. The intrinsic rewards of self-generated improvement activities are potentially powerful motivators for subordinates.
   3b. Subordinates will have to motivate hierarchical forces in order to bring about some improvements.
4. Policy elites and other managers must be accessible to subordinates so that major agency predicaments can be resolved and errors mitigated at early stages.
5. Proactive initiatives on the part of subordinates are encouraged recognizing that the process of influence usually involves stress and contention.

While this list may, at first glance, seem consistent with other employee participation movements, it has radical implications which reach well beyond current manager thought and practice. Item 1 replaces the private sector profit motive and negates the bastion mentality that drives most agencies. Item 2 brings the ethical responsibilities of subordinates into visible, logical prominence and makes internal contention permissible. Item 3 legitimizes proactive behavior by redefining power sharing. Items 4 and 5 help to establish the groundwork for supportive managerial behavior beyond conventional line authority relationships. Uniting these specifics is the major premise regarding management-subordinate relationships: *Managers are accountable to their subordinates*, accountable to prevent waste and temper error as much as subordinates are to their organizational superiors. Once this core belief is accepted, then the ambiguity of agency democracy can become more readily incorporated into public service management thought and action.

A unique public service management ethos does not deny orientations stressing leadership, mission clarification, design and delegation. Rather, the intention is to adapt the necessities of government operations to the rights of citizen employees to initiate well-reasoned change. By recognizing that professionals have very special perceptions and skills that can be put to better advantage, managers can fulfill their goals and contribute to the effectiveness of political institutions in a more creative and meaningful way. Interestingly enough, when both professionals and managers have the legitimate right to feelings of tentative trust and contingent loyalty one in the other, this raises the probability of more effective joint cooperation. As mutual influence is enhanced within agencies, the need for covert "hot lines" and outside monitoring should decline. Whistle-blowing should decrease in frequency and become less subject to destructive retaliation. As political institutions become more effective through the empowerment of professionals, the public service will be seen as a more gratifying career, so a steady influx of capable employees will be better assured. All revolves around the capacity of major actors to accept the normal, beneficial presence of paradox and use it in a creative manner.

SOME PROMISING RESEARCH DIRECTIONS

The need for a variety of studies was touched upon in previous chapters. For example:

- Major failures of government agencies should be analyzed as case studies in order to better understand (a) when professionals became aware of looming disasters, (b) what actions on the part of subordinates could have attenuated adverse impacts and (c) what perceptions, beliefs and interactions prevented proactive initiatives by subordinates.
- Relationships between agency productivity improvement endeavors and political institutional effectiveness require more examination. What kind of "savings" are translated into what kind of political improvement action? Under what circumstances is productivity progress dissipated?
- Further investigation of interlocking and contending interests between intermediary professionals and others could help refine the model of agency democracy.
- The social psychological aspects of the arousal of proactive behavior, its connection with learning, personality and appropriate levels of paratelic energy should be better understood.

At a more general level it may be possible to model conditions of overload in order to understand when certain intensities and combinations of proactive organizational change could result in operational failure. Systems dynamics approaches combined with stakeholder analysis, have the potential for better defining (a) the nature of dysfunctional change actions, (b) interactive reinforcing factors leading to deterioration, (c) the nature of agency "chaos," (d) ways of implementing change in order to avoid failures and (e) limits upon change content and frequency.[11]

Predicament resolution techniques also require further development. Chapter 8 showed how it is possible for lower-level professionals to engage successfully in such endeavors, but new ways of increasing the level of awareness of predicaments and promoting a joint commitment to their resolutions will emerge. More sophisticated methods of scanning action and designing the sequencing of change are needed; of central interest is the cyclical, reiterative process of first taking advantage of intuitive assessments and then entering design and implementation action phases.

A host of opportunities for systematic investigation revolve around the socialization and orientation of professionals. Little is known about the actual and potential interactions between professionals educated in public administration and other professionals. Are there ways that trained professional public administrators can become more influential in orienting their peers regarding the unique characteristics of public agencies and the opportunities for proactive initiatives? How can professional administration associations become less fixated upon policy elite perceptions and more open to the needs of members at lower positions in hierarchical ladders?

Parallel to these research initiatives is the need to rethink aspects of professional education so as to help students experience as well as learn how to more effectively cope with the ambiguity of their careers. Competing demands to define the content of professional knowledge are constantly present; yet very little thought has gone into understanding processes of transmitting knowledge as shapers of future attitudes toward organizational power. Faculty members seem to have settled for rather conventional bureaucratic relationships with students, but the conditions for a more proactive educational environment are not well understood. How capable are students, as classroom subordinates, of engaging in constructive proactive behavior? What is the nature of cultural conditioning that creates preoccupations with grades and status, too often at the cost of reflecting upon the intrinsic, satisfying aspects of public service careers? How can faculty be adequately rewarded for making innovations in what might be called educational democracy? Better approaches are needed to prepare professionals, ethically and psychologically, to meet the demands of action in the public service. There are pressing requirements to reconcile individual simplistic, essentially innocent moral reasoning with the paradoxical aspects of group realities and experiences.[12] Educational programs must provide these opportunities more consciously and deliberately.

Research into ways of providing better legal protection for those who engage in out-of-role behavior is necessary, though there has been some progress along these lines. More has to be known about not only the promise of legal protection, but, as importantly, its limitations. While laws and judicial processes represent agreements regarding the settling of conflicts, and standards of decency and fairness among community members, there are logical boundaries as to what can be codified and enforced. Consequently great reliance must be placed upon less tangible norms which define what is appropriate, but we need to know more about the relationships between legal controls and less formal normative guides.

Clearly, public agency democracy promotes sizable opportunities for action-oriented applied theoretical research aimed at improving the effectiveness of agencies and exploring ways to make careers in the public service more rewarding. Of equal importance is the effect upon the way that public administration will be valued as a field of endeavor.

REVITALIZING THE PUBLIC SERVICE

What has been discussed promises to open new avenues for the renewal and energizing of professional people in the public service. Thoughtful readjustments in power relationships will make it possible for subordinates to better respond to ethical imperatives. Untapped talent and energy will be released so as to contain costs, correct errors and maintain the integrity of agency operations. A truly distinctive public service professional identity will emerge based upon the need to actively support political institutions. As professionals become better able to define and articulate what is, or should be, at the heart of their calling to the public service, then the prospects for attracting qualified, motivated individuals to the field of public administration will be more assured.

Greater empowerment along with a more robust identity will create pressures by large numbers of students and practitioners to reform professional association and educational goals and practices. As academia discovers new ways for students to become more reflective about authority relationships, this will increase the potential for initiating change from subordinate levels. At the same time better applied theories of public management will integrate the perplexities of ethical considerations and so encourage proactive behavior on the part of students. While intermediary professionals and educators have been emphasized as beneficiaries of these revitalization efforts, managers at all levels can share in the returns as they think through the special nature of public administration and become less attached to inappropriate orthodox administrative convictions. Throughout, professionals as key actors in the network of stakeholders in a democratic society, will develop mutually supportive relationships at the workplace in order to maintain their integrity and strengthen democratic political institutions. They can take the lead by acknowledging that principles of tentative trust and contingent loyalty need not threaten the benefits of, nor the necessity to respond to, appropriate hierarchical direction. In the face of many pressures to do otherwise, the importance of reflection, of an examined life, of the necessity to express essential values through their careers and work, these must not be denied.

At the heart of such matters, what has more meaning than other concerns is the necessity to preserve and improve American democratic institutions. These promise a special kind of freedom for citizens, an appropriate sense of self, an identity that seeks to learn from and thrive in the face of life's ambiguities. All involved in government have an opportunity to play a significant part in the renewal of American society by striving for public agency democracy.

NOTES

1. James B. March and Johan P. Olsen, *The Organizational Basis of Politics* (New York: Free Press, 1989), chapter 7.

2. Ian I. Mitroff, *Stakeholders of the Organizational Mind* (San Francisco, CA: Jossey-Bass, 1983). See chapter 3 for some basic assumptions and methodological approaches.

3. Joseph L. Bower, *The Two Faces of Management* (Boston, MA: Houghton Mifflin, 1983), chapters 1-5.

4. Charles Levine, B. Guy Peters and Frank J. Thompson, *Public Administration* (Glenville, IL: Scott, Foresman, 1990), pp. 53, 54, 128.

5. Shan Martin, *Managing Without Managers* (Beverly Hills, CA: Sage Publications, 1983).

6. The activities of Ernest Fitzgerald as a whistle-blower, for example, put into jeopardy a variety of informal arrangements between agencies, the legislature and the defense industry. Some of the more tenuous relationships were probably rationalized as necessary because of the need to deliver equipment on schedule so as to counter the Soviet armament buildup. Consequently matters of cost, irregularities, inferior quality and malfeasance could have been seen at times as matters of secondary importance to prevailing in the cold war.

7. See the *Public Administration Times*, September 1, 1994, p. 15, for a proposed revision of the ASPA Code of Ethics.

8. Hugh Heclo, *A Government of Strangers* (Washington, D.C.: Brookings Institution, 1977). See chapter 2.

9. Rosabeth M. Kanter, "Power Failure in Management Circuits," in *Harvard Business Review* (July/August 1979): 65-75.

10. Robert T. Golembiewski, "Toward Excellence in Public Management," in *The Revitalization of the Public Service*, ed. Robert B. Denhardt and Edward T. Jennings, Jr. (Columbia, MO: University of Missouri Press, 1987), chapter 11.

11. Peter M. Senge, *The Fifth Discipline* (New York: Doubleday, 1990).

12. Stuart Hampshire, *Innocence and Experience* (Cambridge, MA: Harvard University Press, 1989), chapter 5, p. 170.

Selected Bibliography

Amabile, Teresa M. *The Social Psychology of Creativity*. New York: Springer-Verlag, 1983.

Apter, Michael J. *The Experience of Motivation*. London: Academic Press, 1982.

Astley, W. Graham and Andrew H. Van de Ven. "Central Perspectives and Debates in Organization Theory." *Administrative Science Quarterly*. Vol. 28, 1983.

Balk, Walter L., Ed. "Symposium on Productivity in Government." *Public Administration Review*. Vol. 38, No. 1, January/February 1978.

Bandura, Albert. "Self-Efficacy Mechanism in Human Agency." *American Psychologist*. June 1982.

Barnard, Chester. *The Functions of the Executive*. Cambridge, MA: Harvard University Press, 1968.

Barnes, Louis B. "Managing the Paradox of Organizational Trust." *Harvard Business Review*. March/April 1981.

Bellah, R.N. et al. *Habits of the Heart*. Berkeley: University of California Press, 1985.

Blau, Peter M. *Exchange and Power in Social Life*. New York: Wiley, 1964.

Bower, Joseph L. *The Two Faces of Management*. Boston, MA: Houghton Mifflin, 1983.

Bruce, Willa and Dorothy Olshfski. "The New American Workplace," in Holzer, Marc, ed. *Public Productivity Handbook*. New York: Marcel Dekker, 1992.

Caiden, Gerald E. "The Challenge to the Administrative State," in Frederick Lane, ed. *Current Issues in Public Administration*. New York: St. Martin's, 1986.

Cameron, Kim S. "Effectiveness as Paradox: Consensus and Conflict in Conceptions of Organizational Effectiveness." *Management Science*. Vol. 37, No. 5, May 1986.

Cooper, Philip J. *Public Law and Public Administration*. Englewood Cliffs, NJ: Prentice Hall, 1988.

Denhardt, Robert B. *Theories of Public Organization*. Monterey, CA: Brooks/Cole, 1984.

Denhardt, Robert B. and Edward T. Jennings, Jr., eds. *The Revitalizaiton of the Public Service*. Columbia, MO: University of Missouri Press, 1987.

Downs, George W. and Patrick D. Larkey. *The Search for Government Efficiency*. New York: Random House, 1986.

Etzioni, Amitai. *The Moral Dimension: Toward a New Economics*. New York: The

Free Press, 1988.

Frederickson, H. George. "Minnowbrook II: Changing Epochs of Public Administration." *Public Administration Review.* Vol. 49, No. 2, March/April 1989.

Fry, Brian R. *Mastering Public Administration.* Chatham, NJ: Chatham House Publishers, 1989.

Glazer, Myron and Penina Glazer. *The Whistleblowers.* New York: Basic Books, 1989.

Graber, Doris A. *Processing the News.* New York: Longman, 1988.

Gulick, Luther and Lyndall Urwick, eds. *Papers on the Science of Administration.* New York: Institute of Public Administration, 1937.

Hampden-Turner, Charles. *Maps of the Mind.* New York: Macmillan, 1982.

Hampshire, Stuart. *Innocence and Experience.* Cambridge, MA: Harvard University Press, 1989.

Harmon, Michael. *Action Theory for Public Administration.* New York: Longman, 1981.

Heclo, Hugh. *A Government of Strangers.* Washington, D.C.: Brookings Institution, 1977.

Held, David. *Models of Democracy.* Cambridge, UK: Polity Press, 1987.

Henerson, Verne E. "The Ethical Side of Enterprise." *Sloan Management Review.* Vol. 23, No. 3, Spring 1982.

Holzer, Marc, ed. *Public Productivity Handbook.* New York: Marcel Dekker, 1992.

Hummel, Ralph. "The Crisis in Public Administrative Theory." *Dialogue,* Vol. 11, No. 4, Summer 1989.

Jos, Philip H., Mark E. Thompkins, and Steven W. Hays. "In Praise of Difficult People: A Portrait of the Committed Whistleblower." *Public Administration Review.* Vol. 49, No. 6, November/December 1989.

Kanter, Rosabeth M. "Power Failure in Management Circuits." *Harvard Business Review.* July/August 1979.

Kekes, John. *Facing Evil.* Princeton, NJ: Princeton University Press, 1990.

Kets de Vreis, Manfred F.R. *Organizational Paradoxes.* London: Tavislock, 1980.

Larson, Magali S. *The Rise of Professionalism: A Sociological Analysis.* Berkeley: University of California Press, 1977.

Levine, Charles, B. Guy Peters, and Frank J. Thompson. *Public Administration.* Glenville, IL: Scott, Foresman, 1990.

Levinson, Harry. *Executive: The Guide to Responsive Management.* Cambridge: Harvard University Press, 1981.

Lincoln, Yvonna S., ed. *Organizational Theory and Inquiry: The Paradigm Revolution.* Beverly Hills: Sage Publications, 1985.

Lipsky, Michael. *Street Level Bureaucracy.* New York: Russel Sage Foundation, 1980.

Lynn, Laurence E., Jr. *Managing the Public Interest.* New York: Basic Books, 1981.

Lynn, Naomi B. and Aaron Wildavsky, eds. *Public Administration, The State of the Discipline.* Chatham, NJ: Chatham House, 1990.

March, James B. and Johan P. Olsen. *The Organizational Basis of Politics.* New York: The Free Press, 1989.

Marini, Frank. *Toward a New Public Administration.* Scranton, PA: Chandler, 1972.

Martin, Shan. *Managing Without Managers.* Beverly Hills, CA: Sage Publications, 1983.

Marx, Fritz M., ed. *Elements of Public Administration.* New York: Prentice-Hall, 1946.

Meier, Kenneth J. *Politics and Bureaucracy.* Monterey, CA: Brooks/Cole, 1987.

Mintzberg, Henry. *Structure in Fives: Designing Effective Organizations*. Englewood Cliffs, NJ: Prentice-Hall, 1983.

Mintzberg, Henry. *The Nature of Managerial Work*. New York: Harper & Row, 1973.

Mitroff, Ian I. *Stakeholders of the Organizational Mind*. San Francisco, CA: Jossey-Bass, 1983.

Morgan, Gareth. *Images of Organization*. Beverly Hills: Sage Publications, 1986.

Mosher, Frederick C. *Democracy and the Public Service*. New York: Oxford Press, 1982.

Muller, Robert K. *The Innovation Ethic*. New York: American Management Association, 1971.

Nader, Ralph. *Whistle-Blowing. The Report of the Conference on Professional Responsibility*. New York: Grossman, 1972.

Newland, Chester A., ed. "Symposium on Productivity in Government." *Public Administration Review*. Vol. XXXII, No. 6, November/ December 1972.

Nuttin, Joseph. *Motivation, Planning and Action*. Hillsdale, NJ: L. Earlbaum Association, 1984.

Okun, Arthur. *Equality and Efficiency*. Washington, D.C.: Brookings Institution, 1975.

Osborne, David and Ted Gaebler. *Reinventing Government*. Reading, MA: Addison-Wesley, 1992.

Ostrom, Vincent. *The Intellectual Crisis in Public Administration*. Alabama: University of Alabama Press, 1973.

Pateman, Carole. *Participation and Democratic Theory*. New York: Cambridge University Press, 1981.

Perrow, Charles. *Normal Accidents*. New York: Basic Books, 1984.

Pfeffer, Jeffrey and Gerald R. Salancik. *The External Control of Organizations*. New York: Harper & Row, 1978.

Reich, Robert B. *The Power of Public Ideas*. Cambridge, MA: Balinger, 1988.

Robey, Daniel. *Designing Organizations*. Homewood, IL: Irwin, 1982.

Rohr, John. *Ethics for Bureaucrats: An Essay on Laws and Values*. New York: Marcel Dekker, 1978.

Rosenbloom, David H. *Public Administration*. New York: Random House, 1989.

Schöen, Donald A. *The Reflective Practitioner*. New York: Basic Books, 1983.

Scott, William G. "Organizational Revolution: An End to Managerial Orthodoxy." *Administration and Society*. Vol. 17, No. 2, 1985.

Senge, Peter M. *The Fifth Discipline*. New York: Doubleday, 1990.

Simon, Herbert A. *Administrative Behavior*. New York: Free Press, 1965.

Tapscott, John and Art Caston. *Paradigm Shift*. New York: McGraw Hill, 1993.

Thompson, Victor A. *Bureaucracy and the Modern World*. Morristown, NJ: General Learning Press, 1976.

Torbert, William. *The Power of Balance*. Newbury Park, CA: Sage, 1991.

Waldo, Dwight. *The Enterprise of Public Administration*. Novato, CA: Chandler and Sharp, 1980.

Warwick, Donald P. *A Theory of Public Bureaucracy*. Cambridge, MA: Harvard University Press, 1975.

Weisband, Edward and Thomas Franck. *Resignation in Protest*. New York: Grossman Publishers, 1975.

Whyte, William F. *Organizational Behavior: Theory and Applications*. Homewood, IL: Irwin, 1969.

Wilson, James Q. *Bureaucracy.* New York: Basic Books, 1989.
Wright, Dale N., ed. *Papers on the Ethics of Administration.* Provo, UT: Brigham Young University, 1988.

Subject Index

Action: and mental constructs, 107-8; preferences and data gathering, 111-12. *See also* Borderline-role performance

Accountability of professionals, 7-8, 13, 17, 42-43, 70

Administrative state, 36-37. *See also* Professionals in government

Administrative thought: generic, 69-70, 89-94

Agency democracy. *See* Public agency democracy

American Society for Public Administration, 31, 168-70; code of ethics, 147-48, 184, 189-90

Artificial and natural systems, 90, 132-33

Authority: democratic opposition to, 8, 9; organizational, 89-105. *See also* Orthodox management

Behavioral approach, 107-8

Borderline-role behavior, 53-54, 57

Borderline-role performance, 123-43; case and field studies of, 124-27, 131, 134-36, 138-40

Bureaucracy, 23, 36-38, 52, 177. *See also* Overhead democracy

Business: experience, 81-82; and management values, 47, 96-100. *See also* Orthodox management; Productivity

Citizen feelings toward government, 3-4, 36-37, 39, 77-78

Coalition formation, 54-55, 153-55

Conflicts and tensions, 6-7, 9, 25-26, 156, 158-59

Commanders, 111-12

Corruption, 3-4, 151, 165

Creativity, 124. *See also* Innovation and intuition

Cutback management, 78

Decision analysis, 91-92

Democratic management, 61

Education of professionals, 20-22, 25, 30, 48, 170-72

Effectiveness, 69-87; meanings of, 83-85. *See also* Productivity

Errors of commission and omission, 3, 4, 145, 167

Ethics: managerial and bureaucratic, 100-4; and moral reasoning, 146-51; and reform initiators, 151-55. *See also* Out-of-role performance

Evil, 148. *See also* Ethics

Focal organization, 132-35

Harmony. *See* Loyalty and harmony values

Hierarchical relationships, 9, 26-29. *See also* Reactive and proactive reasoning

Name Index

About the Author

WALTER L. BALK is an emeritus professor, Department of Public Administration and Policy, Graduate School of Public Affairs, at the State University of New York, Albany. He has held various industrial engineering and production management positions with IBM, and now as a consultant he specializes in public administration organization, design, and behavior. Author of numerous book contributions and articles, Dr. Balk is an authority in the area of public agency productivity. He serves on the editorial board of two journals.